A LITTLE HISTORY OF ARCHAEOLOGY

BRIAN FAGAN

A LITTLE
HISTORY

of

ARCHAEOLOGY

YALE UNIVERSITY PRESS
NEW HAVEN AND LONDON

For information about this and other Yale University Press publications, please contact:
U.S. Office: sales.press@yale.edu   yalebooks.com
Europe Office: sales@yaleup.co.uk   yalebooks.co.uk

Set in Minion Pro by IDSUK (DataConnection) Ltd
Printed in the United States of America.

Library of Congress Control Number: 2017959448

ISBN 978-0-300-22464-1

A catalogue record for this book is available from the British Library.

10 9 8 7 6 5 4 3 2 1

To
Vernon Scarborough
Water expert extraordinaire
Who told me about Bali and offers
encouragement at every turn

Contents

CHAPTER 1

The 'Backward-Looking Curiosity'

On 24 August AD 79, Italy's Mount Vesuvius erupted like a great cannon. An enormous fountain of ash, red-hot lava, rocks and smoke burst from the volcano. Daylight turned into darkness. Ash fell like heavy snow, blanketing the nearby cities of Herculaneum and Pompeii.

About midnight, an avalanche of scalding gases, mud and rocks slid down the mountain slopes and cascaded through the two Roman towns. Herculaneum vanished completely. Only the roofs of Pompeii's larger buildings poked through the volcanic debris. Hundreds of people perished. Wrote an eyewitness, the author Pliny the Younger: 'You could hear the shrieks of the women, the wailing of infants, and the shouting of men.' Then there was silence.

Soon only a large, grassy mound marked the site of Pompeii. More than sixteen centuries passed before anyone disturbed the two buried cities. Then, in 1709, a peasant digging a well on top of Herculaneum uncovered some sculpted marble. A local prince sent workmen underground. They recovered three intact female statues. This chance discovery led to treasure hunting in the heart of the buried city. From this casual looting of Roman artefacts buried deep in volcanic ash emerged the science of archaeology.

Gold-laden pharaohs, lost civilisations, heroic adventures in remote lands – many people still believe that archaeologists are romantic adventurers who spend their lives digging into pyramids and lost cities. Today's archaeology is far more than hazardous journeys and spectacular discoveries. It may have begun as treasure hunting – and alas, the looting of sites continues alongside serious archaeology today. But treasure hunting isn't proper archaeology: it's fast-moving, ruthless digging with one objective – to uncover valuable objects to sell to wealthy collectors. Contrast this with archaeology, the scientific study of the past, of human behaviour over 3 million years.

How did archaeology develop from uncontrolled searches for astonishing finds and forgotten peoples into the serious pursuit of the past that it is today? This book tells the story of archaeology through the work of some of the most famous archaeologists, from the casual observers of four centuries ago to the close-knit research teams of the twenty-first century. Many pioneering archaeologists were colourful individuals who spent months working alone in remote lands. At some point in their lives, all of them developed a fascination for the past. One early scholar called archaeology the 'backward-looking curiosity'. He was right. Archaeology is curiosity about what's behind us.

I first experienced archaeology as a teenager on a rainy day in southern England, when my parents took me to Stonehenge (see Chapter 38). The massive stone circles towered above us. Low, grey clouds swirled in the gloom. We walked among the stones (you could in those days) and looked out at silent burial mounds on nearby ridges. Stonehenge cast its spell over me, and I have been fascinated by archaeology ever since.

I became curious about Englishman John Aubrey (1626–97), who often visited Stonehenge and discovered another dramatic stone circle at nearby Avebury, when he galloped into it while foxhunting in 1649. Aubrey puzzled over both Avebury and Stonehenge, both of them said to have been built by 'Ancient Britons'. Who were these savage people who wore skins? They were, Aubrey supposed, 'two or three degrees less savage than the [Native] Americans'.

Aubrey and his successors knew little of Europe's past before the Romans. Certainly, there were burial mounds, stone circles and other monuments for them to examine; also a confusing muddle of stone tools, pottery and metal objects that appeared from ploughed fields and the occasional digging of crude trenches into burial mounds (see Chapter 9). But these had belonged to completely unknown people – not Romans from a city like Pompeii, buried on an exact date that is recorded in historical documents.

Serious digging began at Herculaneum in 1748. King Charles II of Naples commissioned Spanish engineer Roque Joaquín de Alcubierre to probe the depths of the city. Alcubierre used gunpowder and professional miners to blast and tunnel his way through the ash to uncover intact buildings and magnificent statues. The king displayed the finds in his palace, but nevertheless, his excavations were a closely guarded secret.

A German scholar, Johann Joachim Winkelmann (1717–68), was the first serious researcher. In 1755, he became librarian to Cardinal Albani in Rome (which required him to convert to Catholicism, much to the horror of his Protestant friends). This gave him access to books, and also to the objects uncovered by Alcubierre. Seven years passed before Winkelmann could actually visit the secret excavations. By then, he had unrivalled knowledge of Roman art – more like the knowledge of modern archaeologists than of his contemporaries. He was the first scholar to study artefacts from the towns in their original positions.

Winkelmann pointed out that these objects were vital sources of information about their owners and about daily life in Roman times – about the people of the past. In an era of uncontrolled looting, this was a revolutionary idea. Unfortunately, Winkelmann could never test his theories with his own excavations: he was murdered by thieves for some gold coins while awaiting a ship in Trieste in 1768. This remarkable scholar was the first to establish a basic principle of archaeology: all artefacts, however humble, have a story to tell.

Sometimes the stories are unusual. I once visited an abandoned Central African village dating to the 1850s. The site was a jumble of tumbledown cattle enclosures, grinding stones and pot fragments. There appeared to be nothing of any great interest. Then I picked up a 500,000-year-old stone axe lying among the pottery. I realised at once that the axe must have been carried to the village from elsewhere, for there were no other stone tools or signs of very early human occupation around.

This was perhaps the first time that I thought about tools from the past as storytellers. I imagined a villager, perhaps a child, picking up the beautifully shaped axe in river gravel about 8 kilometres away and carrying it home. Back home, people looked at it, shrugged and threw it away. Perhaps an elderly villager remembered coming across another such axe in his youth, and so the finder kept it for years. There was a story here; but alas, it had long vanished. Only the stone axe remained.

The story of archaeology begins with the curiosity of landowners and travellers. Wealthy Europeans with a taste for classical art often took what was called the 'Grand Tour' to Mediterranean lands. They returned laden with Roman, and sometimes Greek, works of art. Stay-at-home landowners started digging into barrows (burial mounds) on their properties. At dinner parties back home, they would proudly display 'rude relics of 2,000 years'. The diggers were amateurs, people with no archaeological training whatsoever; their ancestors were antiquarians (people interested in the ancient past) like John Aubrey, who had puzzled over Stonehenge.

Archaeology was born about 250 years ago, at a time when most people believed in the biblical creation. Then large-scale archaeological excavation began when French diplomat Paul-Émile Botta and English adventurer Austen Henry Layard searched for, and found, the biblical city of Nineveh in northern Iraq. Layard was no expert digger. He tunnelled into the great mounds of Nineveh and followed the carved walls of Assyrian King Sennacherib's palace deep underground in a search for spectacular finds for the British Museum. He even discovered the ruts left by chariot wheels in limestone slabs at the palace gates.

Layard, John Lloyd Stephens, Heinrich Schliemann and many others: these were the remarkable amateurs who discovered the world's earliest civilisations, described in the chapters to follow. There were other amateurs too – people who puzzled over stone axes and the bones of extinct animals, over the primitive-looking skull of Neanderthal man. They showed that the human past stretched back far further than 6,000 years (the figure that had been calculated by the Christian Church from the Bible – see Chapter 7). Professional archaeologists were virtually unknown until the late nineteenth century. And, indeed, the number of professional archaeologists worldwide remained in the hundreds until the years before the Second World War.

Archaeology revolves around human lives. No discovery brought this home to us more than the famous opening of the Egyptian pharaoh Tutankhamun's tomb by Lord Carnarvon and Howard Carter in 1922. Carter's painstaking clearance of the tomb painted a unique portrait of a young man from over 3,000 years ago. It took Carter eight years to complete the work and he died before he published it. Experts have studied the life of this little-known pharaoh ever since.

A much humbler story comes from a sandy clearing near Meer, Belgium, where a small group of hunters camped in 7000 BC. One individual walked over to a boulder, sat down and fashioned some stone tools using a lump of flint that he (or she) had brought along. A short time later, a second person joined the stoneworker and also made some tools. Belgian archaeologist Daniel Cahen carefully pieced together the waste flakes from the toolmaking. The direction of the hammer blows revealed a remarkably intimate detail: the second stoneworker was left-handed!

Modern, scientific archaeology is not just about finding sites and digging. It unfolds as much in the laboratory as it does in the field. We've become detectives who rely on all kinds of tiny clues from many often unlikely sources to study the people of the past – whether an individual like an Egyptian pharaoh or an entire community.

As we'll see, archaeology began in Europe and the Mediterranean world. Now it has become a global quest. There are archaeologists working in Africa and Mongolia, Patagonia and Australia. The crude diggings of a century ago have become highly controlled and carefully planned. Today, we focus not only on individual sites, but on entire ancient landscapes. We rely heavily on remote sensing, using lasers, satellite imagery and ground-penetrating radar to find sites and to plan very limited excavation. We move less earth in a month than many earlier excavations did in a day. In collaboration with professional researchers, amateur archaeologists with metal detectors have also made remarkable discoveries in England. These include a hoard of 3,500 pieces of Anglo-Saxon gold and silver found in Staffordshire in central England, dating to about AD 700. This is modern, scientific archaeology, which surveys and excavates in search of information, not goodies.

Why is archaeology important? It's the only way we have of studying changes in human societies over immensely long periods of time, over hundreds and thousands of years. We add fascinating details to written history, such as the findings from the rubbish dump of a nineteenth-century sauce manufacturer's factory, discovered while excavating in central London. But most of our work is concerned with human history before writing – that is, prehistory. Archaeologists are uncovering the unwritten past of African societies that flourished long before Europeans arrived. We're tracing the first peopling of the remote Pacific islands, and studying the first settlement of the Americas. In some countries like Kenya, we're writing unrecorded national histories with the spade.

Above all, archaeology defines us as human beings. It reveals our common ancestry in Africa and shows the ways in which we are different and similar. We study people everywhere, in all their fascinating diversity. Archaeology is people.

The development of archaeology is one of the great triumphs of nineteenth- and twentieth-century research. When our story begins, everyone assumed that humans had been on earth for a mere 6,000 years. Now the timescale is 3 million years and counting. But for all the serious scholarship, we still marvel at astounding, and often unexpected, archaeological discoveries that bring the past alive. The terracotta regiment of Chinese emperor Shihuangdi, found during the digging of a well (Chapter 31); a 3,000-year-old village in eastern England destroyed so rapidly by fire that an uneaten meal survives in a pot (Chapter 40); or finding out that 2 million years ago some humans were left-handed. These are the discoveries that make our blood quicken – and we make new finds every day.

And so, the actors are on the stage and the curtain is about to rise. Let the historical play begin!

CHAPTER 2

Donkeys and Pharaohs

People forget that 200 years ago Egypt was a remote land about which little was known. Today, the pharaohs and their tombs and pyramids are familiar to everyone. In 1798, when French General Napoléon Bonaparte arrived at the Nile, it was almost like visiting another planet. Egypt was far off the beaten track. It was a province of the Ottoman (Turkish) Empire that was based in Constantinople (now Istanbul); it was an Islamic country and hard to reach.

A few European visitors wandered through Cairo's bustling markets or visited the nearby Pyramids of Giza. A handful of French travellers journeyed far up the Nile River. (I actually own a remarkably accurate map of Egypt drawn by Robert de Vaugondy, France's royal geographer, in 1753.) Some visitors purchased powdered ancient Egyptian mummy – prized as a powerful medicine, even by the King of France. A few ancient Egyptian sculptures reached Europe, where they caused considerable excitement.

No one knew anything about ancient Egypt and its spectacular monuments, although it had long been recognised as a centre of early civilisation. A few diplomats realised that there was money to be made from its exotic artworks, but the remoteness of the country was against them – until Egypt moved centre stage in the 1790s. The Isthmus of Suez (the Suez Canal was not built until 1869) was a natural gateway for those with an eye on British possessions in India. In 1797, the twenty-nine-year-old Napoléon Bonaparte defeated Italy, whereupon he developed a taste for classical art. His restless mind was filled with visions of military conquest, and he had a deep curiosity about the land of the pharaohs. On 1 July 1798, his army of 38,000 men reached Egypt in 328 ships. Among them were 167 scientists charged with mapping and studying Egypt, both ancient and modern.

Napoléon had a passion for science, and especially for archaeology. His scientists were talented young men – agricultural experts, artists, botanists (plant experts) and engineers. But none were archaeologists, for Egyptology, the study of ancient Egyptian civilisation, did not exist. Napoléon's soldiers called the scientists 'donkeys' – because, it is said, during a battle both donkeys and scientists would be placed in the middle of infantry groupings. Their leader was Baron Dominique-Vivant Denon, a diplomat and gifted artist. He was the ideal leader, and his fine drawings, excellent writing and infectious enthusiasm put ancient Egypt on the scientific map.

Napoléon himself was preoccupied with reorganising Egypt, but he took time to visit the pyramids and the Sphinx, the statue of a mythical creature with the head of a human and the body of a lion. His interest in science was genuine, marked by his founding of the Institut de l'Egypte in Cairo. Here, Napoléon attended lectures and seminars and kept track of his 'donkeys'. He was fascinated when, in June 1799, French soldiers building defences near Rosetta in Egypt's Nile Delta found a mysterious stone in a pile of boulders. It was covered in three different types of writing. One was formal ancient Egyptian script; the second a freehand version of the same writing; and the third was Greek. This stone would prove to be the key to unlocking the strange code that the French had seen covering the temples and tombs along the Nile.

The soldiers sent what became known as the Rosetta Stone to scientists in Cairo, who soon translated the Greek text. The stone bore an order issued by Pharaoh Ptolemy V in 196 BC. The order was nothing exciting, but the experts realised at once that the Greek lines could potentially be the key to unlocking the unintelligible hieroglyphs (a word that comes from the Greek, meaning 'sacred symbol') that were used by the ancient Egyptians. It would be twenty-three years before the code was cracked (see Chapter 3).

Meanwhile, the scientists travelled throughout the country in small groups. They accompanied the army, sometimes fighting alongside the infantry. Denon and his colleagues sketched under fire. At the temple of the cow goddess Hathor at Dendera in Upper Egypt, Denon wandered among the columns, ignoring the sunset and darkness falling, until his commanding officer led him back to the army. Denon's enthusiasm was infectious. His engineer colleagues would abandon their work to sketch temples and tombs and loot small objects. When pencils ran short, they made more from melted-down lead bullets.

The architecture was exotic and totally unlike Greek or Roman temples. Even the humblest private was overcome with wonder. And when the army sighted the temples of the sun god Amun at Karnak and Luxor in Upper Egypt, the soldiers formed ranks and saluted as their bands played in tribute to the ancient Egyptians.

Napoléon may have been a military genius, but his Egyptian campaign ended in defeat when British naval commander Admiral Horatio Nelson destroyed the French fleet at Abukir Bay, near Alexandria, on 1 August 1798. Napoléon fled to France.

When the French army surrendered in 1801, the scientists were given safe passage back home. The British allowed them to keep most of their Egyptian finds, but ensured that the Rosetta Stone went to the British Museum.

Though militarily a failure, the Egyptian expedition was a scientific triumph. The general's 'donkeys' examined the passageways of the Pyramids of Giza and measured the Sphinx. Aside from sketching the Nile, they also drew the interiors of the great Egyptian temples at Karnak, Luxor and Philae, far upstream. The drawings of the great columns with their hieroglyphs and of temple walls with gods and pharaohs were remarkably accurate for the day. Their twenty-part

Description de l'Egypte depicted scarabs (a sacred beetle) and jewellery, statues, elegant jars and gold ornaments. Delicate lines and skilfully used colour brought exotic Egyptian art and architecture to life. The volumes caused a sensation. When people saw the riches of ancient Egypt, there for the taking, they went wild for them.

The excitement unleashed a frenzied scramble for Egyptian antiquities in a Europe hungry for anything exotic. Inevitably, a steady stream of collectors, diplomats and shady characters descended on the Nile in search of valuable discoveries. No one was seeking knowledge – just spectacular finds that could be sold at top price. Serious research, such as that undertaken by Napoléon's scientists, took a back seat to treasure hunting.

Egypt remained part of the Ottoman Empire and was ruled by Muhammad Ali, an Albanian soldier in Turkish service. He did much to open his domains to merchants and diplomats – and also to tourists and dealers in antiquities. There was big money to be made from well-preserved mummies and fine art objects – so much so that governments got into the collecting business. Both Henry Salt and Bernardino Drovetti, the top British and French diplomats in Cairo, were urged to collect spectacular objects for museums at home. They did so eagerly – which is how a circus strongman-turned-tomb robber came to be one of the founders of Egyptology.

Giovanni Battista Belzoni (1778–1823) was born in Padua, Italy, the son of a barber. He made a living as an acrobat, performing across Europe. In 1803, he arrived in England, where he acquired a contract as a strongman at Sadler's Wells theatre (then a lowbrow music hall). Belzoni was a handsome, imposing figure. Standing nearly 2 metres tall, he was a man of remarkable strength. He became the 'Patagonian Samson', a brightly dressed weightlifter, who strode across the stage carrying twelve performers on a massive iron frame.

During his years as a performer, Belzoni acquired practical experience of weightlifting, the use of levers and rollers, and 'hydraulics' – stage acts involving water. All these were useful skills for a tomb robber. A restless traveller, Belzoni and his wife Sarah arrived in Egypt in 1815. British diplomat Henry Salt recruited him to recover a massive statue of Rameses II from the pharaoh's temple on the west bank of the Nile, opposite Luxor. This well-known figure had defied the best efforts of Napoléon's soldiers to move it to the river. Belzoni assembled eighty workers and built a crude wooden wagon, which moved on four wooden rollers. He used poles as levers and employed the weight of dozens of men to raise the heavy statue, then to move the wagon and rollers beneath it. Five days later, the pharaoh was on the river bank. He floated the statue downstream and returned to Luxor. Today, you can see the Rameses statue in the British Museum.

Whenever local officials gave him trouble, Belzoni's height and strength proved to be powerful weapons (he was also prepared to use firearms if need be). His determination and ruthlessness, combined with his expertise at bargaining, served him well, and he acquired a dazzling haul of antiquities.

Now Belzoni targeted the cemeteries located on the west bank, where he befriended the tomb robbers of Qurna. They took him deep into the narrow passages in the cliffs where hundreds of bandaged mummies were to be found. Mummy dust, he noted, was 'rather unpleasant to swallow'. The people lived in the tombs, ignoring piles of mummified hands, feet and even skulls. They used mummy cases, and the bone and rags of the bandaged dead, as firewood on which to cook meals.

Belzoni's French rival, Bernardino Drovetti, responded to his success by claiming digging rights everywhere near Luxor. He caused so much trouble that Belzoni preferred to sail away to tackle the Abu Simbel temple far upstream. Despite having to deal with rebellious workers and dodge sand cascading down the cliffs, with the help of two British naval officer travellers Belzoni succeeded in opening the doorway. He found himself in a pillared hall with eight figures of Rameses II, but few small artefacts to take away.

Back at Luxor, he found Drovetti's men digging at Qurna. Their leader threatened to cut his throat, so Belzoni moved on to the Valley of the Kings, burial place of Egypt's greatest pharaohs. The valley had been explored since Roman times, but Belzoni had brilliant archaeological instincts. He located three tombs almost immediately. Shortly afterwards, he made his most astonishing discovery: the sepulchre (tomb) of Pharaoh Seti I, father of Rameses II and one of Egypt's most important rulers, who reigned from 1290 to 1279 BC. Magnificent paintings adorned the walls. In the burial chamber lay the king's translucent, but empty, alabaster (soft rock) sarcophagus, in the shape of his body. Unfortunately, the tomb had been robbed soon after the pharaoh's death.

Belzoni was on a roll. He had opened four royal tombs, and, ever restless, back in Cairo he succeeded in penetrating the interior of the huge pyramid of Khafre at Giza, the first person to do so since medieval times. He painted his name in soot on the wall of the burial chamber, where it remains visible today. Ever the showman, he decided to make an exact copy of Seti's tomb to be exhibited in London. He and an artist lived in the tomb for a summer. They copied the paintings and numerous hieroglyphs, and made hundreds of wax impressions of figures. By this time, Drovetti was so jealous that his men threatened Belzoni with firearms. Fearing for his life, the showman left Egypt forever.

Back in London, he put on a wildly successful exhibition of the tomb and his finds in the aptly named Egyptian Hall, close to today's Piccadilly Circus, and wrote a bestselling book about his adventures. Inevitably, the number of visitors fell and the exhibition closed. But the former strongman still craved fame and fortune. In 1823, he went on an expedition to find the source of the Niger River in West Africa, only to die of fever in Benin.

Giovanni Belzoni was a larger-than-life character who ultimately was a showman and tomb robber. One could describe him as a ruthless treasure hunter, but he was more than that. He certainly began as a booty-seeker, out for fame and fortune; but was he an archaeologist? There is no question that he had superb instincts for discovery. Today, he might well have been a successful archaeologist. But in his day, no one could read hieroglyphs, or had any clue how to excavate and record the past. Like others at the time, Belzoni measured success by the value of his finds. Nevertheless, the flamboyant Italian did lay some of the rough-and-ready foundations of Egyptology.

CHAPTER 3

Reading Ancient Egypt

'I've got it!' a panting Jean-François Champollion cried out as
he fainted at his brother's feet. Champollion had discovered the
complex grammar of ancient Egyptian hieroglyphs and had solved
a centuries-old mystery.

Napoléon's scientists, Giovanni Belzoni and many others had
studied the inscriptions on the Rosetta Stone without success. The
ancient Egyptians and their pharaohs were anonymous, people
without history. Who were the kings depicted in temple inscriptions? Who were the gods and goddesses receiving their offerings?
Who were the important people buried in richly decorated tombs
close to the Pyramids of Giza? Belzoni and his contemporaries
operated in an archaeological fog.

At first, the experts wrongly assumed that the glyphs were
picture symbols. Then in the 1790s, a Danish scholar called Jørgen
Zoëga came up with the theory that the scripts represented not
objects, but sounds: that they were a way of turning human speech
into writing – a phonetic script. The discovery in 1799 of the

Rosetta Stone, with its two hieroglyphic texts, was a major step forward. One text was in a formal writing system that no one could unlock. But the other was a simplified script used by ordinary people. This was clearly an alphabetic version of hieroglyphs, and is now known to have been widely used by scribes.

The Rosetta Stone was the first breakthrough. A second was the work of Thomas Young, an English doctor and expert in languages and mathematics. His knowledge of ancient Greek allowed him to read one inscription. This enabled him to go on to identify the pharaoh Ptolemy V's name within six cartouches (a group of hieroglyphs within an oval, representing the name of a monarch) in the Rosetta inscriptions. He then matched the hieroglyphs to the letters of the Greek spelling of the pharaoh's name. Unfortunately, though, Young assumed that most hieroglyphs were non-phonetic, and so his efforts to read them ultimately failed.

Young's great rival was Jean-François Champollion (1790–1832), a linguistic genius with a volcanic personality. The son of an impoverished bookseller, Champollion didn't begin formal education until he was eight years old. But he soon displayed a remarkable talent for drawing and languages. By the age of seventeen he had mastered Arabic, Hebrew and Sanskrit, as well as English, German and Italian. The young Champollion was obsessed with hieroglyphs. He also learned Coptic, believing that the language of Christian Egypt might have retained some ancient Egyptian elements.

In 1807, Champollion and his brother Jacques-Joseph moved to Paris, where they lived in poverty. The young linguist turned his attention to the Rosetta Stone. He studied it for months and pored over numerous Egyptian papyri (documents written on papyrus-reed stems). The research was frustrating and full of dead ends. Unlike Young, Champollion became convinced that Egyptian script was phonetic. He widened his study to include both Egyptian and Greek papyri, as well as an obelisk from Upper Egypt with cartouches of Queen Cleopatra.

In 1822, he received accurate copies of the hieroglyphs at Abu Simbel, which allowed him to identify the cartouches representing Rameses II, and then another pharaoh, Thutmose III. He realised that hieroglyphic writing did not include vowels: there were twenty-four symbols that represented single consonants (much like letters in English) and that functioned like an alphabet. The script was usually, but not always, written from right to left. No blanks or punctuation marks separated words. By the time Champollion rushed into his brother's room, he had deciphered a script that he called 'at times figurative, symbolic and phonetic'.

On 27 September 1822, Champollion presented his findings to the French Academy of Inscriptions and Literature. The discovery was considered so important that the King of France was informed. However, years were to pass before Champollion's work was universally accepted. In 1824, he published a summary of hieroglyphs that was savaged by his critics. It seems likely that his argumentative personality and inability to tolerate criticism added to his difficulties.

Champollion became curator of the Egyptian section at the Louvre, where his knowledge of hieroglyphs allowed him to arrange the collections in their correct time order. This was a major advance.

But the man who had unlocked the formal script of ancient Egypt had never visited the Nile. In 1828, influential supporters persuaded the king to back a joint French and Tuscan expedition under Champollion's leadership. Thirty years after Napoléon's experts sailed for Alexandria, Jean-François Champollion, Egyptologist Ippolito Rosellini and a team of artists, draughtsmen and architects – all wearing Turkish clothing, which was more comfortable in the heat – embarked on a journey up the river.

The expedition was a triumph. For the first time, the master and his companions could read the inscriptions on temple walls and understand the significance of some of the oldest monuments in the world. At the goddess Hathor's temple at Dendera, excited members of the expedition jumped ashore one bright moonlit night. For two glorious hours, they wandered through the ruins, only returning to their boats at three o'clock in the morning.

After brief stays at Luxor, Karnak and in the Valley of the Kings, the expedition rode the summer flood down to Cairo in triumph.

Champollion was the first scholar to identify tomb owners and to translate the inscriptions on temple walls of pharaohs making offerings to gods. Exhausted, he returned to Paris in January 1830. He would die of a stroke two years later at the age of just forty-two, but the controversy surrounding hieroglyphs continued long after his death. And fifteen years would pass before everyone agreed that his translations had been correct.

A flock of less scrupulous visitors descended on the Nile. The success of Belzoni and Drovetti encouraged other treasure hunters to seek fame and fortune there. Ancient Egypt rapidly became a money-making enterprise. Champollion was disgusted at the destruction: people were openly robbing tombs for their treasures, digging up statues and hammering art off temple walls, all with a view simply to make a profit.

He wrote to Muhammad Ali to complain about the antiquities trade and the damage being done. Champollion's letter was the trigger for Ali to pass a law that forbade the export of antiquities, to authorise the construction of a museum, and to make it illegal to destroy monuments. Without officials in place, the law meant nothing. But it was a move in the right direction, even if Ali and his successors did give or sell most of the museum exhibits to prominent foreigners. Fortunately, a few visitors now started to come to the Nile in search of information rather than artefacts.

Champollion's dramatic claims to have deciphered the hieroglyphs encouraged a move towards research rather than collecting. At last there was a way of learning the secrets of ancient Egyptian civilisation. Influential scholars like the classical archaeologist and traveller Sir William Gell encouraged promising young men. One was John Gardner Wilkinson (1797–1875), whose parents had died when he was young and left him modest private funds. While awaiting an officer's commission in the army, he went on a tour to Mediterranean lands. In Rome, he met Sir William Gell, who probably knew more than anyone about ancient Egypt at the time. Young Wilkinson arrived in Alexandria in late 1821, armed with a little Arabic and boundless enthusiasm. This was shortly before Champollion deciphered Egyptian script. But Wilkinson knew enough of Thomas Young's approach to hieroglyphs and of Egyptian artefacts to be better prepared than anyone before him. He travelled upstream and threw himself into Egyptology.

Here was a different kind of archaeologist. While Belzoni and his kind were excavators, digging for art and artefacts, Wilkinson took a much broader view of Egyptology. In this, he was far ahead of his time. He realised that the civilisation and people of ancient Egypt could only be understood by combining archaeological finds and inscriptions.

Wilkinson had no interest in acquiring artefacts. He was a copyist of inscriptions, monuments and tombs – a true student of the past. Though done freehand, his work was remarkably accurate by modern standards – especially his drawings of hieroglyphs, which were better than those of Napoléon's experts.

For the next twelve years, Wilkinson travelled widely throughout the Nile Valley and into the desert. Sometimes he was alone or just with his friend James Burton. At other times a small number of like-minded archaeologists and artists would join him. To ensure their safety in this remote land, they adopted Turkish ways and passed themselves off as Muslims, even to their servants.

Wilkinson worked at first without any knowledge of the glyphs. But in 1823, Gell sent him a copy of Champollion's summary. This made him realise just how much progress the young Frenchman had made. But as he got better at comparing Coptic and ancient Egyptian words, Wilkinson came to realise that Champollion was careless. He had made 'terrible mistakes' with inscriptions that he deciphered.

Wilkinson never met Champollion, but he disliked the way the Frenchman sought fame while tolerating no criticism of his work. He was secretive, quarrelled violently with other scholars and made false claims about his research. Wilkinson, by contrast, preferred to stay in the background, quietly sketching, recording and working on the dating of temples and tombs.

Once he had acquired a working knowledge of hieroglyphs, the ever-curious Wilkinson moved on to other research. From 1827, he spent most of his time on the west bank of the Nile, at Luxor. There he occupied the tomb of a high official named 'Amechu (fifteenth century BC), living in considerable style and enjoying magnificent views across the Nile Valley. He put down carpets, erected partitions to create rooms and installed his personal library. He would entertain his friends, burning wooden mummy cases in the hearth to keep warm, as everyone did – not the done thing today!

Wilkinson was not a morning person – he would breakfast at half past ten. But he accomplished an astonishing amount, including creating the first maps of the west bank cemeteries. He numbered the tombs in the Valley of the Kings, and his system is still used today. He concentrated on the tombs of nobles, realising that they provided rich insights into Egyptian life. The monuments offered a chance to travel back in time and to live, as it were, among the people – as though you were a spectator watching the events unfolding on the walls.

I love exploring Egyptian tomb paintings, even if they are often very faded today. You can witness life on the nobles' estates – labourers gathering in the harvest under the watchful eye of a scribe, cattle being butchered, and brightly clothed guests gathering for a feast. There is even a charming painting of a nobleman fishing, accompanied by his cats.

Wilkinson was one of a small group of scholars who placed Egyptology on a firm footing during the 1820s and 1830s. They were serious researchers with a passion for their work and for the knowledge that came from it. They worked both together and independently. Wilkinson himself left Egypt in 1833 with an idea for a book about the lives of the ancient Egyptians. *Manners and Customs of the Ancient Egyptians* appeared in 1837 and sold well, its reasonable price bringing it within reach of the middle class.

The book took readers on a journey in time through ancient Egypt, providing a wealth of information. Its people were brought alive thanks to details acquired from paintings, papyri and inscriptions. Wilkinson had the rare gift of being able to communicate important, original research to a wide audience. He became a household name and was knighted by Queen Victoria.

Champollion and Wilkinson were a new breed of scholar. They painted a vivid portrait of a colourful, vigorous civilisation. And both realised that archaeology alone could not reconstruct ancient civilisations. Any serious research depended on teamwork between excavators and the people who worked on inscriptions and written records.

Wilkinson's brilliant popular account of the Egyptians placed the serious study of the world's earliest civilisations centre stage. Wholesale destruction along the Nile slowly gave way to more disciplined research.

Six decades were to pass before new copyists came to the Nile. But thanks to Champollion and Wilkinson, they were professionals.

CHAPTER 4

Digging into Nineveh

Babylon and Nineveh: these great biblical cities were the stuff of romance. The Old Testament told of King Nebuchadnezzar (who reigned from about 604 to 562 BC), the greatest king of ancient Babylon (in today's southern Iraq). He was a ruthless conqueror, famous for holding Jews captive in his capital. The proceeds from his mighty empire created a magnificent capital. According to later Greek accounts, thousands of slaves erected city walls so thick that chariots could race along the top.

Nebuchadnezzar allegedly created fabulous hanging gardens for his terraced palace which became one of the Seven Wonders of the Ancient World. Whether they ever existed is an open question. His capital vanished when Assyrian civilisation collapsed. The few European travellers who reached Babylon found themselves in an arid wilderness of dusty mounds. Centuries passed before German archaeologists could reconstruct parts of it (see Chapter 20).

Nineveh lay far upstream in what is now northern Iraq. In 612 BC, it was a major Assyrian city, mentioned in the Book of Genesis in the Bible. According to the prophet Isaiah, God doomed the arrogant Ninevites. He made Nineveh 'a desolation, and dry like a wilderness'. No buildings or temples remained to be seen above the ground. Later European visitors remarked that God's wrath had indeed destroyed the Assyrians.

Babylon and Nineveh passed into the historical shadows, known only from the Bible. There they remained until amazing archaeological finds confirmed biblical history. In 1841, a group of influential scholars in the French Asiatic Society seized on Nineveh as another opportunity for dramatic excavations that would reflect well on France. In 1842, the government appointed Paul-Émile Botta (1802–70) as its consul (representative) in Mosul. Botta had been a diplomat in Egypt, and it was his fluent Arabic that led to this new appointment. His unofficial task was to excavate Nineveh, even though he had no relevant experience.

Botta's unsophisticated diggings were largely fruitless, since he was penetrating only the sterile upper layers of Nineveh's Kuyunjik mound (that is, layers with no bones or tools). City mounds like Nineveh's were formed gradually, layer by layer – the earliest, often most important, levels were at the bottom. But Botta knew nothing of such sites. He dug around near the surface and found some inscribed bricks and alabaster fragments, but nothing spectacular.

Then, after months of labour, his luck changed. A villager from Khorsabad, some 22 kilometres north of Kuyunjik, showed Botta some inscribed bricks. He told stories of numerous finds around his house, in an ancient mound. The consul sent two men to investigate. A week later, one of them returned in great excitement. A little digging had revealed walls carved with images of exotic animals.

Botta rode to Khorsabad at once. He was astounded by the elaborate carvings exposed in the walls of the small pit that had been dug. Unfamiliar bearded men wearing long gowns walked alongside winged animals and other beasts. Botta quickly moved his workers to Khorsabad. Within a few days, the excavators uncovered a series of sculpted limestone slabs from the palace of an ancient and unknown king.

Botta wrote to Paris in triumph, claiming to have revealed a biblical truth. 'Nineveh is rediscovered,' he proudly reported. The

French government gave a grant of 3,000 francs for further excavations. Botta employed more than 300 workers, knowing that he had to dig on a large scale to make important finds. He started a tradition of enormous excavations in Mesopotamia (from the Greek, meaning 'the land between the rivers') that continued well into the twentieth century.

Wisely, the French also sent out Eugène Napoléon Flandin, an experienced archaeological artist from Paris. The two men laboured on the mounds until late October 1844. They unearthed the outline of an enclosed palace compound that covered over 2.5 square kilometres. The workmen merely followed the walls of the palace wherever they could. They uncovered scenes of a king at war, besieging cities, hunting game and engaging in elaborate religious ceremonies. Human-headed lions and bulls guarded the palace gates. Never had an excavation yielded such treasures.

Flandin arrived in Paris in November 1844 with drawings that filled French scholars with joy. This was an entirely new art tradition, quite unlike that of Greece, the Nile or Rome. Botta also returned to Paris. He completed a report on the excavations, accompanied by four volumes of Flandin's drawings, and this caused a sensation. Botta claimed, wrongly, that he had rediscovered Nineveh at Khorsabad. You can't blame him. Like Belzoni in Egypt, he was unable to read the palace inscriptions. We now know that he had excavated Dur-Sharrukin, the palace of Assyrian King Sargon II (722–705 BC), an aggressive, successful conqueror. Years were to pass before so-called 'cuneiform' (from the Latin for 'wedge', because of its shape) inscriptions identified his capital (see Chapter 5). In that time, Botta retreated from view, being assigned to an obscure post in Lebanon, and never returning to archaeology.

But just as Botta was starting work at Nineveh in 1842, a young Englishman by the name of Austen Henry Layard (1817–94) was becoming fascinated by archaeology in Mesopotamia. He had spent two weeks at Nineveh in 1840, studying the site. Blessed with insatiable curiosity and outstanding powers of observation, he became determined to excavate ancient city mounds. Archaeology became his passion.

Like many great archaeologists, Layard was always restless. He went off to spend a year among the Bakhtiari nomads in the mountains of Persia (now Iran), becoming a trusted adviser to the tribe. He knew so much about local politics that the British envoy in Baghdad sent him to Constantinople to advise the ambassador there. At this point, in 1842, he spent three days in Mosul with Botta, who encouraged him to dig. Layard, however, was penniless.

He spent three years as an unofficial intelligence officer in Constantinople. Then the British ambassador, Sir Stratford Canning, reluctantly allowed him two months to excavate at Nimrud, a series of mounds downstream from Mosul. Layard gambled that he would get to the heart of the city from the bottom, and so he tunnelled into the mounds. Almost immediately, the workers uncovered a large chamber lined with cuneiform-inscribed slabs. We now know that this was the North Palace of Assyrian King Ashurnasirpal (883–859 BC). That same day, Layard moved men to the south and unearthed the Southwest Palace, built by King Esarhaddon (681–669 BC). Layard remains the only archaeologist ever to have found two palaces within twenty-four hours.

His excavations simply followed the decorated walls of the palace rooms. Layard found stockpiled carvings from an earlier palace, including scenes of a battle and of a siege. These finds soon overshadowed those at Khorsabad.

Layard worked with one objective in mind: to discover breathtaking artworks and artefacts that could be shipped to London. He knew that exotic finds sent to the British Museum would place him firmly in the public eye. By no stretch of the imagination could his work be described as careful recording.

Layard and his Assyrian assistant Hormuzd Rassam set up camp atop the Nimrud mound, which gave them a superb view of the surrounding plains. Layard was constantly on his guard against sudden raids from neighbouring tribesmen in search of treasure. He lavished the local chiefs with gifts to buy their loyalty, but did not hesitate to use violence if needed. Eventually, he became a kind of chief himself, settling disputes and arranging marriages.

Extraordinary discoveries followed, including three winged-bull sculptures which guarded the palace. Layard threw a three-day party for his workers to celebrate these finds. In the North Palace, his men unearthed a magnificent carved pillar depicting a king receiving tribute. It recorded the military triumphs of King Shalmaneser III (859–824 BC), who fought constantly with neighbouring states, including the Hittites (see Chapter 20). Layard built a large wagon and hauled the heavy finds to the Tigris. The artefacts were floated downstream to Basra on rafts supported by inflated goatskins, identical to those shown on Assyrian reliefs. Next, Layard dug into the Kuyunjik mound at Nineveh, where tunnels soon exposed nine chambers adorned with bas reliefs (sculptures where the figures barely stand out from the surface).

The first load of Nimrud sculptures reached the British Museum on 22 June 1847, and when Layard arrived in England he found himself the hero of the hour. In 1849, he published *Nineveh and Its Remains* – 'a slight sketch' of his work that became a bestseller.

Excavations at Kuyunjik resumed in 1849. Layard dug a labyrinth of tunnels which followed decorated palace walls, and ignored the precious room contents. Again, he spent days underground sketching the carvings as they appeared, by the light of ventilation shafts and candles. Dimly lit tunnels led to great lion figures that guarded palace gates. The limestone slabs of the entrances still bore the ruts of Assyrian chariot wheels. Layard's workers exposed the entire southeast façade of the palace of King Sennacherib (705–681 BC), who campaigned in Mesopotamia, Syria, Israel and Judea.

The palace inscriptions offered a chronicle of conquests, sieges and royal achievements. Lifelike monarchs and gods appeared in relief, as if they were stepping forward to question the intruding visitors. Many Kuyunjik reliefs are now on display in the British Museum, and I always make a point of visiting them. The carving is stunning. A set of reliefs shows nearly 300 labourers dragging a great human-headed bull from a river raft to the palace. A man seated astride the bull directs the work. Meanwhile, the king supervises from his chariot, shaded by a parasol.

Layard's most sensational discovery came when he uncovered the siege and capture of an unknown city – unknown, that is, until the accompanying cuneiform inscriptions were deciphered in the 1850s (see Chapter 5). Reliefs were his primary concern: small finds, unless valuable, were of little interest.

The excavations yielded the occasional clay tablet with a cuneiform inscription, but many of these fell to dust, being unfired and fragile. Then Layard struck gold, although it was some time before he realised it. Towards the end of the dig, he shovelled hundreds of inscribed clay tablets into six crates. These had formed part of the royal library and turned out to be one of his most important discoveries. After the 1850 excavations, he shipped more than a hundred crates down the River Tigris.

After an unsuccessful excavation attempt at Babylon and another early southern city (which failed because his methods were too crude to handle the unfired brick), Layard returned home.

The British Museum has many sketches in Layard's hand – the only record of the finds that he could not ship. He had the great archaeologist's instinct for the important rather than the trivial; and, like Giovanni Belzoni, he had a nose for discovery that led him to royal palaces and spectacular finds. But his methods were appallingly crude, and much was lost. Half a century was to pass before German scholars turned archaeological excavation in Greece and Mesopotamia into a scientific discipline (see Chapter 20).

Layard is hard to figure out. By any standards, he was a hurried, ruthless excavator in search of exciting discoveries and treasure. He dug entire cities with only one or two European assistants and hundreds of local workers. Ultimately, all he cared about was fame and dazzling Assyrian finds for the British Museum. He did excel, however, at dealing with local people, many of whom became firm friends – unusual among the early archaeologists.

For all his eloquent writing and fluent descriptions, Austin Henry Layard was ultimately an adventurer as much as an archaeologist. But he did bring the biblical Assyrians into the spotlight and showed that much of the Old Testament was based on historical events. The deciphering of cuneiform script soon made his finds even more important (see Chapter 5). Exhausted after his demanding excavations and fed up with the constant struggle to obtain funds, Layard gave up archaeology at the age of thirty-six. Instead, he changed gears and became a politician, then a diplomat – a job that drew on his expertise at dealing with people from other cultures. Eventually, he was to become the British ambassador in Constantinople, at the time one of the most important diplomatic posts in Europe. Not bad for an adventurer archaeologist.

CHAPTER 5

Tablets and Tunnelling

Even during the 1840s, archaeology was more than just digging for lost civilisations. Layard made brilliant discoveries at Nimrud and Nineveh, but he was working with one hand tied behind his back: he couldn't read the cuneiform inscriptions that accompanied the magnificent carvings on Assyrian palace walls. Who were these powerful monarchs who went to war, besieged cities and erected human-headed lions in front of their palace gates? The young excavator was aware of the problem, but was no expert in ancient languages. He needed someone who could read the wall inscriptions and tiny writing on the clay tablets that came from his trenches. In his first book, *Nineveh and Its Remains*, he had assumed that Nimrud was ancient Nineveh. But that was sheer guesswork, and he was about to be proved wrong.

Investigation of the Kuyunjik mound and Nimrud was very much on his mind – and on that of Henry Rawlinson, a British diplomat in Baghdad. Henry Creswicke Rawlinson (1810–95) was a brilliant horseman, a crack shot and a skilled linguist. He joined the Indian Army at the age of seventeen as an officer in the Bombay Grenadiers. Rawlinson worked hard to learn Hindi, Persian and other languages.

In 1833, he joined a military mission based in the Kurdish town of Kermanshah. He found time to ride out to the Great Rock of Behistun. King Darius the Great of Persia (550–486 BC) had commissioned a huge carved relief that covered 111 square metres of smoothed and polished Behistun rock face. A huge Darius stands in triumph over Gaumata, a rival for his throne in 522 BC, 90 metres above the ground. Three inscriptions in Old Persian, Elamite (a language once spoken in modern southeastern Iran) and Babylonian announce his triumph.

Like others before him, Rawlinson realised that this virtually inaccessible inscription on a limestone cliff was the Rosetta Stone of Mesopotamia. The Old Persian script, which was alphabetical, had been deciphered in 1802. He scaled the cliff and copied it. But the Babylonian and Elamite texts lay across a deep chasm. Rawlinson threw together makeshift scaffolding and risked his life perched high above the ground to make copies of the Elamite text.

Rawlinson's military duties were demanding, leaving him little time for the texts, and so his research slowed until he got his diplomatic job in Baghdad in 1843. His new post allowed him to spend time on cuneiform and on making further accurate Behistun copies. He got in touch with others puzzling over cuneiform, notably Edward Hincks, a country priest in Ireland, and Jules Oppert, a French-German linguist. The three of them were the eventual architects of decipherment.

The breakthrough came in 1847, when Rawlinson made a third trip to Behistun to copy the inaccessible Babylonian inscription. A young Kurd, nimble as a mountain goat, hung ropes from pegs and clawed his way across the face. Eventually the boy rigged up a simple cradle seat for himself. He then pressed wet paper into the carved writing. The paper dried into moulds that could be used to duplicate the symbols. With the entire inscription, Rawlinson could now use the Persian translation to decipher the Babylonian text.

Rawlinson's research now extended to the inscriptions found by Layard at Kuyunjik and Nineveh. As he pored over the reliefs on the walls of King Sennacherib's palace at Kuyunjik, he identified the siege and capture of a city. A huge Assyrian army is encamped before the city walls. Soldiers fight their way through the fortifications. Despite ferocious resistance, the city falls. King Sennacherib sits in judgment on the defeated citizens, who become slaves. Rawlinson could read the accompanying inscription: 'Sennacherib, the mighty king, King of Assyria, sat on the throne while the booty of Lachish passed before him.' This was sensational – the siege of Lachish in 700 BC is described in the Bible's Second Book of Kings.

Londoners flocked to view the carvings when they arrived in the British Museum. They are still on display there, and are well worth a visit. All these discoveries raised public interest in archaeology to fever pitch at a time when biblical teaching was prominent in schools.

Rawlinson encouraged others to dig in southern Mesopotamia, including J.E. Taylor, a diplomat at Basra in the south. Rawlinson sent him to explore possible biblical cities, including some low mounds near the town of An Nasiriyah, which were often flooded by the nearby Euphrates. Taylor found an inscribed cylinder that enabled Rawlinson to identify the place, which was known locally as Muqayyar, as the biblical city of Ur of the Chaldees, associated in Genesis with Abraham (see Chapter 20). Compared with the cities of the north, those in southern Mesopotamia yielded few spectacular finds until excavation methods improved dramatically. The unbaked mud brick was simply too fragile for the diggers to handle.

In 1852, the British Museum appointed Hormuzd Rassam (1826–1910) as director of excavations under Rawlinson's supervision. Rassam was himself an Assyrian with local connections, and he had worked as Layard's assistant (see Chapter 4). He was ambitious, ruthless, sneaky and quarrelsome. He desperately wanted to be recognised as a great archaeologist and assumed that wonderful finds were the way to success. When he resumed work at Kuyunjik, he dug into an area that had been assigned to the French, and so he worked secretly at night. His tunnelling revealed a carving of an Assyrian king hunting lions from his chariot. Ultimately the dig uncovered the whole story of a carefully managed royal lion hunt, complete with cheering spectators and a dying lioness. Like the Lachish siege, you can see the hunt up close in the British Museum.

Unfortunately, Rassam's excavations of the palace were so hasty and slapdash that only some drawings of the building survive. These were made by a skilled artist, William Boutcher. Rawlinson divided the carvings between France and King Friedrich Wilhelm IV of Prussia. The French packed 235 crates for the Louvre in Paris. Their shipment and that bound for Berlin were floated downstream on goatskin-supported rafts. South of Baghdad, marauding tribesmen attacked and plundered the rafts, tipping the crates into the Tigris and killing several of the crew. Only two crates of French discoveries at Khorsabad, upstream of Nineveh, ever reached Paris. Fortunately, the lion hunt was shipped separately and arrived safely in London.

Henry Rawlinson left Baghdad in 1855. He became active in Indian affairs and was a frequent visitor to the British Museum. The museum had already decided not to sponsor any more Assyrian excavations. So much sculpture had been found that there were almost too many Assyrian kings in London. Public interest faded during the years of the Crimean War (1853–56) between Britain, France and Russia. Only a few scholars maintained an interest in the hundreds of tablets shipped from Mesopotamia by Layard, Rassam and others, or in the collections purchased by dealers from illegal excavations.

When Rassam cleared the floor of the Kuyunjik lion chamber, he also found a huge cache of clay tablets. Considering them unimportant, he stacked them hastily in packing cases. How wrong could he have been? Three years previously, Layard had recovered part of King Ashurbanipal's royal library in two small rooms (see Chapter 4). Now Rassam had found the rest, which had landed on the floor of the great hall when the ceiling collapsed. The king's archive contained records of wars as well as administrative and religious documents. One tablet records how he ordered his officials to collect tablets throughout his kingdom. Over a century and a half later, the 180,000 tablets in Ashurbanipal's library are still being deciphered. They have yielded enough information to allow an entire dictionary of Ancient Assyrian to be compiled.

The focus of Assyrian research passed from the field to the museum and library. A small band of cuneiform scholars sifted through the tablets from King Ashurbanipal's library. They worked in a cramped study room without the aid of dictionaries or grammars. One was George Smith (1840–76), a quiet, shy engraver's apprentice who was passionately interested in cuneiform, having read Rawlinson's work at an early age.

By 1872, Smith had already sorted many tablets into categories, one of which was 'myths'. He came across half a tablet and found a reference to a ship on a mountain, and mention of a dove being sent out to find a resting place and being forced to return. Smith realised at once that he had part of the flood story contained in Genesis. The tale is familiar to everyone who has read the Bible: Noah gathered the animals into an ark, survived the rising waters, then sent out a dove and a raven to look for land. Noah and his ark saved humanity from destruction. The normally calm Smith jumped up and rushed around the room in a state of high excitement.

On 3 December 1872, George Smith addressed the Biblical Archaeological Society, an organisation of the day concerned with excavations to study the scriptures. The prime minister, William Gladstone, attended the meeting. Smith's lecture was a triumph. He translated key parts of the narrative that bore a startling resemblance to the biblical story. Smith suspected that they could be traced back to much earlier myths. The story was part of a classic of early Mesopotamian literature, *The Epic of Gilgamesh*. Gilgamesh, a king of the city of Uruk in about 2600 BC, long before the Bible, undertakes epic journeys in search of immortality, but fails to find it.

The flood tablets seemed to prove that the Bible was true. The *Daily Telegraph* newspaper offered the British Museum 1,000 guineas for a new excavation at Nineveh to find the missing gaps in the story, provided Smith led the investigation. Amazingly, in just a week of excavating at Kuyunjik in Layard's dumps Smith found the crucial missing seventeen lines about the beginning of the flood.

After only a month of digging, Smith set off home. Four months later, the British Museum sent him back to try to find more of the royal library. Smith recovered more than 3,000 tablets in three months, mainly by excavating the contents of rooms where Layard had tunnelled around the walls. At times, Smith had 600 men working on the excavations. In 1875, while returning from a third trip, he died of a stomach infection – a great loss to the British Museum.

The Kuyunjik excavations resumed under Hormuzd Rassam. His team cleared the floors of palace rooms and recovered yet more tablets. One 1,300-line inscription on a clay cylinder described Ashurbanipal's conquests. Rassam moved on to Babylon, but, like Layard, his methods were too unsophisticated to find unbaked brick palace walls.

He hurried from site to site, ending up at Abu Habbah, formerly an ancient city called Sippar, where he excavated around 170 rooms and recovered as many as 70,000 tablets. One of them described how a Babylonian king named Nabonidus became interested in archaeology and dug into the cities of his predecessors. When Rassam departed for England, dealers moved in and caused an unseemly scramble for cuneiform tablets that pitted museum against museum across Europe. The damage was incalculable.

Layard, Rassam and Rawlinson were pioneers, working in remote lands in conditions of tribal unrest. This was rough-and-tumble archaeology, without any careful forward planning; but it was archaeology that validated much of the history set down in the Old Testament and placed ancient cities firmly within recorded history. In those days, when archaeology was in its infancy, many archaeologists were as much opportunists as excavators. And yet some of them were giants in their field. It is on their broad shoulders that succeeding generations of professional archaeologists have stood.

CHAPTER 6

The Maya Revealed

Copán, Honduras, 1840. Monkeys were on the move in the tree tops. The crackling of the dry branches they broke shattered the silence of the forest and disturbed the peace of the deserted city across the river. Forty or fifty of the apes moved in procession, like the spirits of those unknown people who had once dwelt in the mysterious ruins. Overgrown pyramids towered up among the trees.

John Lloyd Stephens (1805–52), an American traveller and lawyer, and Frederick Catherwood (1799–1854), a talented English artist, were transfixed by their first glimpse of ancient Maya architecture. They pushed their way through the undergrowth and stumbled across some elaborately carved upright stones. They had never seen architecture or art like this before.

Both men were experienced adventurers. Stephens had been born in New Jersey. He entered Columbia University at the age of thirteen and graduated top of his class in 1822. His training was in law, but he preferred politics and travel.

Stephens cut his teeth on a trip out west as far as Pittsburgh and beyond. In 1834, he set off on a two-year expedition that took him across Europe as far as Poland and Russia. Then he explored the Nile Valley and Jerusalem. He also went to Petra, at the time a remote and dangerous place. The great camel-caravan city with its rock-cut temples electrified him. Petra gave Stephens a passion for ancient civilisations almost overnight.

A gifted storyteller, he started writing to his family about his travels. Some of his letters appeared in New York newspapers and were widely enjoyed. He wrote two books about his adventures, both called *Incidents of Travel*. One was about Egypt and the Holy Land, and the other was an account of Poland, Turkey and Russia. Stephens had a direct, entertaining writing style, and he was a perceptive observer of people and places. Both books became best-sellers and established him as a first-rate travel writer.

Through his fellow authors he met the artist Frederick Catherwood. London-born Catherwood had superb artistic talent, which came to the fore when he visited Italy in 1821. Like Stephens, he was a restless wanderer. Between 1822 and 1835, Catherwood travelled widely in the Middle East. In Egypt, he worked with traveller Robert Hay, who visited and studied numerous sites. He also visited Jerusalem, where he drew the virtually inaccessible decorated roof of the eleventh-century Islamic Dome of the Rock shrine. To do so, Catherwood used a camera lucida – basically a mirror that reflected the image of the roof onto his drawing board.

Back in London, Catherwood created an enormous panoramic scene of Jerusalem, which proved hugely popular. Stephens and Catherwood met for the first time at the exhibit in 1836. Later that year, Catherwood brought it to New York and set up business as an architect. By then, the two men had become friends, sharing an enthusiasm for adventure and ancient civilisations. An unsmiling man, Catherwood had an entirely different personality from Stephens.

Constantly searching for new opportunities, the artist drew his friend's attention to two little-known publications that described mysterious ruins in the forests of Central America. They agreed that they would look for them one day. Fortunately, both Catherwood's architecture and the exhibit made good money, as did Stephens' books, and so they were able to travel. To smooth their passage, Stephens managed to land a job as an American diplomat in Central America. On 3 October 1839, the two friends left New York for a small, isolated coastal town named Belize, now in the country of the same name. From there, they would travel inland to ruins at a place called Copán.

The overland journey through the forested Yucatán Peninsula was tough. The political situation was chaotic. Their mules sank into the mud on the narrow trail. Eventually they reached the village of Copán, with its half-dozen rundown huts. The next day, a guide led them through fields and dense forest to a river bank. On the opposite side, they spotted a wall of the Maya city.

Stephens and Catherwood arrived not knowing what to expect. They crossed the river on horseback and found themselves in a complex of terraces and pyramids. Unexpectedly they came across a square stone column sculpted in high relief with the figure of a man and elaborate hieroglyphs. It was instantly clear to them that the architecture and art styles at Copán were different from anything in the Mediterranean world. The builders had erected pyramids (now overgrown), separated by courts and plazas. Elaborate hieroglyphs carved into stucco (fine plaster) covered the buildings, and there was a series of richly decorated, individual columns (known technically as 'stelae'). Copán's stelae – which depicted portraits of rulers – lined processional ways in the central plaza. They were also to be found near a large royal complex of overlapping, stepped pyramids, plazas and palaces that formed the main core of the city. The tallest pyramid, now known as Temple 16, once stood more than 30 metres high.

Stephens was moved to eloquence about the brooding forest and the plazas, as perfect as any Roman amphitheatre. 'The city was desolate,' he wrote. 'All was mystery, dark impenetrable mystery.' Who had built these amazing monuments, he wondered? The hieroglyphs were quite unlike those of the Egyptians, and the local Indians had no idea who had constructed Copán. Stephens compared it to a shipwreck: 'It lay before us like a shattered bark.' With a compass and a tape measure, they mapped the ancient city by cutting straight lines through the forest. This was the first plan of any Maya site. Unlike Layard in Mesopotamia, they did no digging, but instead relied on measurements and careful observations to tell Copán's story.

Catherwood settled down to draw the elaborately decorated stelae and reliefs – a complex task that tested his artistic ability. Meanwhile, Stephens pondered who had built Copán. He realised at once that it was not the work of ancient Egyptians, or of some other civilisation that had sailed across the Atlantic many centuries earlier. This was an exotic, unique city. If they could transport even a small portion of the ruins to New York, it would make a wonderful exhibit. After much bargaining, Stephens bought Copán from the local owner for $50. Fortunately for future archaeologists, the river would not support barges, and so he could not actually move anything.

Stephens spent only thirteen days at Copán, but Catherwood stayed much longer. He worked in heavy rain, with mud up to his ankles, plagued by mosquitoes. The reliefs were hard to see except in strong light. His task was enormous, for Copán extended over nearly 3 kilometres and had three main courts, pyramids and temples.

Eventually, Stephens and Catherwood met up in Guatemala City. Stephens now abandoned any thoughts of a diplomatic career. The two men decided to check out reports of another overgrown city known as Palenque in southern Mexico, said to be as spectacular as Copán. The journey took them through very rough terrain. By this time, they had switched to broad-brimmed hats and loose-fitting clothing for comfort, just like the locals.

The final stages of the journey were appalling, despite the assistance of forty native porters. They often had to cut their way through dense undergrowth. But finally, Palenque loomed out of the forest. This centre was much smaller than Copán. It had been ruled by Pacal the Great from AD 615 to 683, and his funeral monument was the magnificent Temple of the Inscriptions. He was buried under the temple pyramid, which was finally excavated in 1952.

Stephens and Catherwood set up camp in Pacal's palace complex. It was so wet that candles were useless, and Stephens amused himself by reading a newspaper by the light of fireflies. Besieged by mosquitoes and heavy rain, the two men stumbled through buildings that were practically invisible because of the clinging vegetation. While Catherwood sketched, Stephens built crude ladders and cleared the walls of the palace for the artist. The thick-walled and elaborately decorated structure enclosed several court-yards and measured 91 metres in length. The men made a rough plan in a few weeks, but the humidity and swarms of insects drove them away.

Aware of the money-making and scientific potential of Palenque, Stephens attempted to buy the ruins for $1,500 – far more than the $50 for the much remoter Copán. But when he discovered that he would have to marry a local woman to seal the deal, he backed off hastily. The two men fled in search of another Maya centre, Uxmal. Unfortunately, Catherwood fell seriously ill with fever and only managed a single day at that magnificent site.

In July 1840, the two men returned to New York, where Stephens started work on *Incidents of Travel in Central America, Chiapas and Yucatan*, which became a bestseller a year later. The book show-cased Stephens at his best, being written in an easy narrative style. It was, of course, a travel book, but Stephens approached the three great sites from the perspective of someone who was thoroughly familiar with the local Indians. He recognised that the people who had built Copán, Palenque and Uxmal shared a common culture. Their art rivalled the finest works of the Mediterranean civilisa-tions and was of local origin. Stephens ended the book with a clear statement based on his observations and conversations with the local people: the ruins he had seen had been built by the ancestors of the local Maya.

Stephens was not alone in writing about the Maya. His book appeared two years before the Boston historian William H. Prescott published his classic *Conquest of Mexico* in 1843. Prescott drew on Stephens' work, ensuring that it was widely read by fellow scholars. Meanwhile, only fifteen months after their return to New York,

Catherwood and Stephens went back to Central America, determined to spend more time at Uxmal.

From November 1841 to January 1842, they stayed at the ruins, mapping, surveying and drawing perhaps the most magnificent of all Maya centres. Uxmal is famous for its temple pyramids and long palace buildings. It controlled a local state from AD 850 to 925. Once again, the men did not excavate, but concentrated on getting a sense of the site and of its main building, the so-called Nunnery. Catherwood tried to make as accurate a record as possible so that he could create a replica back in New York.

Despite attacks of fever, Stephens managed to visit other sites in the vicinity, such as Kabah. He recovered a few wooden door beams inscribed with hieroglyphs, which he eventually took to New York. Travelling light, they rode across the Yucatán. They spent eighteen days at Chichén Itzá, already famous for its great stepped pyramid, the Castillo, and its huge ball court. They also met some local scholars who shared valuable historical information with them.

Catherwood and Stephens visited Cozumel and Tulum, places noted by the first Spanish explorers, where there was little to see except clouds of mosquitoes. With that, the two travellers returned to New York in June 1842. Another bestseller, Stephens' *Incidents of Travel in Yucatan*, duly appeared nine months later. In the final chapters of the book, he reaffirmed that the Maya ruins were the work of local people, who prospered until the Spanish Conquest. All subsequent research on Maya civilisation is based on his forthright conclusion.

This was the end of the two men's archaeological adventures. Both returned to Central America to contribute to railroad projects. When malaria caught up with them, they left. Stephens died in New York in 1852, weakened by years of tropical fever. Catherwood perished in a collision at sea off Newfoundland two years later.

Forty years were to pass before any scientific work was done at the sites they had recorded in words and sketches. Like Austen Henry Layard, John Lloyd Stephens was content to describe and record, leaving excavation to his successors. Apart from the difficulties of travel, he had no funds for digging. And in any case, he was writing a travel book.

Ancient Maya civilisation was swallowed up by the forest after the Spaniards arrived in the fifteenth century. However, the modern descendants of those who built Palenque and the other great centres still maintained many elements of the old Maya culture, including ancient ritual traditions. With their drawings and publications, Catherwood and Stephens ensured that Maya civilisation never again vanished into historical oblivion.

CHAPTER 7

Axes and Elephants

According to the Book of Genesis, 'In the beginning God created the heavens and the earth.' He completed that task in six days. Then he formed a man – 'a living being'. God placed the first human in the Garden of Eden. Four rivers flowed from Eden, two of them being the Euphrates and the Tigris in Mesopotamia, 'the land between the rivers'.

So how old is humanity? How long has the earth been in existence?

Two centuries ago, Christian teaching considered the creation story in the Old Testament to be an actual historical event, calculated from the scriptures to have occurred in 4004 BC. To suggest otherwise was to challenge Christian belief, a serious offence.

But there was a major problem with this: could all human history have unfolded in a mere 6,000 years?

The question of human origins had surfaced in scholars' minds as early as the sixteenth century. Antiquarians throughout Europe puzzled over the collections of stone tools discovered in ploughed fields. Many called them natural objects formed by thunderbolts. Then John Frere came along and everything changed.

John Frere (1740–1807) was an English country landowner and a graduate of Cambridge University, where he had studied mathematics with some success. He became the high sheriff of Suffolk and a member of parliament from 1799 to 1802, but his major interests in later life were geology (the study of rocks and the earth) and archaeology. His political and social connections were excellent, and he was elected a fellow (member) of the Royal Society and of the Society of Antiquaries of London, both major learned societies of the day. By all accounts he was a charming man, blessed with a deep curiosity about the countryside around his home at Roydon Hall in Norfolk, eastern England.

In 1797, some brick workers uncovered stone axes and the bones of large animals in a clay-mining pit at Hoxne, a small village some 8 kilometres from Frere's home. He rode over and dug carefully into the walls of the brick pit, recovering more axes and the bones of long-extinct elephants (now, of course, tropical animals) sealed between sterile layers.

Frere realised that this was something extraordinary. He did what most antiquarians did at the time: he wrote a short letter to the Society of Antiquaries of London, knowing that most people interested in the past were members. As was the custom, on 22 June 1797 his brief report was read aloud to the membership and was published three years later. A trivial event, one might think; but what Frere wrote was truly memorable. He described his finds as 'weapons of war, fabricated and used by a people who had not the use of metals'. So far, there was nothing particularly astonishing as many of his fellow members believed that the ancient Britons had no metal. But what he wrote next was really remarkable: 'The situation in which these weapons were found may tempt us to refer them to a very remote period indeed, even beyond that of the present world.'

Frere's words were fundamentally at odds with religious teachings and must have struck the Society of Antiquaries like a thunderclap. The members were cautious, respectable folk, and numbered among them many priests. And so they quietly published Frere's letter. . . and set it aside. John Frere's discovery was ignored for sixty years.

Even before the Hoxne finds, there had been a few discoveries of elephant bones alongside stone tools fashioned by humans in Europe. This was surprising, for there were no elephants there in the nineteenth century. As more elephant remains and stone tools came to light, it gradually became obvious that humans had lived in Europe long before anyone had used metals, and had dwelt along-side long-extinct animals. Apparently, they had even hunted them. Did they do this before the biblical creation of 6,000 years ago?

Those six millennia of human existence were becoming more crowded. For instance, how could one explain the mysterious stone circles of Avebury and Stonehenge? These were already ancient when the Roman general Julius Caesar invaded Britain just over 2,000 years ago. People started pondering a hitherto unthink-able question: had the world existed before divine creation? Christian teaching considered such a thought both irresponsible and criminal.

We tend to think of archaeology as just the study of ancient human societies, but such a narrow viewpoint is wrong. You can't rely on archaeological excavations and artefacts alone to recon-struct the past. Archaeology developed alongside other disciplines, such as biology and geology. And they all came together when scientists started to confront such tough issues as human begin-nings. There was no way of understanding our origins without studying both fossil animals and the geology of the earth. To show that humans had flourished long before 4004 BC required proof that they had lived alongside the long-extinct animals found in the layered rocks of the earth.

Geology and religion came into sharp conflict. Christian teachings of the day proclaimed that God had created earth's geological layers in a series of divine acts. There were several crea-tions, separated by catastrophes. Some of these events led to the extinction of animals – the last of them being Noah's flood. As far as the Bible was concerned, humans and extinct animals had nothing to do with one another. Yet with increasing frequency, archaeology was turning up evidence of their coexistence in obviously very ancient geological levels.

John Frere unearthed his stone axes and elephant bones at Hoxne during a time of major change across Britain. Cities were booming. Canals and other large-scale construction activities exposed many feet of geological layers in all kinds of places. While the Society of Antiquaries forgot Frere's work, a humble canal expert named William Smith (1769–1839) revolutionised geology with his field observations while designing the routes of waterways across the countryside. Smith mapped rock formations over long distances. And he identified long sequences of them, clearly formed over lengthy periods of time. His enthusiasm for geological formations was infectious, and he soon became known as 'Strata Smith' ('strata' being the geological term for layers or levels).

This remarkable geologist was also a keen fossil collector. His vast experience of geological layers helped him realise that many layers of the earth contained distinctive fossils, and that changes in fossils represented changes in time. This was an entirely different way of looking at the world. There were no snapshots of sudden catastrophes or dramatic divine acts. It became increasingly hard to assume that God had all of a sudden created these complex strata. Surely they had been formed by such natural processes as rainfall, flooding, blowing sand or earthquakes. . .?

A new scientific doctrine emerged, that of 'uniformitarianism'. In other words, the same slow-moving geological factors that had formed the earth in the past were still in operation. The earth as we know it had developed from a continuous process of constant change that extended far back into a remote past.

A celebrated British geologist, Sir Charles Lyell (1797–1875), took over where Smith left off. He studied geological sequences all over Europe and wrote one of the classics of nineteenth-century science. His *Principles of Geology* was an attempt to explain changes in the earth that resulted from natural processes that were still in progress. This, of course, made it possible to argue that humans had originated over a far longer span of time than 6,000 years. But the Church was still all-powerful, and Lyell was careful not to discuss the thorny issue of human origins in his book.

Like so many great scientific advances, Lyell's brilliant study influenced field researchers in other disciplines. Among them was the young biologist Charles Darwin, who read *Principles of Geology* while on a five-year scientific voyage around the world on HMS *Beagle* in 1831–36. Darwin observed geological layers in South America that had clearly been formed over long periods of time. He also recovered fossils and observed modern animal species, especially birds, that had changed gradually over time. These observations were to lead him to his revolutionary theory of evolution and natural selection.

Interest in extinct animals intensified, especially when their bones emerged from buried layers in caves. Cave excavations became a fashionable way of finding long-extinct animals. In Belgium and France, stone tools started showing up in the same cave layers as the bones of extinct animals. In Britain, a Catholic priest, Father John MacEnery (1797–1841), excavated Kents Cavern, a large cave near Torquay in southwestern England, in 1825 and 1826. There he found stone artefacts and extinct rhinoceros bones sealed in the same level, under a layer of stalagmite (a limestone deposit formed on cave floors by drips from the ceiling). MacEnery may have been a priest, but he became convinced that people and (now extinct) animals had lived alongside one another longer ago than 6,000 years. Prominent churchmen disagreed, and some even claimed that later people had dug pits into the older levels and left their tools alongside fossil animal bones.

Nevertheless, thanks to the Kents Cavern finds, the leaders of the scientific establishment started to take notice of the human artefacts and extinct animals that were now routinely being found together. They were particularly interested in the discoveries of Jacques Boucher de Perthes (1788–1868), a minor customs official, at Abbeville in northern France's Somme Valley. Boucher de Perthes visited the gravel pits around the town almost daily. He unearthed finely made stone axes in the same levels as the bones of extinct elephants and other bygone beasts. He became obsessed with his tools and said they were the work of people who had lived before the biblical flood.

Unfortunately, Boucher de Perthes was given to delivering long, dull lectures about his finds. And in 1841, he wrote a book, *De la Creation*, a five-volume discourse on human origins that caused scientists to label him a crank. By 1847, when he published the first volume of another long-winded essay, Boucher de Perthes was convinced that his Somme axes were very ancient indeed. His persistence paid off. A few French experts visited the pits and concluded that he was right. Their influential opinions reached both Paris and London. Had Boucher de Perthes not been such a bore, his discoveries might have been recognised for what they were much sooner.

In 1846, the Torquay Natural History Society set up a committee to explore Kents Cavern anew. They employed a schoolmaster and talented geologist, William Pengelly, to lead new excavations. His discoveries confirmed Father MacEnery's conclusions. Another cave came to light during quarrying above the town of Brixham, across the bay from Torquay, in 1858. A distinguished committee of the Royal Society observed Pengelly's investigations there. Beneath a thick layer of stalagmite on the cave floor, he unearthed numerous bones from extinct animals. These included cave lions, mammoths (a long-haired cold-loving elephant), ancient forms of rhinoceros and reindeer, alongside human-made stone tools. The association between human tools and extinct animals was now beyond doubt.

In 1859, just before Charles Darwin published *On the Origin of Species*, two leading members of the scientific establishment paid a brief visit to the Somme sites: geologist Joseph Prestwich and antiquarian John Evans, the leading expert on stone tools. Evans himself dug a stone axe from the same level as a bone from an extinct elephant. The two scientists returned to London convinced that humans had lived on earth long before the biblical creation. They published their findings in papers that were read to the Royal Society and the Society of Antiquaries of London, where John Frere's brief letter about Hoxne had been presented six decades earlier. Times had finally changed, and the scientific evidence was beyond dispute. There was no longer any doubt that humans had a very long history indeed.

The Brixham and Somme finds raised serious questions about human ancestry. Obviously, humans had first appeared far earlier than 6,000 years ago. But how much earlier? Charles Darwin's famous theory of evolution and the discovery of an exotic-looking human skull in Germany would set the stage for the study of an open-ended human past.

CHAPTER 8

A Huge Turning Point

The bombshell exploded a few months after John Evans and Joseph Prestwich returned from their visit to the Somme gravel pits with axes and elephant bones. Charles Darwin's *On the Origin of Species* placed archaeology at the centre of the debates on human origins. The archaeologists and geologists had proved that human beings had lived on earth alongside extinct animals. Now Darwin's theory of evolution and natural selection provided explanations for how animals and other living things had developed over time.

Darwin's new theory removed all possibility of a boundary between the modern world and any previous world inhabited by extinct animals. No terrible floods or great extinctions separated mid-nineteenth-century scientists from the landscapes inhabited by earlier animals or humans. There could no longer be any doubt that now-extinct animals and people had lived on earth at the same time.

The year 1859 was a huge turning point in archaeology – and in science generally. New questions confronted archaeologists and biologists alike. Were there earlier forms of humans on earth before ourselves? If so, how long ago did they flourish? And how could you account for the great differences between living human societies and their ancestors? The Darwin bombshell sent archaeologists on a search for answers to these questions – and for early humans and their tools.

Charles Darwin (1809–82) had become an enthusiastic biologist while still an undergraduate at Cambridge University. His lengthy voyage around the world aboard HMS *Beagle* from 1831 to 1836 provided him with data on numerous plants and animals. Soon he began keeping notebooks on changes in animals over time. He observed geological layers in South America and realised that Charles Lyell's arguments about the theory of uniformitarianism were correct. But the clincher came when Darwin read the scholar Thomas Malthus's *Essay on the Principle of Population*, published in 1798. Malthus argued that animal populations, including humans, expanded to the limits of their food supplies. Darwin took the argument a stage further and wrote that human progress was a product of nature, and the mechanism was the gradual process of natural selection.

Natural selection causes changes in the properties of organisms from generation to generation. Animals display individual variation in their appearance and behaviour, such as body size, number of offspring and so on. Some traits are inherited – they pass from parent to offspring. Others are strongly influenced by environmental conditions and are less likely to be passed on. Individuals who had traits well suited to competition for local resources – what Darwin called 'the struggle for existence' – survived. Natural selection preserved small, beneficial changes that members of different species passed on to their offspring. The advantaged individuals survived and multiplied as the inferior ones died out. Natural selection applied to all animals, including humans.

Charles Darwin brought the mechanism of natural selection to the table. But he did not take up the issue of human evolution, for he felt it would prevent the book from getting a fair hearing. He merely remarked that his theory would 'throw light' on the development of humans. Twelve years passed before he published *The Descent of Man*, which explored the relationship between natural selection and human evolution.

Darwin also theorised that humans originated in tropical Africa, where many apes flourished. Today, we know he was right. His brilliant research provided a convincing reason for archaeological research into early humans. Evolution made it certain that humans had descended from apes. Respectable Victorian households were horrified. Mothers drew their children to their skirts and whispered to one another that they hoped the rumours were untrue. Satirical magazines mocked human ancestry among the apes with cartoons showing Darwin with a chimp's body, and a gorilla upset at Darwin's claims to be one of his decendants. Clergymen preached against evolution in their sermons.

Fortunately, Darwin had powerful allies, among them Thomas Henry Huxley (1825–95), one of the greatest biologists of the nineteenth century. Huxley was a striking man with lion-like features, black hair and whiskers. A brilliant public speaker, he made the case for evolution and natural selection so forcefully that he became known as 'Darwin's Bulldog'. Gradually the opposition to Darwin's ideas faded, except among the most committed Christians.

No one had any idea what an ancestral human would have looked like. Three years before the publication of Darwin's *Origin of Species*, quarrymen working in the Neander Valley near Düsseldorf, Germany, had discovered a thick-set skull and limb bones in a cave. The primitive-looking skull had a massive, rugged brow and was bun-shaped – quite unlike the smooth, rounded heads of modern people. The experts puzzled over the find. A well-known biologist, Hermann Schaaffhausen, proclaimed that the remains were those of an ancient and savage inhabitant of Europe. Schaaffhausen's colleague Rudolf Virchow, also a distinguished surgeon, dismissed the bones as those of a deformed idiot.

But Darwin's Bulldog had a different opinion. He realised that the Neander skull was that of a primitive human who had lived before modern humans, ourselves. He made a detailed study of the remains and compared them bone by bone with a chimpanzee skeleton. The similarities between the two were striking. Huxley wrote a classic of human evolution about his findings. In *Man's Place in Nature*, published in 1863, he declared that the Neanderthal

skull was from the most primitive human ever found and one
clearly related to our apelike ancestors. Here was the proof that
humans were descended from apes, as Darwin's theory hinted. All
modern studies of early human fossils originated in this short but
beautifully and clearly written book. Huxley was heavily influenced by recent findings in geology and archaeology, as well as by
evolutionary theory.

More Neanderthal skeletons came to light in caves and rock
shelters in southwestern France during the 1860s and 1870s. With
jutting jaws, heavy brows and sloping foreheads, the compactly
built Neanderthals looked primitive, almost apelike. They became
caricature cave people, armed by cartoonists with heavy clubs.
Many more fossil discoveries were needed to establish even the
basic details of human evolution.

Increasingly there was talk of a 'missing link' between apes and
humans, the link being the ultimate human ancestor. Many people
believed Darwin was correct that such a link would be uncovered
in tropical Africa. Since that was where the most forms of apes
flourished, it was logical to assume that humans originated there.
Instead, the next important human fossil discoveries after the
Neanderthals were elsewhere.

Eugène Dubois (1858–1940) was a Dutch physician who became
obsessed with human origins. He believed that our ancestors came
from Southeast Asia, where many apes were also to be found.
Dubois was so intent on discovering them that he wangled a job as
a government medical officer in Java in 1887. For the next two
years he patiently searched in the gravels of the Solo River, near the
small town of Trinil. There he unearthed the top of a skull, an
upper leg bone and the molar teeth of an apelike human. He
named it *Pithecanthropus erectus*, meaning 'Ape-human who stands
upright', but it was popularly known as 'Java Man'. It was, he said,
the missing link between apes and humans. Today, it is known as
Homo erectus.

The European scientific community scorned Dubois's claims,
partly because all early human fossils had hitherto come from
Europe. The scientists laughed at him. They were mesmerised by

the Neanderthals, who 'looked' primitive. Dubois was devastated, returned to Europe, and is said to have hidden the fossils under his bed.

By the turn of the century, for most people the Neanderthals had become the shambling, savage cave people depicted in newspaper cartoons. Instead, scientists became obsessed with a remarkable 'discovery' made by a lawyer and fossil hunter, Charles Dawson, in a gravel quarry at Piltdown in southern England in 1912.

Dawson also claimed to have found the 'missing link' – but it was a forgery. It had been fashioned from a medieval skull, a 500-year-old human lower jaw and carefully filed fossil chimpanzee teeth, all the bones stained with an iron solution to look ancient. It was almost certainly Dawson, hungry for scientific recognition, who created this outrageous fake. Dawson knew that scientists of the day believed that the development of a large brain came before the consumption of a broad-based diet by modern humans. And so (it is thought) he quietly created a fossil human with a large skull from an anatomically modern person, and then added suitably modified chimpanzee teeth to create the primitive 'Piltdown Man'.

Astonishing though it may seem, no one questioned the find. But it should be remembered that at the time there were not the analytical tools required to verify its age. Chemical analysis of the bones finally exposed the forgery in 1953. By that time, however, other fossil finds from both Africa and China were casting doubt on Piltdown, which did not look anything like them.

Dubois's *Pithecanthropus erectus* was more or less forgotten until the 1920s when a Chinese geological survey excavated a deep cave at Zhoukoudian, southwest of Beijing. There a Swedish fieldworker and Chinese scholar Pei Wenzhong unearthed human bones. The specimens proved to be virtually identical to Dubois's Trinil find. Soon the two forms of *Pithecanthropus* were united under the single label of *Homo erectus*, 'the human who stood upright'.

Despite the discovery of the Neanderthals and *Homo erectus*, enormous gaps remained in the story of the past. Many thousands of years separated the stone axes from Hoxne and the Somme

Valley from later human fossils and much more recent archaeological sites such as Stonehenge. No one could date either Dubois's
fossils or the Neander finds. All that filled the gap between the Java
fossils and the Neanderthals were museum drawers full of undated
stone tools. And they showed only that technology had become
more complex over time – nothing else.

One pressing question was who the earliest humans had been.
Another was how the widely differing human societies had lived
together.

Theories of human social evolution appeared, notably in the
works of a social scientist called Herbert Spencer (1820–1903). He
worked at a time of rapid industrialisation and major technological
change. Hardly surprisingly, Spencer argued that human societies
had developed from the simple to the complex and the highly
diverse. Such a theory allowed archaeologists to imagine orderly
progress from simple ancient societies to complex modern ones.

But what had the ancient societies been like? Spencer was
writing at a time when knowledge of non-Western societies in
Africa, the Americas, Asia and the Pacific was becoming widely
available. Using explorers' descriptions of hitherto unknown tribes,
as well as the work of Catherwood, Stephens and others, you could
easily imagine a tree of progress. At the base were the Neanderthals,
as well as hunting peoples like the Australian and Tasmanian
aborigines. Higher up were the sophisticated civilisations of the
Aztecs, Maya and Cambodians. And at the top, of course, was
Victorian civilisation.

People were trying to slot both human fossils and archaeological
finds into a framework that was easily understood and that made
sense. Theories of human progress brought a convenient framework to the little-known past uncovered by archaeologists. But
some people went further.

Another British social scientist, Sir Edward Tylor (1832–1917),
thought of human societies in three stages: savagery (hunting and
foraging societies), barbarism (simple farming societies) and civilisation. A simple, stepwise perspective on the past appealed to
Victorian audiences, who believed strongly in technological

progress as a mark of civilisation. And who can blame them? At the time, almost nothing was known of archaeology outside the narrow confines of Europe. These simple theories reflected the common assumption that nineteenth-century civilisation represented the peak of humankind's long history. As it appeared in the 1860s and 1870s, the evolution of humanity did seem ladderlike and orderly.

But all that was to change when archaeological discoveries in Africa, the Americas and Asia revealed a far more diverse and fascinating prehistoric world.

CHAPTER 9

The Three Ages

Early nineteenth-century European archaeology was a confusing mystery. For most students of the European past, real history began with Julius Caesar and the Romans. This was nonsense, of course, for there were many earlier archaeological sites. But everything earlier than Caesar – polished stone axes, bronze swords and often elaborate ornaments – was a jumble of finds stacked in the drawers and cabinets of museums and private collections. The chaos of artefacts and archaeological sites made no historical sense.

The scriptures, a commonly used historical source, had nothing to offer. How could you create a framework for the remote past? Had different peoples used stone tools or developed metal swords? What were they like? Were there people living in Britain and other European countries who had resembled the Native Americans, as John Aubrey had suggested (see Chapter 1)? No one knew what human societies had lived in Europe before the Romans.

Few Europeans took archaeology as seriously as the Danes. The Romans had never conquered Denmark, which meant that its people felt a strong attachment to the country's ancient inhabitants.

Archaeology was the only way of studying them, and developed alongside a strong patriotic interest in pre-Christian artefacts. But Danish excavators, like their English and French counterparts, wrestled with a confusion of archaeological finds. It was no coincidence that the first attempts to create order out of chaos arose in Scandinavia.

In 1806, the Danish government set up a Commission on Antiquities to protect archaeological sites and to found a national museum. In 1817, its members appointed Christian Jürgensen Thomsen (1788–1865) to set the national collections in order and put them on display (at the time, they were stacked in a church loft). Thomsen was the son of a wealthy merchant and was an enthusiastic coin collector. His tidy and precise mind made him the ideal person to put the museum in order. Anyone who collects coins seriously becomes a classifier, accustomed to placing objects in sequence according to their style. By all accounts, Thomsen also enjoyed meeting people and engaging in conversation. Add to this a gift for letter-writing, which gave him contacts throughout Denmark and beyond, and you have an ideal museum official.

The industrious Thomsen began by entering the collections into a ledger or logbook, just as in business. Each object received a number. New acquisitions were catalogued and numbered as well. This gave him immediate access to any object in the museum. Within a few months, he had catalogued 500 artefacts. The dull process of cataloguing and ledger entry gave him familiarity with a broad range of prehistoric artefacts. The Copenhagen collections included thousands of stone tools from early hunting sites, and rows of stone axes and adzes (a cutting tool with a blade set at right angles to the handle) used for woodworking far back in the past. There were beautifully made stone daggers, bronze swords and numerous brooches.

Cataloguing was one thing, but making sense of the jumble of stone axes and small knives, bronze adzes, shields and occasional gold ornaments was quite another. Thomsen observed that much of the collection came from burials, where people had been laid to rest alongside clay vessels or stone axes, and perhaps with brooches and pins. The groups of grave offerings varied from each other, marked by changes in the artefacts. After examining numerous burials, Thomsen noticed that some of the graves contained metal, but others only artefacts of bone or stone. He decided to employ the raw materials used to manufacture tools as the basis for classification.

In 1816, he divided Danish history into three phases. The earliest, corresponding to what today we call prehistory, the time before written history, was the 'Heathen Period'. He subdivided this into three ages: the Stone Age, the Bronze Age and the Iron Age. Thus was born the famous Three-Age System, which transformed perceptions of prehistoric times.

The Three-Age System was based entirely on Thomsen's museum collections. The Stone Age was a period when only stone and antler, bone and wood were used for tools and weapons. The Bronze Age followed, with bronze and copper artefacts. Then there was the Iron Age, when iron tools came into use. Thomsen thought of the three ages as a timeframe for the prehistoric past. He developed it carefully, using different groupings of finds in undisturbed burials and living sites.

One might expect Thomsen to have been an object-obsessed museum curator, but he was not. His museum galleries did display artefacts from the three ages; but they offered far more, for he made sure that his visitors knew that archaeology was not about objects, but about people.

Thomsen told museum visitors of burial mounds that dotted the countryside where once living men and women lay; of gold and bronze ornaments that had glittered on a woman's chest or glowed in the sunlight on a long-forgotten battlefield. The museum was open for two days a week, and then for longer periods. Every Thursday at two o'clock, Thomsen would show visitors around, full of enthusiasm, even placing ancient gold necklets around young girls' necks. He made the past come alive.

Thomsen wrote only one book, a short *Guidebook to Northern Antiquity*, published in 1836 and read throughout Europe. In this, he described his Three-Age System, which was simple and based on well-documented museum collections. Thomsen's three ages cut through the confusion. Within a surprisingly short time, the

Three-Age System became the framework used to subdivide the prehistoric past.

Archaeology is based on excavations and field surveys, but indoor research in laboratories is equally important. No one would call Thomsen a fieldworker: he was, above all, a museum man. His career was in museum galleries. He only excavated once, in 1845, when he and a colleague investigated a Bronze Age burial. The dead man had been cremated, his sword and a fine brooch laid out on an ox hide. Thomsen's excavation was remarkable for his accurate recording, a reflection of his precise mind and passion for detail.

Thomsen spent much of his time on small finds and tiny artefacts. But he also revolutionised the big picture of the past. With the development of the Three-Age System, the modern science of archaeology and archaeological classification was born.

It still needed to be proved that the three ages followed one another in time, and they still needed to be dated. In 1838, a young university student, Jens Jacob Worsaae (1821–85), came to meet Thomsen. He had long been interested in archaeology and had acquired a large collection of antiquities. The highly intelligent Worsaae became an unpaid museum volunteer, but soon offended Thomsen because he was not afraid to express his opinions and was a fluent writer.

Fortunately, King Christian VIII thoroughly approved of Worsaae's work and sponsored the young man's research. Worsaae's first book, *The Primeval Antiquities of Denmark*, was published in 1843 and translated into English in 1849. It was a brilliant essay on the Three-Age System. Worsaae insisted that excavating archaeological sites was the only way to write Denmark's earliest history, using artefacts in the same way as a historian uses documents. The king was so impressed with young Worsaae that he sent him on a tour of the British Isles to study the remains of the Vikings, Scandinavian seafarers and traders between the eighth and the eleventh centuries. This yielded another book, and on the strength of that the king appointed Worsaae inspector for the conservation of antiquities.

Worsaae travelled constantly, recording sites and saving many from destruction. Above all, he excavated numerous sealed Stone and Bronze Age burials, recovering the dead themselves as well as their possessions, which included swords and shields, clay vessels and the remains of leather garments. Such finds provided snapshots of different people and their technologies – glimpses of the Three-Age System unfolding in the past. Worsaae's excavations were highly significant. His careful observations confirmed that Thomsen's three ages were in the correct time order. Until Worsaae's digs, the scheme had depended entirely on museum collections. Now it was based on excavations as well.

As he worked, Worsaae showed that archaeological research could produce facts about the past. When a well-preserved corpse of a woman came to light in a bog in southern Denmark, traditionalists who believed in legends claimed that it was the body of the legendary Queen Gunnhild of early medieval times. Worsaae publicly disagreed and showed her to have been an Iron Age individual.

Much of Worsaae's research was concerned with burial mounds. Indeed, a great deal of Denmark's past was preserved in such monuments, but by no means all of it. Along the country's coastlines lay hundreds of large shell heaps from earlier times – enormous piles of oysters and other mollusc shells. Some were simply rubbish heaps. But on others people had lived and built houses. The first person to investigate these was Japetus Steenstrup (1813–97), professor of zoology (the study of animals) at the University of Copenhagen. He called all such sites *kjokkenmoddinger*, or 'kitchen middens' (midden comes from the Danish word meaning 'kitchen scraps').

The only way to understand the middens was by studying still-living non-Western societies whose diet was mainly shellfish. Steenstrup and his colleagues, notably the English archaeologist John Lubbock, were particularly interested in the Fuegian Indians who lived at the southern tip of South America. Charles Darwin had described them during his *Beagle* voyage. He – and indeed Lubbock and Steenstrup – had a low opinion of their abilities and commented on the primitive lifestyles of shellfish collectors.

The Danish government now appointed a three-scientist commission – including both Steenstrup and Worsaae – to examine the middens. Other scientists were also brought in, including a zoologist to identify shells. Worsaae examined many shell heaps. His largest investigation was of a shell midden found during road works at Meilgaard. A large cross-section of the mound revealed thick layers of oyster shells and mussels. He also recovered antler spearheads, stone tools, hearths and evidence of long-term occupation. He described Meilgaard as 'some kind of eating place'.

Steenstrup and Worsaae were years ahead of their time. They not only studied artefacts, but also recorded the mollusc species found in the middens – this was the earliest known research into how people lived.

Meanwhile, Worsaae's colleagues studied ancient climate change, using layers of peat bogs and the plant remains in them. As the Ice Age ended, open country around ice sheets had given way to cold-tolerant birch forests. Then, as the climate warmed further, oak forests replaced birch. Steenstrup even identified the bones of migratory birds to establish the seasons in which the middens were in use. This was truly revolutionary archaeology, which emphasised ancient environments. Steenstrup published his work a century before such approaches became commonplace.

Worsaae was a major force in Scandinavian archaeology for decades. He taught prehistory at the University of Copenhagen, the first such teacher in Scandinavia. He left to become director of the National Museum in 1866, a post he held until his death in 1885.

At the time of his death, Scandinavian archaeology was years ahead of its competitors. Worsaae's rigorous application of the Three-Age System and his careful observation of occupation layers provided a general framework for archaeology in Northern Europe. His outline was much refined in later decades, as the Three-Age System and detailed classifications of all kinds of prehistoric artefacts became routine throughout Europe.

Thomsen and Worsaae laid the foundations for European prehistoric archaeology – indeed of archaeology generally. The Three-Age System brought a broad order to the prehistoric past. The Stone Age included the Somme axes and Frere's finds, *Homo erectus* and the Neanderthals, as well as early farming societies. The

Bronze and Iron Ages covered the more recent periods of the past, up to the appearance of civilisation in the Middle East and elsewhere, and beyond.

This general framework provided a kind of orderly bridge that linked the earliest known sites with much more recent times. But there remained significant gaps. Important discoveries in the river valleys of southwestern France and by the Swiss lakes would soon fill in the empty spaces with remarkable hunting societies and sophisticated farming communities.

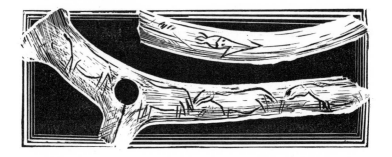

CHAPTER 10

Stone Age Hunters in an Icy World

In 1852, a road worker accidently stumbled across a cave in the foothills of the Pyrenees mountains, near the small village of Aurignac in southern France. The labourer dug into the soft cave earth, looking for buried treasure. Instead of gold, he uncovered the remains of seventeen people buried with shell beads and mammoth teeth. The local priest promptly reburied them in the village cemetery.

The news finally reached Édouard Lartet (1801–71), a country lawyer with a passion for geology, fossils and ancient stone tools. Some eight years after the original find, he rode over to Aurignac and poked about in what remained of the cave filling. His hasty dig exposed a hearth of ashes and charcoal, as well as nicely made stone tools that were clearly very ancient. Lartet puzzled over his finds. Who were these ancient toolmakers? The Aurignac tools were completely different from the stone axes found by Boucher de Perthes along the River Somme (see Chapter 7).

Lartet's geological training kicked in, and he realised that the best chance of finding the answers lay in humanly occupied caves and rock shelters (rocky overhangs in cliffs). If many generations of people had visited the same location, the chances were that there would be layers of human occupation extending over long periods of time. He turned away from geological fossils and became an archaeologist. In the process, he pioneered a new approach to excavation that involved not burial mounds, like those in Scandinavia, but caves and rock shelters.

Lartet excavated several other caves and found both animal bones and stone tools. His contacts among geologists led him to the tiny, and at the time remote, village of Les Eyzies in southwestern France's Dordogne region. This is a wonderful part of France to explore. The Vezère and other rivers flow through deep valleys carved out by ancient floods. I always love visiting this well-watered countryside, with its green fields, thick woods and riverside meadows. High limestone cliffs tower above you. These are riddled with deep caves and rocky overhangs in sheltered gorges that would have provided welcome protection during sub-zero winters.

Lartet had no funds himself, but he joined forces with Henry Christy (1810–65), a wealthy English banker, who was involved in numerous businesses (including one that experimented with woven silk instead of the traditional beaver fur for top hats). Christy was also an enthusiastic collector of antiquities and became interested in Native American societies. In 1853, he visited Scandinavia, where the museum collections in Copenhagen and Stockholm fascinated him. While in America in 1856, he met Edward Tylor, an anthropologist (a person who studies living non-Western societies), and travelled with him to Mexico.

Hearing stories of Les Eyzies, Christy visited the Dordogne caves with Édouard Lartet. The two men became friends and collaborators. Christy provided the funds and acquired most of the finds; Lartet carried out the excavations.

By the standards of today's cave excavations, this was primitive digging. Lartet was a geologist used to examining layers with changing fossil animals. He knew that the earliest occupation would be at the bottom. The excavations yielded numerous antler, bone and flint artefacts. Drawing on the distinctive stone tools and the different animals found in each layer, such as reindeer and wild horses, Lartet identified several levels of human occupation. His diggings explored caves and rock shelters that are household names for today's archaeologists – Le Moustier and La Ferrassie, as well as La Madeleine.

La Madeleine rock shelter lies at the water's edge on the Vezère River. Here Lartet unearthed the finest antler and bone artefacts of all – delicate antler points, harpoons with barbs on one or both sides, and needles. To his astonishment, he also found bone fragments decorated with fine engravings. Some bore simple patterns, while others were more intricate. Yet others had been carved into lovely animal shapes. One carving of a bison licking its flank was so detailed that the tear duct in the eye could be seen.

But who had been the artists of La Madeleine? After several years of excavations, Lartet and Christy had discovered a sequence of changing Stone Age societies. The earliest was the Neanderthal occupation at Le Moustier cave. The Neanderthals, with their heavy brows, were quite different from modern people. They were not like us at all. So who were our ancestors?

The answer came in 1868, when workers digging foundations for the new Les Eyzies railway station uncovered a buried rock shelter at a cave called Cro-Magnon. Lartet dug into the back of the shelter. He excavated five human skeletons, including the remains of a foetus and several adults. One was a woman, who may have been killed by a blow to the head. The skeletons lay among a scattering of shell beads and ivory pendants. These were no Neanderthals with heavy brow ridges: they had round heads and upright foreheads. Their appearance was identical to that of modern people. Lartet believed, correctly, that he had found the remote ancestors of modern Europeans.

The skeletons came from the same layer as the bones of reindeer and other cold-loving animals. This was proof that modern humans lived in Europe at a time of intense cold, during the last Ice Age (now known to have been about 18,000 years ago). Lartet and Christy wrote of an 'Age of Reindeer', but was this a reality? The Swiss geologist Louis Agassiz had spent many years studying the movement of glaciers high in the Alps. In periods of intense cold, ice advanced far down mountain valleys. During warmer periods, the glaciers shrank, just as they are doing during today's global warming. Agassiz wrote of a Great Ice Age, which ended with rapid warming before written records began. The last cold period of the Ice Age coincided with Lartet and Christy's Age of Reindeer.

What were these late Ice Age people like? Before Darwin's *Origin of Species*, people had turned to the classics and the Bible for explanations of the past. Now there was a new source of information: anthropology. The immediate and obvious living equivalents to the Cro-Magnons were the Eskimos, who had adapted brilliantly to extreme cold and found solutions to living in sub-zero conditions. There were indeed many parallels. For example, Eskimo hunters preyed on migrating caribou herds in spring and autumn; the Cro-Magnons harvested reindeer during the same seasons. Also, the ivory and bone needles that were found showed that the inhabitants of the Dordogne rock shelters probably wore tailored clothing, such as trousers and anoraks, just like living Arctic peoples.

The Cro-Magnons became Eskimos in the popular and archaeological imagination. They were often depicted wearing Eskimo-like garments, including hooded parkas. Despite the huge time gap between the Cro-Magnons and living Eskimos, the comparison at least gave an impression of what life might have been like. Just as Darwin had compared Fuegians to very primitive ancient hunters, so Sir John Lubbock and the early anthropologists used contrasts with living non-Western societies. They gave birth to a new archaeological method. Such similarities, known to archaeologists as 'analogies', are a fundamental part of archaeology today.

Lartet and his contemporaries excavated crudely, with picks and shovels (occasionally with something smaller). Their work was somewhat like fossil hunting, but instead of fossils they were looking for people, which required much greater care. Everyone was searching for finely decorated tools and weapons made of reindeer antler and stone tools. Layer after layer, they dug rapidly through the remains of one short visit after another, through the hearths and other traces of temporary dwellings.

Contrast this approach with today's, when expert cave excavators adopt the mindset of the original visitors. They always dig with trowels, dental tools and fine brushes, so that they can distinguish each thin layer that represents just a brief visit. Everything is passed through fine sieves, and even the smallest seeds, fish bones and beads are recovered. A square grid laid out over the floor and electronic survey devices guarantee that every object of significance is recorded in place.

The changing forms of tools provided Lartet with a record of developing Neanderthal and Cro-Magnon societies. Antler and stone implements recorded technological changes through time. There were close similarities in the ways in which tools changed over time at many of his sites. Lartet, being a geologist, had a somewhat impersonal approach to ancient peoples. But he was at least aware that people had made the tools and had hunted animals.

Others were thinking about the French cave discoveries as well. In 1865, the British archaeologist Sir John Lubbock published *Prehistoric Times*, the first general account of the subject. In his book, Lubbock divided the Stone Age into the Palaeolithic period, or Old Stone Age (Greek: *palaeos*, old, and *lithos*, stone), and the more recent Neolithic period, or New Stone Age (Greek: *neos*, new, and *lithos*, stone), when Europeans became farmers. These terms are still used today.

Lubbock produced a very general framework, just as Christian Jürgensen Thomsen had done with the three ages in Scandinavia. Lubbock, with his interest in living non-Western societies, was very much a people person. Others were not, obsessed as they were with the enormous numbers of stone tools in the French caves, rather than with the people who made them. Their changing artefacts became signposts of human progress, notably in the hands of Gabriel de Mortillet, a French geologist turned archaeologist.

Gabriel de Mortillet (1821–98) joined the National Museum of Antiquities at Saint-Germain as overseer of the Stone Age collections in 1863. He was fascinated by artefacts and brought his geological ideas to them. He had a fanatical belief in inevitable human progress that could be measured by changing tool forms.

And he adopted this approach after organising displays about the history of labour for the 1867 Universal Exhibition in Paris, a celebration of human progress through the past and present.

Mortillet borrowed from geology and wrote of changing 'type fossils', using what was a geological term to refer to tools like antler spear points and harpoons. Distinctive 'type fossils' marked different periods of Stone Age technology. Humans and their societies had evolved in almost the same way everywhere. Mortillet believed there was a 'universal law' of human progress.

This rigid-minded, geologically trained archaeologist's ideas dominated Stone Age archaeology for generations. The approach persisted, because it created an impression of orderly progress through ancient times and was simple to understand.

You can still see Mortillet's approach in the new museum at Les Eyzies. The upstairs gallery displays rows of antler, bone and stone tools, arranged in order through time. I find the beautiful displays depressing: it all seems as coolly detached as it was in Mortillet's day. Fortunately, other displays talk of the Neanderthals and Cro-Magnons as people, but the tool displays highlight a problem with archaeology. Finds like knives, scrapers and spear heads are excavated, classified and stored in boxes. They become impersonal symbols of human behaviour. You tend to forget that they were made and used by once-living people. We lose the human connection.

For all this, Mortillet did leave one legacy. He subdivided the different archaeological levels and their artefacts, using cultural labels for each one. He named the layers after the archaeological sites where they were found. One culture with split-based antler points he named Aurignacian (after the Aurignac cave), another Magdalenian (after the La Madeleine rock shelter), marked by antler harpoons. This was all very geological: he forgot that stone tools were fashioned by humans, whose behaviour varied constantly. Despite this limitation, Mortillet's rigid approach persisted, especially in French circles, well into the twentieth century.

The French cave excavations may have been crude, but they launched a new era in Stone Age archaeology. They revealed Neanderthals with simple technology, followed by the reindeer-hunting Cro-Magnons with much more elaborate weapons. Lartet and Christy's Palaeolithic discoveries revealed vanished European societies that adjusted brilliantly to bitter cold. But they raised questions about the people who lived in Europe immediately after the Ice Age. Were they also hunters in a much warmer world, or did they become farmers? As we'll see in the next chapter, their settlements first came to light in the picturesque setting of the Alps.

Across the Ages

Fishermen on the shores of the Swiss lakes had complained for years. Their lines caught on the bottom, then snapped, and they lost the hooks. Their nets mysteriously clung to the bottom. Fragments of torn netting tangled up with branches would occasionally float to the surface. There was talk of sunken underwater forests.

No one took any notice of their complaints until 1853–54, when a major drought reduced lake levels dramatically. The 'forests' turned out to be wooden posts, or 'piles', sunk into layers of dark sediment. These had once supported huts built above the water. Local antiquarians followed up, and by 1869 they had located more than 200 such lakeside sites.

The finds came to the attention of Ferdinand Keller (1800–81), a professor of English at the University of Zürich and president of the Zürich Antiquarian Society. He led major excavations at a maze of piles visible in the exposed bed of Lake Zürich near the village of Obermeilen in 1854.

This was an entirely new kind of archaeology for Switzerland, involving organic materials that normally never survived. Unless kept wet, such finds soon dry out, crack or even crumble into dust. The damp mud had preserved an astounding range of objects that would usually have perished: axes and adzes with timber handles, wooden wheels, fishing nets, baskets and ropes. There were lots of cattle, sheep and goat bones, and the remains of red deer, beaver and boar. There were numerous wheat and barley seeds, wild fruit, hazelnuts, peas and beans.

Keller's methods were crude. He dug around the posts and recovered as many objects as he could. However, he had no way of dating the site and its contents.

The lake dwelling discoveries came just as Gabriel de Mortillet and others brought a ladderlike order of human progress to the Palaeolithic period. But many people interested in the remote past wondered about later prehistoric societies. What had happened in Europe as temperatures rose after the Ice Age? When did farming begin in Europe? What crops did such people grow? Keller's discoveries at Obermeilen drew back the curtain on some of Europe's early farmers.

Keller knew from his finds that his lake dwellings were occupied over several thousand years. But why did the inhabitants build houses on the water? Like Lartet and Christy with the Cro-Magnons, Keller turned to anthropology. He thought immediately of French explorers' descriptions of New Guinea villages, comprising stilt houses built in shallow water. Thus, Keller imagined that the wooden piles were from similar prehistoric stilt houses, whose inhabitants had dropped the tools and food remains into the water beneath their dwellings. He referred to the houses as 'pile dwellings'.

Much later, more careful excavation proved Keller wrong. Some Swiss lake dwellings lay on swampy land that had been flooded by rising lake levels. Others had been built above the water and had had posts sunk into the ground to stabilise the structures. As the water rose, fine silt covered the house floors and hearths between the posts, preserving numerous perishable remains of early farming life.

Ferdinand Keller's discoveries hit the headlines. Artists painted reconstructions of the villages. They located them (wrongly) on platforms joined to dry land by gangplanks, as if the settlements were on humanly made wooden islands. Unlike the Cro-Magnons, who moved around constantly, these villagers lived at the same location for long periods of time. They had to, because they were farmers tied to their fields. The remains of their crops survived at the sites.

Today, we know that most lakeside settlements like these date to between 4000 BC and somewhere after 1000 BC. Similar kinds of villages occur by alpine lakes in France, Germany, Italy and Slovenia. In the late nineteenth century, Obermeilen and sites like it became a benchmark for the study of early European farmers. They provided such rich archives of tools and food remains that they became a kind of dictionary for understanding such people, even those who dwelt far from the Swiss lakes.

Farmers crave salt – to supplement their diet of mainly cereal grains, but also for preserving fish and meat for later consumption. Rock salt was like gold dust for those lucky enough to live close to a source and who were able to trade in it. The Salzkammergut Mountains contain vast quantities of rock salt. People were mining it near Salzbergtal, a small village above the lakeside town of Hallstatt, close to Salzburg, Austria, by at least 1000 BC, and probably earlier. Generations of miners worked the Salzkammergut Mountains, among them Johann Georg Ramsauer (1795–1874). He became a mining apprentice at the age of thirteen. Soon an expert, he rose to the position of Bergmeister, manager of all mining activity.

Ramsauer was quite a character. He lived in a medieval fort called the Rudolfsturm, close to the mine. Very much a family man, he raised twenty-two children who survived to adulthood. His other passion was archaeological excavation. He devoted his leisure time to excavating 1,000 or so graves in an enormous Iron Age cemetery, discovered during construction between Rudolfsturm and the mine. The dead were the Hallstatt people, their culture named by Ramsauer after the local town. They were miners, who had dug into the hills by the light of pine torches. The salt had preserved their leather backpacks, gloves and hats.

Ramsauer excavated the cemetery between 1846 and 1863 – a period that coincided with the first Neanderthal discovery and the excavations of Swiss lake villages. To assist him, Ramsauer employed a painter, who spent years sketching and recording the finds and the graves. His watercolours show the positions of vessels, metal objects and other grave furniture relative to the human bones or cremated remains.

As the graves were cleaned, they were sketched and described in comprehensive notes. About half were cremations and half were burials. The dead were not chieftains or important people. They were miners and metalworkers, buried with ornaments and their tools and weapons. These were expert traders, whose metal products and salt spread across wide areas of Europe. They were clearly in touch with long-distance trade networks: some of them owned ivory ornaments from distant Africa, while others wore amber (fossilised tree resin) beads from the Baltic Sea area.

Unfortunately, in 1874 Ramsauer died before publishing his work. Nor did he record the bones or details of the objects found in the graves. His handwritten notes vanished, only to be found in a second-hand bookstore in Vienna in 1932. How reliable they are as a record of the work is uncertain. But they were finally published in 1959. It is a miracle just how much valuable information survived from the enormous excavation. Sadly, however, it represents just a fraction of what could have been learned from the cemetery today.

But how old were the lake villages and the Hallstatt cemetery? Today we know that the Hallstatt culture flourished from the eighth to the sixth centuries BC. But in the mid to late nineteenth century there was no way of guessing this. The new geology, the theory of evolution and the Neanderthal discovery had all opened up a vast, unknown landscape of the past. Worsaae's excavations and the Three-Age System provided a general framework, but still no actual dates for any pre-Roman European society. Fortunately, a Swedish archaeologist, Oscar Montelius (1843–1921), took over where Jens Jacob Worsaae and others had left off. He devoted his career to building chronological frameworks (records of events as they occurred in time) across Europe.

It takes a special kind of personality to be an expert on artefacts, especially when almost nothing is known about them. The work requires endless patience, a passion for obscure, often tiny details, and a love of the past. Montelius possessed these qualities in abundance. A brilliant linguist, he was easy-going and personally engaging. In demand as a lecturer, he did much to keep archaeology in the public eye.

Montelius was born in Stockholm and spent his entire professional life at the Museum of National Antiquities there, rising eventually to become its director. He was one of the first museum archaeologists. Such scholars spend their careers totally immersed in collections and artefacts.

Accurate chronologies (timelines) based on artefacts and the positions in which they were found were Montelius's passion. He realised from the start that the only way to achieve such timelines was to travel throughout Europe, the Mediterranean and the Middle East. There, one could find objects dated by the known age of the sites where they were found or by historical records. These artefacts would be the chronological anchors for similar objects found hundreds of miles away in prehistoric Europe.

And travel he did. Montelius visited hundreds of museums, many of them in small towns far from big cities. There were no cars, only railways and endless journeys by horse-drawn coach or on horseback. Electric lighting was still unknown, and of course there were no typewriters or computers. Everything had to be recorded by hand. Montelius acquired information not only from his own travels, but also from a wide network of colleagues whom he encountered during his journeys or contacted by letter.

Over many years of research, Montelius developed his 'cross-dating' technique. Using objects of known age from the ancient Egyptians and other Mediterranean civilisations, he linked artefact after artefact across Europe by comparing their minor details and stylistic features. He also compared them to dated objects. Bracelets, daggers, clay vessels and pins – all formed part of Montelius's chronologies. He ended up with interconnected networks of dated artefacts of all kinds that extended from one end of Europe to the other.

In 1885, Montelius published his masterpiece, *On Dating in the Bronze Age*. This brilliant work, based on his study of thousands of objects and the sites where they came from, produced the first timeline for ancient Europe. Using axes, brooches, swords and other artefacts, he subdivided the European Bronze Age into six time periods. His evidence for these stages, based on huge numbers of finds, was so convincing that it was very soon almost universally accepted. Sometime later, Montelius dated the beginning of the Bronze Age back to 1800 BC. Many of his colleagues thought this too early. But more than three-quarters of a century later, in the early 1970s, radiocarbon dating, unknown in Montelius's day, proved him correct (see Chapter 27).

Montelius also believed that archaeologists should share their discoveries with the public. To this end, he lectured and gave guided tours of the museum, talking to a wide variety of audiences. He spoke eloquently in English, French, German and Italian – all without notes. Numerous popular articles and books flowed from his pen. Influenced by his wife, he also fought for women's rights. In many ways, the leading European archaeologist of his day was far ahead of his contemporaries.

By the time Montelius became director of Sweden's Museum of National Antiquities, archaeology had come a long way. Thanks to his thorough research, and that of his Scandinavian predecessors, many Europeans were now well aware of the importance of the prehistoric past. However, excavation methods (with a few notable exceptions) were still rough and ready, especially in Mediterranean lands. The lust for museum specimens and spectacular finds continued unabated. But for the first time, there was a framework for Europe before the Romans, based on artefacts and their contexts, and not just on a few great discoveries.

In the late nineteenth century, professional archaeologists were a rare breed. Much archaeology was still little more than casual collecting. And almost all of it was still done in Greece and Italy, the Middle East and Europe. But archaeology was on the move elsewhere, and especially in the Americas. There, the sensational discoveries of John Lloyd Stephens and Frederick Catherwood helped direct other archaeologists' minds towards three fundamental questions. What was the ancestry of the Native Americans? Where had they come from? And how had they crossed into the Americas?

CHAPTER 12

The Myth of the Mound Builders

On 12 October 1492, Italian explorer Christopher Columbus, Spain's Admiral of the Ocean Sea, set foot on an island in the Bahamas. There he found people whom he thought would make ideal servants. Within a few generations, however, unfamiliar diseases and mistreatment had drastically reduced the island populations of the Caribbean. Few paused to wonder where these native people had come from or how they had reached their homeland.

The debate over Native Americans began when Columbus paraded some of his captives before the Spanish king. Who were these strange people? Were they human beings? It was assumed that they were simple, uncomplicated souls until Spanish conqueror Hernán Cortés and the soldiers under his command revealed the dazzling, sophisticated world of the Aztecs in 1519. The Aztec capital, Tenochtitlán ('the place of the prickly pear cactus'), which stood where Mexico City is now, was home to more than 200,000 people, with a great market that rivalled those of Constantinople and Seville.

The staggering diversity of Native American societies, from simple hunting bands to wealthy civilisations, posed challenging questions in a Europe raised on the biblical creation story set in the Middle East. How had the Indians reached the Americas? Had they come by land, or from Asia? Or had some unknown pioneer crossed the Atlantic long before Columbus? American archaeologists are still researching these issues.

In 1589, a Spanish Catholic missionary, José de Acosta, announced that the first settlers had crossed into North America from Asia, with only 'short stretches of navigation'. We now know that Acosta was correct and that the Native Americans are indeed of Asian origin.

Nearly three centuries later, in 1856, this theory received a boost when a scholar named Samuel Haven affirmed that the Indians had crossed the Bering Strait in ancient times. Haven was a lone voice at a time when thousands of settlers were moving westward across the Allegheny Mountains into unknown territory. Most of them were farmers eager for fertile land. They were astounded to find hundreds of large mounds, earthen enclosures and banks in the Ohio Valley and from the Great Lakes and Nebraska to Florida. Lusting after gold and buried wealth, many farmers went treasure hunting. They found numerous human skeletons, shell ornaments and weapons, but no gold.

The mysterious earthworks (artificial banks of soil) emerged from often thick woodland as pioneer farmers cleared their lands. Some of the mounds stood alone; others were in tightly arranged groups. Great enclosures surrounded some of them. The earthworks were clearly ancient, for no modern Indian peoples constructed anything of the kind. Some were obviously burial mounds, with well-defined layers of skeletons or elaborate log-lined burial chambers. When the farmers trenched (dug) into the mounds, they recovered stone pipes, finely hammered copper axes and ornaments, well-made pottery and other tools that were clearly the work of skilled craftspeople. The few experts who looked at the finds saw no similarities with Egyptian or other artworks. The Mound Builders became something unknown and mysterious.

So who were the Mound Builders? Almost everyone assumed that the Indians were too primitive. And so tales of gold, valiant warriors and exotic civilisations spread like wildfire. These were the stuff of dreams for adventurous settlers in an unfamiliar land. Tall tales entertained farmers on winter evenings. In the early 1830s, popular writer Josiah Priest wove stories of great armies of white warriors, of war elephants charging over the plains, and of larger-than-life heroes. He gave the North Americans an entirely fictional, heroic past, usually known today as the Myth of the Mound Builders.

Treasure hunting was commonplace, but there were relatively few spectacular finds. The digging was quick and destructive. Mounds were flattened by ploughs, and few of the settlers examined the earthworks and mounds at all systematically. But there were one or two exceptions.

Caleb Atwater, postmaster of Circleville, Ohio, surveyed and excavated large numbers of mounds in the early nineteenth century. He found hundreds of burials and numerous fine ornaments made from mica (a transparent mineral), some in the form of bird claws or humans. The deeply religious Atwater insisted that those who had built the mounds were shepherds and farmers from Asia who had crossed the Bering Strait soon after the biblical flood. As for the Indians, he assumed that they had arrived long after the earthworks were abandoned.

In developing his theory of ancient migration, Samuel Haven had relied on the work of another researcher, Ephraim Squier (1821–88). Squier was an intelligent, well-educated American with a serious interest in the past. He began his career as a journalist in New York State, then worked for a small-town local paper in Chillicothe, Ohio. Later on, he would become a traveller and successful diplomat, and on assignment to Peru in 1868 he would become one of the first outsiders to describe the breath-taking Inca sites in the Andes. But long before he went to South America, Squier teamed up with a local Chillicothe physician, Edwin Davis. Between 1845 and 1847, the two excavated, surveyed and puzzled over the bewildering array of earthworks and burial mounds in the Ohio Valley.

The major force in the partnership, Squier was responsible for the partners' accurate plans of many major earthworks. His surveys were so precise that they are still used today and appear in several guidebooks. Supported by the American Ethnological Society, the two men hurriedly tunnelled into more than 200 mounds, surveyed many earthworks and enclosures, and assembled a huge collection of artefacts. One important site they surveyed was the Great Serpent Mound, a long, curving mound on a ridge in the shape of a wriggling snake holding a small oval mound in its open jaws.

All this research came together in Squier and Davis's 1848 book, *Ancient Monuments of the Mississippi Valley*. Squier wanted to produce facts to replace wild theories, and the 300-page volume was a handsome publication, with lavish illustrations. It remained the only account of the Mound Builders for generations. The authors attempted to classify the earthworks and mounds into such imaginative categories as 'Mounds of Sacrifice' and 'Temple Mounds', but their inventories of sites and their detailed plans are a delight to examine and can be linked to modern maps. In many cases, the authors recorded features that have since vanished.

Squier carefully described the small finds from his hasty excavations. He even correctly identified the copper ore from near Lake Superior, far to the north, that had been hammered into simple axes and adzes. There were carved soapstone pipes and animal figures. The latter struck Squier as far more sophisticated than anything fashioned by the local Indians.

Squier and Davis wrote of the Mound Builders in general terms, pointing out that the mound people were expert at constructing defensive earthworks. Their ideas were influenced by popular tales of great armies and huge battles in earlier times. They painted a portrait of peace-loving early Mound Builders: when attacked by 'hostile savage hordes', they had frantically built defences to protect themselves. But it had all been in vain: the invaders conquered them and the Mound Builders disappeared. Squier and Davis assumed that the Indians encountered by Europeans were these warlike, hostile newcomers, who were thus no more entitled to Ohio than the Europeans.

Squier and Davis may have been prejudiced, but their catalogues and surveys placed the controversies surrounding the Mound Builders on an entirely new footing. Nevertheless, wild speculation continued. William Pidgeon, who claimed to be a trader in the west with long experience of Indians, announced in 1858 that the biblical Adam had built the first mound in America. Many others had followed, including Alexander the Great and various Egyptians and Phoenicians. Pidgeon made a fortune from his book, which he said was based on conversations with an Indian named De-coo-dah. His informant conveniently died after passing on his secrets.

For all the mythmaking, change was afoot. Archaeological research received a major boost from the publication of Darwin's *On the Origin of Species* and from the Neanderthal discovery (see Chapter 8). A new generation of research began, centred on institutions like Harvard University and the Smithsonian Institution. But despite numerous claims, no one found any Somme hand axes or Neanderthal fossils anywhere in North America. The major controversies still surrounded the Mound Builders of the Midwest and South.

So intense was the speculation about the Mound Builders that in 1881 a group of archaeologists persuaded the US Congress to set aside funds for Mound Builder research. A Division of Mound Exploration attached to the Smithsonian's Bureau of Ethnology set to work under Professor Cyrus Thomas (1825–1910). Little is known about Thomas, who was a geologist by training. However, we do know that he originally believed that a race of Mound Builders – separate from the Indians – had built the mounds.

Thomas and eight assistants fanned out over mound country, especially the Mississippi Valley. Here farmers were digging into mounds in search of treasure, and there was now an active market in artefacts. A paper merchant named Clarence Moore spent his summers floating along the Mississippi and Ohio Rivers on house-boats. He would stop, his labourers would dig, and thousands of artefacts would vanish below deck – to be sold or added to his collection.

Most of Thomas's work concentrated on the country between Ohio and Wisconsin. He spread his team thinly on the ground, and they worked all year round surveying and excavating with the minimum of destruction. He laboured for more than seven years. This was planned archaeological research, collecting accurate data on a large scale. He and his men sampled more than 2,000 mounds and earthworks of every size and complexity. Some 38,000 artefacts came into Thomas's hands via excavation or donation.

In 1894, Thomas published a 700-page report, in which he described hundreds of earthworks and mounds in minute detail. Although Thomas's work is not an easy read, it is based on carefully collected data.

As he described the earthworks and finds, his beliefs about the Mound Builders changed radically. As a careful researcher, he compared the artefacts and artworks from his excavations and from private collections to the objects made by living Native American societies. He found close similarities between ancient and modern tools and weapons. He also studied accounts by European travellers, who described mounds that were still in use as late as the eighteenth century.

No longer did Thomas believe in a vanished Mound Builder civilisation in the Mississippi Valley. Instead he stated that all the sites he had examined were constructed by 'the Indian tribes inhabiting the corresponding area when it was first visited by Europeans'.

Thomas's data-driven book changed the archaeological game, and science came to replace speculation. But prejudice against Native Americans endured and their lands were seized, often on flimsy legal grounds. Gradually, haphazard digging by non-experts gave way to the systematic fieldwork of professional researchers.

Many years were to pass before well-trained archaeologists came along. But the corner had been turned. Tragically, apart from some rare sites in public parks, nearly all the places in Thomas's monograph (a detailed study) have suffered at least some damage.

Thomas's report remains a basic source for archaeologists today. But the legacy of this energetic fieldworker extends even further: he commented on the great diversity of peoples who had lived in Mound Builder country in ancient times. The challenge for future archaeologists was to identify these diverse societies and their relationships with both earlier and later cultures.

Over a century since Cyrus Thomas finally debunked the Myth of the Mound Builders, research has revealed some of this remarkable diversity. Today, we know a lot about the so-called Adena, Hopewell and Mississippian societies who built the earthworks, and about their elaborate ritual beliefs. We also know that many of the rituals and religious beliefs of those who built North America's great earthworks survived into the period of recorded history.

Thomas's work failed to halt the tidal wave of destruction, but he at least managed to persuade a group of Boston ladies to raise $6,000 to buy the Great Serpent Mound, which he restored as a public park for visitors in 1887. It is now an Ohio State Memorial and a National Historic Landmark.

CHAPTER 13

'Stepping into the Unknown'

In April 1883, the soldiers at Fort Apache, Arizona, were astonished when a lone traveller on a mule rode up to the gate. The Apache were on the warpath, and that made travel very difficult.

The rider was Swiss-born Adolph Francis Alphonse Bandelier (1840–1914), who was wandering through the remote Indian territories of the desert studying the 'ruined cities' of the people who had lived there long before Columbus.

Bandelier was travelling through the virtually unknown American Southwest. A few Spanish-led expeditions from Mexico had visited Hopi and Zuni Pueblo Indian villages in search of gold, but they had left empty-handed. There had been tales of crowded, multi-storey Indian settlements, commonly called 'pueblos', but there were few details.

The first lengthy description of the ancient pueblos came in 1849, when US Army Lieutenant James Henry Simpson and artist Richard Kern visited ten ancient pueblos, including the great ruins at Pueblo Bonito, in Chaco Canyon, New Mexico, and the Navajo pueblos in Canyon de Chelly in northeastern Arizona.

The number of outside visitors to the region increased dramatically after the completion of the transcontinental railroad in 1869, as ever more settlers moved westward. The US government organised official expeditions to map and explore what was essentially a huge environmental laboratory. Their tasks included studying the geology of the area and gathering knowledge about the Pueblo Indians and their settlements.

Most government expeditions were more concerned with geology and potential mining opportunities than with Indian pueblos. Adolph Bandelier on his humble mule had quite different interests. A small-town banker in upstate New York, then a coal-mine manager, the quiet and scholarly Bandelier used his spare time to study Spanish records of Mexico and the Southwest at a time of public fascination with the American West.

A skilled linguist, he scoured little-known archives, but learned virtually nothing about Pueblo Indian history. His hobby became an obsession, and he soon realised that he needed to extend his library-based research by going into the field in the Southwest. Bandelier dropped everything to travel to Santa Fe, New Mexico, with only a small grant to his name. Though almost penniless and with few possessions beyond his mule, at least he could now study Pueblo Indian archaeology and history in situ.

Bandelier knew that any investigation of the past would start with existing Pueblo Indian communities. He stopped first at the recently abandoned Pecos Pueblo in New Mexico. As late as the seventeenth century, as many as 2,000 people had lived at Pecos. The last of them had left by the 1830s, fifty years before Bandelier arrived.

Having mastered the local language in an astonishing ten days, he collected vital historical information from elderly residents. He also described and surveyed the ruins of the large pueblo, but did not excavate: he had neither the knowledge nor the money to do so. His Pecos research convinced him that the only way to study earlier Pueblo history was by working backwards from living societies into the distant past, using archaeology. Bandelier wrote a detailed report on his Pecos research, but it attracted little attention.

He now searched for other promising sites. In late 1880, he spent three months living with the inhabitants of Cochiti Pueblo. New Mexico's Catholic priests helped him extensively in contacting Indian informants, especially after he converted to Catholicism.

The pueblos that Bandelier visited consisted of closely packed adobe (mud) rooms, connected to one another by a maze of entrances and narrow passageways. Some of the larger pueblos had two storeys – or even more, like the great semi-circular, multi-storey Pueblo Bonito in Chaco Canyon. Large, circular underground chambers were to be found in the open centre of the semi-circular structure. These *kivas* were places where secret ceremonies were held. Seemingly ramshackle and somewhat untidy, the pueblos were in fact highly organised communities, where extended families had lived for generations.

From 1881 to 1892, Bandelier wandered across Arizona and New Mexico. Though he made extensive notes during his travels, he didn't live to see them in print (they were finally published in the 1960s and 1970s). They contain information of great archaeological and historical importance.

Strictly speaking, Bandelier was not an archaeologist; but he was in all but name. He never drove a spade into an archaeological site. Instead, with his plans and site descriptions, he laid the groundwork for later researchers' excavations.

Bandelier approached the history of the Pueblo Indians using written sources and oral traditions, as well as his own observations. He was the first American archaeologist to use his observations of living Indian tribes to interpret the past. He regarded archaeology as a study not of objects, but of the history and information that the finds supplied. He tracked back from the present to ancient times, using everything from Indian pot designs to local histories passed from generation to generation. As he put it, he worked 'from the known to the unknown, step by step'. Bandelier's remarkable fieldwork formed the foundations for the pioneering archaeological work that was to come a generation later. All those who followed in his footsteps worked from the present back into the past, as Southwest archaeology does to this day.

Bandelier supported his wanderings by writing a Catholic history, magazine articles – and even a novel, *The Delight Makers*, set in prehistoric times. His object in doing so was more than just to make money (although that would have been welcome). He wanted to share Southwest Indian history with a broader public. The novel was not a commercial success, but it was striking for its insights into Indian society. Bandelier left the Southwest in 1892 and spent the rest of his life working in Mexico, South America and Spain.

Unlike archaeology in many other parts of the world, which began with large-scale digging, the Southwest's past began with Bandelier's careful studies of living societies and historic pueblos. He realised that to succeed, archaeologists would have to work back through the centuries by digging into pueblo garbage heaps, with their thousands of broken pot fragments. He could not do so himself, and so he contented himself with maps, surveys and talking to living Pueblo Indians. There was another problem, too. Many of the most promising pueblos for archaeology were still occupied, which made digging impossible.

Alongside Bandelier was another visitor who helped lay the basis for later excavations – a remarkable anthropologist who lived among the Zuni Indians and acquired an insider's knowledge of their society. Frank Hamilton Cushing (1857–1900) was the son of a physician. A smooth-talking scholar, he liked drama and had a taste for carefully managed publicity. In 1875, Cushing was appointed assistant in ethnology (the study of non-Western peoples) at the Smithsonian Institution, where he learned of the Pueblo Indians of New Mexico.

In late 1879, Cushing accompanied US Army Colonel James Stevenson on a Smithsonian expedition to the Southwest. Cushing arrived at Zuni Pueblo as the September sun was setting behind the village. He described the densely inhabited pueblo as 'a little island of mesas [flat-topped hills], one upon another.' He was supposed to stay for just three months. Instead, he remained for four and a half years, after which time he left to attend to his neglected duties in Washington.

Cushing stayed behind after Stevenson and his companions moved on. Even after a few days, he was aware that his work had hardly begun. Bandelier had wandered freely across the Southwest, collecting information and identifying abandoned pueblos. But Cushing took a totally different approach. He realised that a true understanding of the Zuni could only be achieved by living among them, mastering their language and recording their lives in detail. Today, anthropologists call this 'participant observation', but it was a novel idea in Cushing's time. Cushing was not an archaeologist, but he was aware that Zuni culture extended far back into the past. And he knew that his research provided a baseline for studying much earlier history.

At first the Indians threatened to kill him when he tried to record their dances. But his calm response made a deep impression on them and he was never harassed again. The Zuni allowed him to study the structure of their society, and he was even initiated into their secret Priesthood of the Bow. Cushing had his ears pierced and he dressed in Indian clothes. Eventually, the Zunis came to trust him enough to appoint him a war chief. Next to his numerous transcriptions of Zuni folktales and myths, he recorded his own title: '1st War Chief of Zuni: US Assistant Ethnologist'.

Cushing became a passionate supporter of the Zuni and did much to protect their lands against European settlers. But he upset some powerful people in Washington who had their eyes on land in the area, and he was recalled. Despite ill health, he lectured widely on his experiences and wrote about them for popular audiences. Frank Cushing's strong personal magnetism and his public-speaking skills did much to heighten public interest in the Southwest. His books and lectures presented a romantic vision of pueblo life that was often far from reality. Nevertheless, his accounts of Zuni oral traditions and ceremonies are of lasting value, even today.

Cushing would be the first to admit that he was no archaeologist; but he considered archaeology a way of carrying his research on living people back into earlier centuries. Excavation, he knew, was the way to work from modern times into the past. On a later, brief expedition to the Southwest, he did excavate a cemetery in

Arizona's Salt River Valley. A powerful earthquake had destroyed a nearby pueblo, which he also investigated. But his Southwestern researches were over by 1890.

Bandelier and Cushing showed the potential for serious excavation. Dry conditions in caves and pueblos preserved ancient baskets, painted pots, woven sleeping mats and even dried-out human burials. Many of these finds trickled back to America's East Coast and fetched high prices.

Inevitably, pothunters and antiques dealers moved in on the pueblos. Richard Wetherill, a Colorado rancher-turned-trader and artefact collector, was one of those who indulged in treasure hunting, acquiring painted pottery and other artefacts from dozens of archaeological sites.

In 1888, Wetherill and another rancher, Charlie Mason, were looking for stray cattle in the canyons of Mesa Verde in southern Colorado when they came across a large pueblo set in a cave – the largest cliff dwelling in North America. Now known as the Cliff Palace, the pueblo was built of sandstone, with mortar made of soil, water and ash to hold the stone blocks together. About a hundred people dwelt in the Cliff Palace between AD 1190 and 1260, before it was abandoned, perhaps following a long period of drought. This was an important administrative and ceremonial centre, with twenty-three sunken *kivas*.

Mesa Verde and other sites in the region became a gold mine for Richard Wetherill's family. His last years found him at Pueblo Bonito in Chaco Canyon. In 1897, he opened a store near the site selling artefacts and provisions. By 1900, he had cleared more than 190 rooms – over half the site – and had sold their contents. His 'excavations' were sponsored to the tune of at least $25,000 by private individuals, who gave the finds to the American Museum of Natural History in New York. After rumours of huge profits reached Washington, Wetherill's excavations were suspended by official order. In 1907, he signed over ownership of the land to the government.

Meanwhile, the few professional archaeologists in the Southwest, led by Edgar Hewett (1865–1946), a disciple of Adolph Bandelier, lobbied successfully for some laws to protect archaeological sites on public land. The American Antiquities Act of 1906 offered limited protection to key areas like Chaco Canyon and Mesa Verde. Hewitt started a field school to train young archaeologists in proper excavation methods – not those used by pothunters. Much of the work involved cleaning up sites damaged by looters.

Bandelier, Cushing and others established a basic principle about the Southwest: you need to work backwards from the present into the past. Archaeologists have followed this principle ever since.

CHAPTER 14

Toros! Toros!

In 1868, while out fox hunting, a Spanish hunter, Modesto Cubillas, lost track of his dog among some rocks. From below ground came the sound of barking. Cubillas found the hole through which the dog had disappeared, widened it and stumbled upon a long-hidden cave. He didn't explore the cavern, but reported its existence to the landowner, the Marquis de Sautuola (1831–88), a lawyer who owned several estates in northern Spain. Sautuola had many interests, among them books, gardening and archaeology.

But investigating the past was not a high priority for the busy landowner. Eleven years passed before he visited Cubillas's cave (now known as Altamira, meaning 'a high viewpoint'). Wandering through the cavern, he noticed some black marks on the wall, but thought nothing of them. Soon afterwards, however, he visited Paris where he saw a display of beautifully engraved antler and bone fragments – ancient Cro-Magnon artefacts from south-western France. His mind turned to Altamira, and he wondered whether similar finds might lie in the layers of the cave.

Back home, he decided to excavate. His nine-year-old daughter Maria begged to come along too. As father and daughter looked on, labourers dug into the earthen floor with picks and shovels in a hasty search for engraved tools. But Maria soon tired of the muddy work and wandered off to play deeper in the cave. Suddenly, from a low side chamber, the marquis heard a cry: 'Toros! Toros!' – 'Bulls! Bulls!'

Sautuola hurried over and Maria pointed to a polychrome (multi-coloured) bison, one of numerous animal paintings on the rock. Bison, wild boar and deer all appeared in a jumble on the roof. The vivid colours of the paintings made the beasts look as if they had been painted only the day before. Maria had made one of the greatest archaeological discoveries of the nineteenth century.

The Altamira painted chamber, with its low ceiling, is like a zoo of large, Ice Age beasts. Long-extinct bison painted in black and red stand there, their hair bristling, sometimes with lowered heads. Others crouch. A wild pig prances across the rock. There are deer with huge antlers. The animals fill the ceiling, and many seem more alive because of the bulges in the rock that emphasise their bodies. Among the beasts are red handprints. Some of these were made by blowing red powder onto the ceiling, while others were carefully painted in place.

Sautuola recognised at once that the Altamira cave paintings were similar to the engraved figures he had seen in Paris. He published a pamphlet on the cave in which he proposed the idea that the wall art could be from the same period as the artefacts he had seen on display in France. To his dismay, French archaeologists immediately rejected the notion: the fresh-looking paintings were, they said, modern and too sophisticated to be the work of prehistoric savages. Some went so far as to call the paintings forgeries, created by a modern artist, perhaps in collaboration with the marquis. Bitter and heartbroken, Sautuola retired to his estates and died in 1888, still suspected of forgery. It would be many years before his name was cleared.

A few paintings and engravings had also been found in caves in southwestern France. The experts also considered them to be modern. This was hardly surprising, since, at the time, most people believed that 'primitive' ancient hunters could never be artists. Soon, more prehistoric paintings came to light. In 1895, the owner of the La Mouthe cave near Les Eyzies in the Dordogne – Lartet and Christy's hunting ground – removed some of the earthen fill. He found himself in a hitherto sealed gallery, with an engraved bison and other figures covering the walls. They were obviously ancient. More painted caves came to light, at locations that are now popular tourist attractions – Les Combarelles (which is famous for its engravings) and the Font de Gaume cave, close to Les Eyzies (with its woolly mammoth paintings). The case for Ice Age art grew stronger and stronger.

In 1898, a small party of archaeologists visited Les Combarelles. They included an eminent French archaeologist named Émile Cartailhac (1845–1921) and a young Catholic priest, Henri Breuil (1877–1961).

The engravings deep underground left a powerful impression on Cartailhac. Four years later, he and Breuil visited Altamira. The young priest firmly believed that the paintings there dated back to the Ice Age, but Cartailhac had long maintained that they must be modern. Now, however, he changed his mind – the paintings were ancient. Indeed, he found the evidence so strong that he published a famous paper apologising for his previous beliefs. He declared that Altamira was a prehistoric art gallery. The Marquis de Sautuola and his daughter were finally proved right.

Much of the credit for Émile Cartailhac's change of mind must go to Henri Breuil, who was to become a giant of rock art research. A native of Normandy in northern France, Breuil was the son of a lawyer. He was ordained a Catholic priest in 1900. A man of profound faith, Breuil was also an exceptional scientist. The young priest's faith was so strong that the Church ignored his Ice Age research (which was against its teachings) and gave him permission to pursue his studies – not as a priest, but as an independent scholar.

Soon after he became a priest, Breuil met two French prehistorians, Louis Capitan and Édouard Piette, who gave him a thorough grounding in the antler, bone and stone tools from the French caves. Breuil was strong-minded and did not suffer fools gladly – you disagreed with him at your peril. But he was a superb artist at a time when both controlled lighting underground and high-quality photography were near impossible. Copying delicate rock paintings required the artist to make rough sketches and then measure the figures. This obliged him to lie on sacks filled with ferns and straw, using only candles or flickering lamps for illumination. Breuil spent days wedged into narrow passages in near-total darkness, tracing engravings and faint images onto paper. He once calculated that he had spent more than 700 days underground, copying paintings and engravings.

Breuil finished his rough sketches in watercolours, checking them against black-and-white photographs whenever possible. Inevitably, some of his copies were somewhat imaginative; but even today, when colour images are available, they represent an invaluable rock art archive. Unfortunately, many of the paintings he recorded have now vanished because of air changes generated by frequent visitors.

An astonishing discovery came in 1940, when some schoolboys hunting rabbits near the town of Montignac lost their dog down a rabbit hole. On hearing him barking underground, they opened up the rabbit hole and scrambled down. The boys found themselves in a large hall covered in magnificent paintings of wild bulls, bison and other animals. Breuil hastened to what is now known as Lascaux cave. The huge bulls and fierce bison, the colours as vibrant as the day they were painted, astonished him. Thanks to radiocarbon dating (see Chapter 27), we now know that the paintings and engravings had been sealed underground for at least 15,000 years.

After copying the Altamira paintings, Breuil had devised a theory that there were two different Upper Palaeolithic art styles, which evolved from the simple to the more complex. He was convinced that the artworks were a form of what he called 'hunting magic'. The images were a connection to the spirits of the animals painted on the walls, created to ensure hunters' success. He also believed that some of the paintings and engravings, especially on portable objects, were of such artistic merit that they were made for pleasure – evidence of the creativity of Cro-Magnon artists.

Colour and infrared photography, as well as later, often spectacular discoveries, such as Lascaux, has shown that this theory was too simplistic. Another painted cave, Grotte de Chauvet, discovered in 1994, contains magnificent paintings of Ice Age rhinoceroses and other extinct animals, which were painted around 30,000 years ago. The Chauvet paintings are even more elaborate than Lascaux, yet they are earlier.

No one has yet devised a generally agreed sequence for what is obviously a complex and very old art tradition. Nor can the experts agree on what the art means. Soon after the Lascaux discovery, Breuil went out to South Africa, where he stayed until 1952 studying the rock art of the San (indigenous people once known as Bushmen).

He had first seen San rock art during a visit to the country for a conference in 1929. Early travellers and anthropologists had found San paintings long before Altamira was discovered. As early as 1874, South African anthropologist George Stow told of meeting some San hunters who were not painters themselves, but who knew people who were.

San rock art is quite unlike the works in French caves. In southern Africa, there are scenes of the chase during a hunt, of people collecting honey, of dances and ceremonies, and of camp life, as well as signs and symbols. Breuil again considered this art a product of hunting magic, but we now know it had far more complex meanings.

Not that Breuil was the first scholar to puzzle over San rock art. Ironically, not long before Altamira was discovered, a German linguist, Wilhelm Bleek (1827–75), learned several San dialects while living in Cape Town. He did so after persuading the authorities to release twenty-eight San convicts working on the break-waters of Cape Town harbour to act as his teachers. They lived at Bleek's house while he and his sister-in-law Lucy Lloyd compiled not only vocabularies and grammars, but also a valuable body of mythology and folklore. Bleek and Lloyd were well aware of San art, but had only a few copies to show people.

In 1873, another researcher, magistrate J.M. Orpen, travelled through the Maluti Mountains of Lesotho, a short distance from the Drakensberg range. He recorded oral traditions recited by his San guide that were remarkably similar to Bleek and Lloyd's mythologies. Both placed major emphasis on a large antelope, the eland, favoured prey for San hunters.

Bleek became convinced that the paintings illustrated San myths. But researchers who came after him either ignored the carefully assembled accounts he'd gathered or regarded the information as being of dubious value. They focused instead on recording the art systematically.

Breuil himself spent 1947 to 1950 copying art in what is now Namibia and Zimbabwe. Rather than photography, he used a pencil and thick paper, which led to numerous inaccuracies. In Namibia, he copied the famous 'White Lady of the Brandberg'. The 2,000-year-old painting shows a human figure with a partially white-painted face and legs, carrying a bow and arrow and striding along holding a flower. Breuil stated that the painting was of a woman. It was an exotic painting, and he claimed it was not of a San, but of a visitor from a Mediterranean land, perhaps Crete, where ancient female figures were common. Breuil, who seems to have had little respect for the San, was completely wrong. After he died in 1961, research using colour photography showed that the painting is of a man, perhaps a shaman, with white-painted features.

Bleek and Lloyd's nineteenth-century research has helped unlock some of the secrets of both European and African rock art. But fundamental questions remain unanswered. Why did Cro-Magnon artists paint and engrave animals and complex symbols in dark caves? Did the artists experience powerful visions alone and in total darkness, then remember them with their paintings? Why did they work far from daylight, their only illumination coming from animal fat lamps?

San art is mostly in open rock shelters, much of it involving elongated human figures sometimes dancing around dying eland. Without question, their art also had supernatural meaning. Some experts believe that the paintings were a way of communicating with the supernatural, whose powers would pass to humans through their handprints on the cave walls. We will never know exactly what the art meant, but the research continues.

CHAPTER 15

Searching for Homer's Heroes

Heinrich Schliemann (1822–90) is among the most famous – and most controversial – of all early archaeologists. He was the fifth child of a Protestant clergyman from northern Germany. A poor student, he left school at the age of fourteen. In his teenage years, though, he fell in love with the poems of Homer.

Writing during the eighth century BC, Homer created two great epics packed with Greek heroes. *The Iliad* and *The Odyssey* were probably based on tales recited and sung by Greek poet-singers over many centuries. *The Iliad* tells the story of the Greek siege of a city named Troy. *The Odyssey* recounts the adventures of one of the warriors involved, Odysseus, as he returned home. They are some of the finest adventure stories ever written.

If Schliemann is to be believed, his father would recite stories from Homer's epics in the evenings. From an early age, the young Heinrich was desperate to discover Troy, believing the two great poems to be accurate historical accounts.

Did Troy exist and where was it? Did the siege actually take place? Schliemann spent much of his life trying to find out. His obsession with Troy stemmed from his love of Homer, rather than from any scientific basis. Scholars did not even believe that the city had ever existed: experts on the epics held that they were the product of Homer's imagination. At best, Schliemann's fascination with Troy seemed eccentric. And anyway, there was little chance that he could prove the experts wrong – he was dirt poor, lacked education and was apprenticed to a grocer.

In 1841, Schliemann walked away from the grocery business and ended up in Amsterdam. He had a talent for business and languages, and made a fortune from trading dyes in St Petersburg, Russia, from banking in California and from war supplies during the Crimean War. Now a multimillionaire, in 1864 he retired from business to devote the rest of his life to archaeology and Homer.

In 1869, he toured Italy and Greece. He learned modern and classical Greek, the latter in two years. His travels included Odysseus's homeland, Ithaca, the Greek islands and finally the Dardanelles strait in Turkey. There he met Frank Calvert, an English diplomat who owned half a large mound named Hissarlik, near the entrance to the strait. Like Schliemann, Calvert was interested in archaeology, Homer and Troy. He had dug some shallow trenches into Hissarlik, but had found almost nothing. Nevertheless, he firmly believed that this was Troy.

His visitor rode around the dusty mound and its surroundings, *The Iliad* in one hand. He tried to reconstruct the landscape where Homer's battles raged. Schliemann came to share Calvert's conviction that Hissarlik really was Homer's Troy. With deep pockets and restless ambition, Heinrich Schliemann decided to dig for the siege of Troy.

Schliemann had no excavation experience whatsoever. All he brought to the dig was a conviction that Homer had recorded historical fact. He started modestly in April 1870 with a small trial trench and found a huge stone wall. But was the Homeric city at the top of the mound or at its base? The wall merely whetted his appetite for a much larger dig.

He applied for a permit from the sultan of Turkey, which did not arrive until 1871. Meanwhile, he looked for a Greek wife, interviewed several candidates, and finally married the young and beautiful Sophia Engastromenos, the daughter of a shopkeeper. She was seventeen; he was forty-seven. The marriage was a success, and she became a partner in his work.

In October 1871, Heinrich Schliemann started excavating at Hissarlik. He recruited eighty labourers and set them to work on the northern side of the site, searching for the city described by Homer. He was now convinced that it lay at the bottom of the mound. Armed with pickaxes and wooden shovels, the men dug a large trench 10 metres deep in six weeks. This was no archaeological excavation: Schliemann quarried ruthlessly through stone walls and foundations. A jumble of stone blocks, perhaps the remains of the walls of a great city, emerged from the bottom of the cutting.

Schliemann had started work at Hissarlik with no firm plan. He had his copy of *The Iliad*, and pot fragments and partially exposed stone walls suggested that rich pickings might lie below the surface. His methods were direct and simple – move lots of soil using lots of men. He remarked that the scale of his excavations required at least 120 men. Schliemann readily admitted in his account of the excavations that he had been forced to demolish the remains of temples, fortifications and even burials in his single-minded quest for the Homeric city.

In 1872, the Schliemanns returned with a huge stockpile of picks, shovels and wheelbarrows. They built themselves a house on top of the mound. Living conditions there were harsh: strong winds whistled through the thin planks of their dwelling, and once a fire threatened the house.

Schliemann attacked Troy on a huge scale. Three foremen and a surveyor supervised up to 150 men. Large teams peeled away the strata of the mound like a layer cake, and the excavations finally reached the base of the mound at a depth of about 14 metres.

Schliemann renewed his reckless assault, cutting a huge trench through the mound from north to south. At season's end, he had excavated almost 250 square metres of earth and archaeological layers. Even with modern earthmoving equipment, this would have been a stupendous feat; but he did it all by hand. It was no coincidence that some of his supervisors had worked on Egypt's Suez

Canal, which cut through Egypt from the Mediterranean to the Red Sea.

The results were astounding. It turned out that city after city had flourished at Hissarlik. Each had erected its buildings on the foundations of earlier settlements. By the end of the 1873 season, Schliemann had identified no fewer than seven Troys (by 1890, he had added two more). The earliest city was too small, and so Schliemann announced that the third city from the base was Homer's Troy. 'Many treasures' of copper, gold and silver were contained in a dense layer of burnt masonry and ash. This showed that the city had been burnt down. Obviously, said Schliemann, it was the city destroyed by the Greeks. The later cities in higher layers were more recent.

From May 1875, the diggers focused their efforts on this third city. One hot morning, Schliemann spotted gold gleaming 8.5 metres below the surface. Dismissing the labourers, he himself quickly cut into the soft earth and removed the priceless finds. Or so he wrote, for no one witnessed this sensational discovery.

Back at base, Schliemann spread out his 'treasure' of gold pendants and earrings, chains, brooches and other unique ornaments. He seized the opportunity and named it 'Priam's Treasure', after the legendary Homeric King of Troy, claiming it was the monarch's property.

The discovery caused a sensation, but there are real questions as to whether the treasure was in fact all found together. Many experts believe that the Schliemanns assembled it from isolated gold finds made during the excavations. Whatever the truth, Schliemann quietly smuggled all the gold out of Turkey and hid the artefacts in a garden shed in Athens. He later decked out Sophia in part of the treasure, like a Trojan princess. When the Turks learned of the find through a German newspaper, they were furious. The controversy over Heinrich's smuggling was only settled with the payment of a huge sum to the Ottoman government.

Troy and 'Priam's Treasure' made Schliemann an international celebrity. But many scholars were profoundly distrustful of him, some even accusing him of buying the horde's ornaments in Constantinople's bazaars.

Having accomplished so much, many archaeologists would have taken things easy, but not Heinrich Schliemann. For some time, he had had his eye on the walled fortress of Mycenae in the north corner of the fertile plain of Argos, southern Greece. Mycenae was said to be the palace and burial place of the legendary King Agamemnon, leader of the Greeks at Troy. Schliemann was firmly convinced of this, and in 1876 the Greek government reluctantly gave him permission to excavate there.

Once again, Schliemann operated on a huge scale: sixty-three men cleared the famous citadel gate adorned with a lion sculpture; others worked inside a circle of stone slabs (which Schliemann called 'tombstones'). Even before he had dug below them, Schliemann announced that he had found Agamemnon's burial place. After four months, the Schliemanns had unearthed five graves containing fifteen bodies, each dripping with gold. Until the discovery of the Egyptian pharaoh Tutankhamun's tomb in 1922, the Mycenae burials were the greatest ever archaeological treasure. Several gold death masks featuring beards and clipped moustaches came to light. Hammered, embossed gold plates, delicate crowns and vessels, and dozens of small ornaments emerged from the graves.

Schliemann basked in international glory and the entire world followed the excavations. Two ruling monarchs and a prime minister visited the dig. Schliemann announced that he had found the bodies of Homer's heroes. German scholars promptly dismissed the claims. By 1900, archaeologists like Arthur Evans (see Chapter 18) had shown that Schliemann had, in fact, discovered the Mycenaean civilisation, a magnificent Bronze Age society that flourished around 1300 BC – so, later than Homeric times.

Heinrich Schliemann remains something of a mystery. He himself seems to have thought he was God's messenger, sent to bring the truth about Homer to a waiting world. His admirers called him a genius. His enemies labelled him an egocentric lunatic. He may have been single-minded in his pursuit of wealth and Homer, but behind it all, both he and Sophia were gentle, kind people.

The Mycenae discoveries turned Schliemann into a respected elder statesman of archaeology. He returned to Hissarlik in 1878, this time with an esteemed German scholar, Rudolf Virchow, who studied the geology of the Trojan plain and mound. Schliemann was smart enough to realise that his methods were outdated. German archaeologists at Olympia, the ancient site of the Olympic Games, were revolutionising scientific excavation (see Chapter 16). From 1882 to 1890, Wilhelm Dörpfeld, an archaeologist and architect trained at Olympia, excavated alongside Schliemann. They worked closely together and established that the sixth city, not the third, coincided most closely with Homer's Troy – if it had actually existed.

Meanwhile, Schliemann continued to excavate elsewhere. He dug into another Mycenaean palace, on the summit of Tiryns, also on the Plain of Argos. It was famous for its fortified walls made of colossal boulders. But he was now paying closer attention to small finds like potsherds (fragments of ceramics). Many of them bore geometric, painted patterns very similar to those found on Crete.

Schliemann's restless mind then turned to that island, home of King Minos, ruler of Crete in Homer's epics. Legend has it that Minos kept a bull-human, the Minotaur, in a labyrinth beneath his palace. Theseus, son of the King of Athens, was said to have killed the Minotaur with the help of Minos's daughter Ariadne, who guided him out of the labyrinth by means of a thread. The story of Theseus and the Minotaur was the kind of historical mystery that Schliemann found irresistible.

The palace allegedly lay at Knossos, a hillside near the capital, Heraklion. With characteristic boldness, Schliemann tried to buy Knossos. Fortunately, he was unsuccessful and returned to Athens in disgust, leaving the Minoan civilisation for later – and better trained – archaeologists to investigate (see Chapter 18).

A whole new generation of archaeologists was inspired by Schliemann's work and by his ability to make great discoveries. Schliemann died suddenly in Italy, convinced that he had proved that what Homer wrote in his epics was historical truth. In that he was wrong. But he did make thousands of people aware of archaeology.

'Organised Common Sense'

Karl Richard Lepsius (1810–84) became professor of Egyptology at the University of Berlin in 1839. With his ordered and logical mind, and after years of studying ancient Egypt – especially Jean-François Champollion's work on hieroglyphs – he was the ideal candidate for a job that required the careful organisation of field research. Above all, Lepsius was a scholar who collected both artefacts and data.

Three years after his appointment, he became leader of a huge German expedition to the Nile, similar to those mounted by Napoléon's scientists half a century earlier. Then, Giovanni Belzoni and Bernardino Drovetti had plundered Egypt (see Chapter 2). But Lepsius's objectives were high-minded and ambitious. He was to develop the first history and timescale for the pharaohs, who were known only from Greek writings and fragmentary ancient Egyptian records. With Lepsius, we come to the beginnings of a new era in archaeology that stressed scientific recovery of finds and information about the past.

Lepsius began in the Nile Delta in 1842, recording previously unknown pyramids and tombs. He then moved upstream, deciphering inscriptions and carrying out some of the first excavations along the Nile to pay attention to different occupation levels. Lepsius returned to Berlin with 15,000 artefacts, plaster casts of inscriptions, and a mass of information that laid the foundations for serious Egyptology. Between 1849 and 1859, he published a magnificent twelve-volume book on the expedition. This remains a standard source on many sites that have now vanished, and is testament to what can be achieved with an orderly mind.

Careful organisation, responsible, slow-moving excavation, and prompt, detailed publication: Karl Lepsius's report helped trigger a profound change in Mediterranean archaeology. By modern standards, his excavation methods were still rough and ready, but his carefully organised work was pioneering. He surveyed many of the sites he visited and recorded the exact positions of artefacts – something almost unheard of in his day.

Lepsius was well aware of the urgent need for better standards of excavation. He spent much of his later career training a new generation of archaeologists, who were as much concerned with reconstruction and preservation as they were with digging. One of those was Alexander Conze (1831–1914), who was professor of archaeology at the University of Vienna from 1869 to 1877. Another well-organised fieldworker, Conze excavated on the island of Samothrace in the northern Aegean Sea as Heinrich Schliemann was digging into Troy. But while Schliemann excavated as though he were digging potatoes, Conze went to Samothrace to answer important historical questions, not in search of goodies.

Conze's focus was the shrine of the Cabiri, rather mysterious supernatural beings closely associated with the Greek fire god Hephaistos, who protected sailors. In ancient times, a big festival honouring them drew visitors from all over the Aegean every July, with a sacred play that involved a ritual wedding. The sanctuary itself occupied three terraces on a mountain slope. A winged statue, the Winged Victory of Samothrace, discovered there in 1863, became famous when it was moved to the Louvre in Paris.

Conze excavated the sanctuary in 1873 and 1876. He cleared several structures using advanced excavation techniques that were unknown at the time. His main concern was architecture. An architect was on site throughout the dig, while a photographer recorded the excavations. Two lavishly produced volumes detailed the work there.

As Conze's excavations drew to a close, the Germans turned to Olympia, site of the Olympic Games. Another carefully trained archaeologist, Ernst Curtius (1814–96), conducted meticulously planned excavations. In an important gesture of respect, the archaeologists gave up all claims to the finds and built a special museum on the site. Between 1875 and 1881, they cleared the Olympic stadium, with its runners' starting blocks and judges' seats. The excavators uncovered nearby temples with columns that had been shattered by ancient earthquakes, as well as numerous small shrines and lesser buildings. An architect and photographer were always in attendance; records were accurate and complete; and once again the excavations were published in comprehensive detail.

Both Conze and Curtius set new standards for archaeological excavation, and were well ahead of their time. They also paid attention to all finds, both large and small. The Germans realised that the very act of archaeological excavation destroyed sites permanently, which made accurate record-keeping essential.

Curtius and Conze were not alone, for others were increasingly disturbed by the widespread destruction. Unfortunately, the sponsors of excavations were anxious to get exciting results, not necessarily to fund the carefully organised research that recorded even minor details. Much archaeology was still in the hands of people with an interest in the past and some private money, but no formal training. Then, just as Curtius finished his work at Olympia, an English general with a passion for artefacts received a fabulous inheritance. He now devoted much of his time to prehistoric sites on his land, and in the process helped revolutionise archaeological excavation.

Augustus Lane Fox Pitt Rivers (1827–1900) was an unlikely excavator. A conservative Victorian gentleman, he combined soldiering with being a landowner. In 1880, as a little-known army officer named Lane Fox, he inherited from a rich uncle great wealth and a huge estate at Cranborne Chase in southern England – on condition that he adopt the surname Pitt Rivers. Lane Fox's inheritance brought him nearly 11,000 hectares and the leisure to do whatever he wanted.

Pitt Rivers was a formidable man. Ramrod straight, he was always formally dressed, even on an excavation. His military speciality had been firearms, and this led him to spend years researching how these and other artefacts had developed over time.

The general's marriage to Alice Stanley, a baron's daughter, drew him into aristocratic circles, with connections to various intellectuals. Among other things, he proved an expert conference organiser, and this brought him into contact with leading thinkers. He fell under the influence of Charles Darwin's ideas and became obsessed with the notion that, like biological organisms, human tools had evolved. Such evolution produced more efficient and usable tool kits.

With his almost unlimited resources, Pitt Rivers could acquire large collections of objects from non-Western societies in all parts of the world. He founded two museums in his lifetime. The first was the Pitt Rivers Museum in Oxford, which still flourishes. The second was on his estate. Both were intended to teach what he called the 'processes of gradual development'.

The move to excavation was a logical one for a scholarly, well-read man. Pitt Rivers would certainly have heard of the work of Lepsius and other German excavators who stressed the importance of studying changing architecture and artefacts through time. Pitt Rivers' expertise in military organisation made carefully arranged and logically planned excavations quite straightforward.

The general would set up his excavations from scratch. Everything was scrupulously organised and would proceed with military-style discipline. Small teams of trained workers did the actual digging, while six supervisors oversaw the work. They had two assistants – one a draughtsman, the other a model maker. Comprehensive records documented each layer and the finds discovered in them.

Pitt Rivers was a strict taskmaster, who insisted that the exact location of every find, however trivial – even animal bones and seeds – must be recorded. His workers were nervous whenever he visited the dig! Pitt Rivers only dealt with his supervisors, or his 'clerks' as he called them. His eyes would dart to and fro, and he never missed even the smallest detail – an untidy pile of pottery, some tools lying too close to the trench. He would visit, look at some finds or glance through the site notebooks, his black hat jammed firmly on his head in the wind. Then he would ride off, usually without a word.

He began with Bronze Age burial mounds, then moved on to Winklebury Camp, an Iron Age fort in Hampshire, southern England, where he cut cross-sections of the defences to date the earthworks on the basis of the objects found in them. In 1884, he dug a Roman military camp, several hectares of low banks, humps and hollows. Here he had his workers clear off the topsoil, then dig out the dark irregularities in the white chalk subsoil to trace the outlines of ditches and other structures such as hearths and pits. No one had used such discolorations before to identify ancient buildings.

Throughout each excavation, the general thought in three dimensions, something that is a cornerstone of today's methods. He excavated each site down to bedrock, recording each layer and noting human disturbances of the soil.

But he dug narrow trenches, which were filled in as he progressed across the site. Inevitably, then, some features were missed, because larger areas were not exposed at the same time. Nowadays, large trenches, capable of uncovering major features such as hut foundations, are a fundamental feature of any excavation to study the layout of an ancient settlement. But Pitt Rivers was interested in ancient technologies and culture change to the exclusion of virtually everything else. Thus he included food remains, but missed postholes and other evidence of structures.

In 1893, he investigated Wor Barrow, a long Stone Age burial mound that contained six prehistoric burials. Earlier excavators had simply dug carelessly into burial mounds, then removed the human remains and grave furniture. Pitt Rivers excavated the entire mound, including sixteen skeletons. He left a row of earth pillars down the centre, which kept the layers intact, so that they could be recorded accurately. Exposing all the ground under the mound revealed a rectangular outline of discolorations in the underlying chalk over a large area. These were traces of the wooden uprights of a large building that had once protected six burials.

When originally dug by the builders, the Wor Barrow ditches were deep, with steep edges. An archaeologist of infinite curiosity, Pitt Rivers left the excavated ditches exposed for four years. Then he re-excavated them to see how chalk ditches broke down and filled with sediment after they are abandoned. This venture into experimental archaeology was a major advance on any approach seen theretofore. Indeed, it was not repeated in England until the 1960s, when a team of archaeologists built a copy of a prehistoric earthwork to study its decay over centuries.

Pitt Rivers had the funds to publish his excavations in a series of handsome monographs that are now collectors' items. He had no patience with archaeologists who dug to find artefacts rather than information. Science, he said, was 'organised common sense'. So was the logical way in which he conducted his excavations. His contemporaries considered him eccentric and were put off by his energy, his rigid behaviour and his enquiring mind. Even in death, he was unusual: he was cremated, rather than buried – something almost unheard of in 1900.

Almost no one followed up on Pitt Rivers' work until the 1920s. With his military background and passion for organisation, he developed excavation as a highly disciplined process of discovery. But the general was self-taught, as were other excavators in Britain and elsewhere. Except for the Germans in the Mediterranean, archaeology was still a casual business – you learned as you went along. Only a few archaeologists even attempted to train students. And those who did were looking for people who were prepared to work hard, not young men seeking adventure.

According to J.P. Droop, a little-known British archaeologist who wrote a manual on excavation in 1915, excavation was men's work. And on the whole it was, except for a handful of talented women (see Chapter 19). To be an archaeologist near to home required curiosity, at least some interest in the past, and patience.

To work overseas with local people called for the same patience and an ability to supervise large numbers of workers.

If you were lucky, you served an apprenticeship under an experienced excavator. He might not be a good digger, but you learned by watching – and from the mistakes he made. A few better digs, especially on Roman sites, adopted some of Pitt Rivers' ideas. But these were still crude excavations by today's standards.

Young Leonard Woolley, a British archaeologist who later became internationally famous for his excavations of royal graves at Ur in Iraq, found himself in charge of a major Roman excavation even though he had absolutely no experience (see Chapter 20).

Almost everyone who was an excavator learned on the job. There were no field schools or courses in archaeological methods. But with their structured minds and organisation, Conze, Curtius and Pitt Rivers led the way.

CHAPTER 17

The Small and Unspectacular

In the 1880s, Egypt's Pyramids of Giza near Cairo attracted both archaeologists and the eccentric. Imaginative astronomers talked of them as ancient calendars that used the heavens to measure time. Strange visitors with theories about ancient Egyptian units of measurement, such as the cubit, clustered around the Great Pyramid with tape measures. Some even attempted to chip away the edges of boulders to make them correspond to their calculations! Fortunately, two members of the Petrie family of English surveyors became interested in Giza.

The Petrie family had a long history of casual scientific inquiry. Flinders Petrie (1853–1942) was largely self-educated and something of an eccentric. He learned surveying and geometry from his father, and in 1872 the pair of them made the first precise survey of Stonehenge. They always talked of surveying the pyramids accurately, a task no one had attempted before. In 1880, at the age of twenty-seven, Flinders Petrie left for Egypt to survey the Pyramids of Giza, just as General Pitt Rivers was starting his excavations at Cranborne Chase.

Within a week of his arrival in Egypt, Petrie was settled comfortably in a rock-cut tomb near Giza. His survey took two years to complete, during which time he set up accurate survey points and studied the construction of the pyramids. His work attracted numerous visitors, among them Pitt Rivers. Petrie thoroughly enjoyed himself, living simply and padding around the pyramids in bare feet, well clear of the tourists.

His first book, *The Pyramids and Temples of Gizeh*, appeared in 1883 to universal acclaim. His measurements provided a new basis for the study of the pyramids. At the time, Egyptology was in turmoil: it lacked precision and looting was commonplace. Sickened by the destruction, Petrie decided to turn from surveying to excavation. Influential scholars urged the Egypt Exploration Fund to send him to work in the Nile Delta, excavating cities.

From the beginning, there was order and method to his work, although he used huge numbers of workers and proceeded very speedily by modern standards. He employed trenchers, shaft sinkers and stone cleaners, supported by gangs of earth carriers. Work started at half past five in the morning and ended at half past six in the evening, with a noon break in the heat of the day. Unlike his predecessors, Petrie was always on site. He solved the problem of looting by paying his labourers well and by providing housing to ensure their loyalty.

By 1885, Petrie was operating at Naukratis, a commercial centre that had a powerful monopoly on trade between Egypt and the eastern Mediterranean after the seventh century BC. There were 107 men working on the site, with only two European supervisors. They moved tons of earth as they cleared part of a temple and a great enclosure built by the pharaoh Psusennes I of the XXI Dynasty (1047–1001 BC). Petrie also recovered enormous quantities of pottery and baskets of papyri. Some of these he mounted between glass and had translated. This was when he realised that small objects were of great importance. Earlier excavators had largely ignored them.

With his Naukratis excavations, Petrie established a routine that he followed for years. All the finds, however small, were shipped to

England. A report on the excavations appeared promptly at the end of each winter season of excavation, ahead of the next season. He paid his workers fixed sums for their finds, thereby keeping important artefacts from falling into the hands of local dealers.

It was fortunate that he did so. For at Naukratis, many of the objects buried in foundation trenches were easily portable coins with dates, or inscribed ornaments that could be dated precisely. Using these, he could then date the surrounding structures. This was a major innovation that had never before been tried in Egypt.

In 1887, Petrie became an independent excavator. He moved from the Nile Delta to the fertile Faiyum depression west of the Nile. There he tunnelled into the pyramid of the XII Dynasty pharaoh Amenemhat at Hawara (around 1840 BC).

That excavation was unsuccessful, in that he found nothing of any significance, but he became interested in a nearby Roman cemetery dating to AD 100–250 that was filled with mummies adorned with vivid portraits of their owners, painted in coloured wax on wooden panels. The pictures had once hung on house walls and had been lashed to the mummies after death. Petrie found so many that he complained that his tent with filled with stores, cooking utensils – and mummies stored under his bed for safety.

Back in London, he mounted a major exhibition of his finds, including some portraits, in the same Egyptian Hall where Giovanni Belzoni had staged his exhibition some seventy-five years earlier (see Chapter 2). An elderly visitor to the display recalled the original exhibition and the tall figure of Belzoni. Large crowds turned out to view the finds, which contributed to making Egyptology a respected and popular science.

Season after season, Petrie returned to the Nile. In 1888, he investigated a worker's community at Kahun in the Faiyum depression. This XII Dynasty settlement had housed the families of those building the nearby El-Lahun pyramid of Pharaoh Senusret II (1897–1878 BC). The compact, walled town was virtually intact. Petrie cleared numerous houses, recovering many domestic artefacts. These enabled him to reconstruct the existence of an ordinary person at the time – a life of constant, often brutally hard work.

Apart from work in the fields, many commoners laboured on public works for meagre rations. Their skeletons show clear evidence of hard labour. Theirs were lives of anonymous drudgery: they supported the state and its leaders, but to all intents and purposes were invisible. Unlike most of his contemporaries, who were more interested in large monuments and tombs, Petrie realised that ancient Egyptian civilisation was a complex society that depended on the toil of thousands of humble workers.

Next Petrie turned his attention to the small XVIII Dynasty town of Ghurab near Memphis, which dated back to around 1500 BC. After noticing some unusual painted pot fragments on the surface, he cleared a small walled enclosure close to the temple. He soon found more of these fragments in houses. The mysterious finds turned out to be Mycenaean vessels from Greece, similar to those unearthed by Heinrich Schliemann at Mycenae.

Three years later, Petrie himself visited Mycenae, where he recognised vessels imported from Egypt that dated to about the same period as his Ghurab finds. This was a classic example of the cross-dating method that Oscar Montelius had relied on generations earlier – using objects of known age from one area to date sites elsewhere (see Chapter 11). Petrie declared that the later stages of Mycenaean civilisation dated to between 1500 and 1200 BC.

Petrie had a profound knowledge of European and eastern Mediterranean archaeology. He built a reputation based on accurate plans, good excavations, comprehensive records and prompt publication. This made him almost unique among archaeologists of the day and secured him access to a circle of knowledgeable scholars, whose interests ranged far wider than their own excavations.

From Ghurab, Petrie moved to el-Amarna, the capital of Pharaoh Akhenaten in Upper Egypt. This king was a controversial figure, who abandoned worship of the powerful sun god Amun in favour of a new form of sun worship involving the solar disc, Aten. Akhenaten moved his capital downstream to el-Amarna, away from Thebes, in 1349 BC. On his death, this capital was abandoned, providing Petrie with a unique opportunity to examine a sacred city. His large-scale excavations uncovered the royal palace's decorated pavements and wall paintings. Tourists flocked to see these and trampled over the local villagers' fields during the growing season. One farmer was so infuriated that he smashed the priceless floors.

One of Petrie's most important discoveries came when he located the spot where a woman had found some tablets written in cuneiform, the international diplomatic script of the time. He excavated a chamber and two pits filled with tablets in what became known as 'The House of Correspondence of Pharaoh'.

The 300 or more Amarna tablets provide an archive of Egyptian dealings with the little-known Hittite civilisation in Turkey from about 1360 BC into Akhenaten's reign. There are letters about the exchange of gifts, about alliances and diplomatic marriages. And there is correspondence with the unstable patchwork of states to the east, with minor rulers promising to kneel before the pharaoh seven times – and then seven times again. Egyptian officials were also corresponding with independent kingdoms like Alashiya on Cyprus, an important source of copper.

Then, as now, the Middle East was in constant turmoil. There were plots and counterplots, rebellious kings, and military campaigns, usually accompanied by political grandstanding. To describe the archive as priceless is a huge understatement!

Petrie encouraged young archaeologists to excavate with him, and he trained up a generation of future Egyptologists. Among them was a young Englishman named Howard Carter, an artist with the Egypt Exploration Fund. Nothing could have prepared Carter for the excavation camp, where he had to build his own mud-brick house and roof it with reeds. There was no bedding, but newspaper worked quite well. Empty food cans stored small finds. Newcomers received a week's supervision and were then left on their own with a few trained workers. But Carter flourished and worked at the Great Temple of the sun god Aten and elsewhere in the city. His experience under Petrie would prove invaluable in later years (see Chapter 21).

In 1892, without any university degree, Petrie became the first professor of Egyptology at University College London. He promptly celebrated by discovering Predynastic Egypt – societies without hieroglyphic script that had flourished along the Nile before the time of the pharaohs. This occurred when he stumbled upon a vast cemetery near the town of Naqada in Upper Egypt, filled with skeletons accompanied by simple clay vessels. In 1894 alone, Petrie excavated 2,000 burials!

As always, Petrie developed a system for his cemetery excavations. As soon as boys had detected soft patches in the sand and had traced the edge of the burial pit, he moved them on. Then ordinary workers cleared soil away from the pots. Finally, expert excavators with a delicate touch cleared around the skeleton and pots, before leaving the final work to Ali Muhammad es Suefi, Petrie's burial expert, who did nothing but clear graves.

It was all very well that these pots were nice to look at, but there were no inscriptions or papyri to provide a chronology. However, similar jars came to light at other sites nearby, like Diospolis Parva. Eventually Petrie had excavated enough graves for him to be able to study the gradual changes in vessel shape. The handles were especially useful for classification purposes, changing as they did as time passed from functional grips into mere painted squiggles.

Petrie arranged the finds into a series of stages categorising grave furniture groups, starting with Stage 30 (ST30) (he assumed that he had not found the earliest, which would have been ST1). ST80 linked the sequence to the time of the first pharaoh, in about 3000 BC. 'Sequence dating' was one of Petrie's most important contributions to archaeology. It was, of course, no substitute for dating sites in years, but that was not to come until the arrival of radiocarbon dating (see Chapter 27). Nevertheless, Petrie introduced an ordered sequence for the history of Egypt before the pharaohs.

Flinders Petrie's range of work and his legacy were extraordinary. Unfortunately, however, he was tactless and quarrelsome. His lack of formal education would often lead him to insist that he, and he alone, was right – hardly a positive quality in an archaeologist. In 1926, as new and more restrictive regulations came into force in Egypt, Petrie moved his operations to Palestine. There he continued his work until the Second World War began, dying in Jerusalem at the age of eighty-nine.

During his long years along the Nile, Petrie brought order to excavation, established a firm chronology for ancient Egypt, and brought small, inconspicuous objects to the forefront.

CHAPTER 18

The Palace of the Minotaur

It was 1894. The antiques dealers in the Athens city market knew the Englishman well. A short, aggressive man who spoke fluent Greek, he would arrive every morning and walk slowly from stall to stall, sorting through small trays of jewels and seals. Sometimes he would pick up a tiny seal and peer at the almost invisible script in the sunlight. The dealers found him a tough customer. He would haggle and haggle, sometimes walking away, until the price was right. As he wrapped his purchases in paper and slipped them into his leather shoulder bag, he would ask questions. Where did the seals come from? Which site yielded the seals? The answer was always Crete.

Arthur John Evans (1851–1941) is the only archaeologist ever to discover a civilisation thanks to his eyesight. He could read even the tiniest letters without spectacles or a magnifying glass. Like a terrier, Evans followed the archaeological scent to Crete in 1894. The island's major city, Heraklion, was a treasure trove of Cretan gems and seals. Most came from an olive tree-covered hillside named Knossos.

Evans combed the Knossos hillside for hours, collecting arte-facts and copying exotic marks on potsherds. A stone vessel from Knossos was identical to those from Mycenae, and so there was clearly a connection between the two. Without further ado, Evans decided to buy Knossos. He was not the first archaeologist to try: Heinrich Schliemann had done so, believing it to be the palace of the legendary King Minos. But whereas Schliemann had failed, Evans succeeded, although it took him two years of bargaining.

As Evans was to discover, Knossos was indeed the major palace on Crete, and perhaps the home of legendary King Minos, if he ever existed. Evans had no interest in speculation about Minos, and nor did he believe Schliemann's claims about Troy and Mycenae (see Chapter 15). He was no self-taught archaeologist out for sensational discoveries, but rather a scholar in search of reliable information.

Arthur Evans had been plunged into archaeology from childhood. He was the son of Sir John Evans, a wealthy English papermaker. Sir John had supported Boucher de Perthes's claims in the Somme Valley (see Chapter 7) and was an expert on ancient stone tools, as well as on Greek and Roman coins. Encouraged by his father, Arthur was drawing coins by the age of seven. And three years later, he started accompanying John on archaeological trips.

As a student, Arthur was always restless, complaining that his Oxford University lecturers were dull. He spent his summers wandering through Europe on foot and fell in love with the people of its southeast in the Balkans. Known locally as the 'mad Englishman', Evans dabbled in journalism and reported on polit-ical unrest in the Austrian Empire so effectively that he was jailed for six weeks. The authorities expelled him from the empire, and he returned to England in search of a career.

For all his political reporting, Evans was devoted to archaeology. He spent every spare moment collecting artefacts of every kind. He had inherited an instinct for style from his father, and he acquired an encyclopaedic knowledge of archaeology.

In 1884, he became keeper of Oxford's Ashmolean Museum, a post he held for twenty-five years. This was a neglected institution, but the new keeper reorganised the displays and acquired numerous artefacts. He spent most of his time in the Mediterranean, however, collecting and making geological investigations. His assistant would inform visitors that the keeper was 'in Bohemia'. The university did not seem to mind, perhaps because he was less of a nuisance when he was absent.

No one knows when Evans first became aware of Crete. His research started with objects from Mycenae on the Greek mainland. This was such an important trading centre around 1350 BC that artefacts had arrived there from all over Greece and the Aegean. As he examined the hundreds of minute seals and engraved gemstones, Evans realised that the Mycenaeans had their own writing. Symbols like those scratched on Mycenaean pots came from as far afield as Egypt. The search for the unknown script brought Evans to the Athens market, and from there to Crete.

While waiting to close the Knossos deal, Evans had explored the length and breadth of Crete on a mule. He had found seals like those at Mycenae for sale in even tiny village markets and realised that there were at least two writing systems that had belonged to the great civilisation that lay under his feet at Knossos. In fact, there were four!

The palace became his property just as the Cretans rebelled against their Turkish masters. Evans helped the rebels, providing food and medicine at his own expense. The victorious Prince George, the new ruler of Crete, was so grateful to him that an excavation permit for Knossos arrived within a few months. The excavations began in March 1900.

Evans knew a great deal about artefacts and archaeology, but his digging experience amounted to little more than a few small excavations. Now he was to tackle a palace. Fortunately, he had the sense to hire an excavation assistant, a Scot named Duncan Mackenzie, who was to work at Knossos for more than thirty years. Mackenzie managed the workers in fluent Greek with a Scots accent. Evans decided where to dig, examined every find, and kept detailed notes. He also engaged architect Theodore Fyfe to prepare drawings.

Unlike Schliemann's digs, this was a carefully planned excavation from the start. On the second day, Evans found himself gazing at a house with faded wall paintings. The site became a maze of rooms, passages and foundations. There was nothing Greek or Roman about Knossos, which was clearly earlier than Mycenae. Soon the workforce numbered 100 men, all clearing the palace rooms.

Thousands of artefacts emerged from the foundations. Great storage jars, hundreds of small cups and even a complex drainage system came to light. Best of all, Evans had dozens of clay tablets with writing to test his microscopic vision. In April 1900, a magnificent wall painting of a cupbearer with flowing locks and a wasp waist emerged from the soil. Mackenzie carefully backed it with plaster for removal to the Heraklion museum.

Joyfully, Evans announced the discovery of the ancient Minoan civilisation of Crete, although King Minos and Theseus were but myths. The Knossos excavations soon covered 1 hectare. In April 1900, the men unearthed a room where there was still a ceremonial bath, together with a stone throne. Stone benches lined the walls, with fine paintings of wingless griffins behind them. This may have been where a priestess appeared, representing the mother goddess, who was believed to oversee the land.

Evans sent for Émile Gilliéron, a Swiss artist who had long experience of ancient inscriptions. The two men pieced together the Knossos wall paintings. There were olives in flower, a young boy gathering saffron (a spice collected from crocus flowers), and solemn processions on the march. A great painted plaster relief of a charging bull haunted Evans' mind. Bulls appeared everywhere: in frescoes, on vases, on gems, as figurines. He was beginning to form a picture of a long-vanished civilisation.

Evans began each morning by checking the previous day's work. Page after page in his tiny handwriting documented every layer, every find and every room. Day after day, the palace became ever more complex. It was an extraordinary structure. You entered the great central courtyard through a large pillared hall. Rows of narrow storage rooms lay west of the courtyard, each opening onto a narrow passageway. Many had been lined with lead to house valuables as well as huge grain stocks. Evans estimated that nearly 100,000 litres of olive oil were once stored at Knossos.

Two imposing stairways led to a second storey of state rooms above the shrines. A western palace entrance led through a paved courtyard, past huge pictures of young men leaping over bulls. It took Evans and Mackenzie months to decipher the royal chambers with their plastered walls, within which remains of wooden thrones were found. Knossos was far more than a palace: it was a commercial and religious centre, and a workshop where craftspeople fashioned everything from pots to metal objects and stone vessels.

Knossos absorbed the rest of Evans' life. When he inherited great wealth, he embarked on a partial (and somewhat imaginative) reconstruction of some of the buildings to give visitors an impression of the palace. Unfortunately, his reconstructions used concrete, which is impossible to remove without damaging original structures. He was gambling with the past. Any form of archaeological reconstruction is difficult to carry out successfully. How can you be sure that the buildings looked the way you think they did? What was the purpose of each room? What were the different levels of the palace used for?

Evans and Gilliéron wrestled with a set of buildings that were a maze when in use – and even more of one after excavation. On a recent visit, I quickly became confused, and I came to realise why Greek legends refer to a labyrinth: Knossos was not a well-planned structure!

Evans and Gilliéron had a somewhat romantic vision of the Minoans. They thought of the civilisation as colourful, carefree and peaceful. The archaeologist and the architect produced their reconstruction using concrete pillars to replace wooden columns. Thanks to draughtsman Theodore Fyfe's accurate drawings, the workers rebuilt walls and the great stairway at the heart of the palace, even as excavations continued.

Evans spent much time painstakingly restoring the wall paintings from small fragments in the trenches, like a huge jigsaw puzzle. You get a somewhat romantic impression of the Minoans, and undoubtedly Evans added imaginary details to scenes like the bull dance. In one case, he even reconstructed a single kinglike figure instead of the three people preserved in the fragments. These were the mistakes of a man obsessed with Minoan civilisation.

Between 1900 and 1935, Arthur Evans commuted between Knossos and Oxford. He built himself a villa on site where he studied the vast collections of pottery from the excavations. His expertise with artefacts enabled him to identify occasional Egyptian finds that he matched with vessels from the Nile. In addition, English Egyptologist Flinders Petrie had unearthed Mycenaean pottery near Memphis that he dated to between 1500 and 1200 BC (see Chapter 17). Using Petrie's findings to cross-date (the technique used by Oscar Montelius), Evans dated the beginnings of Minoan civilisation to about 3000 BC. It was at the height of its power between 2000 and 1250 BC. But invading Mycenaeans from the mainland finally destroyed the palace.

Years of work produced a magnificent narrative of Minoan civilisation, presented in full in *The Palace of Minos*, published between 1921 and 1935. In this masterwork, Evans put the palace at the centre of a chronological survey of Minoan civilisation. Stage by stage, he built up his story. In the final volume, he bade farewell to his beloved Knossos. He had but one regret: he had failed to decipher the four scripts that emerged from the excavations.

Arthur Evans may have been a romantic who tended to dwell on the positive aspects of Minoan life. But we are fortunate that this remarkable archaeologist with microscopic eyesight had the sense to rely on skilled experts. Nevertheless, the vision of the Minoans and of Knossos was all his.

Every time I visit Knossos, I look around in awe at what Arthur Evans achieved. New excavations, deciphered scripts and radiocarbon dating have, of course, modified his portrait of an almost forgotten civilisation. Today, we know more about the lesser Minoan palaces and can imagine some of the complex political and social relationships that lay below the colourful surface.

Few archaeologists describe a civilisation from scratch, without written records, almost single-handed and to a high scientific standard. But Arthur Evans did just that. He died in 1941 at the age of ninety. By that time, archaeology had changed beyond all recognition.

CHAPTER 19

Not 'Men's Work'

All the archaeologists we have met so far have been men. For quite a long time, archaeology was a male pursuit. But two pioneering women, Gertrude Bell and Harriet Boyd Hawes, proved that it was not just men's work. They blazed a trail for the women archaeologists of today.

The two women were complete opposites: one was a solitary desert traveller, the other an excavator. Most male archaeologists at the time believed that women were most useful as clerks or librarians, yet today many of the world's finest archaeologists are women.

Gertrude Bell (1868–1926) was the daughter of a wealthy Yorkshire ironmaster. In 1886, at a time when few women attended any university, she went to Oxford. She was a brilliant student and graduated with a degree in modern history. Moreover, she emerged with a passion for travel and a reputation for speaking her mind. In 1892, she visited Tehran, Persia – at the time a remote destination. She then travelled extensively and took up mountaineering – very much a male pastime – becoming one of the leading female climbers of the day.

Gertrude was a talented linguist, and in 1899 she moved to Jerusalem for seven months to improve her Arabic. From there she travelled farther afield, to the temples at Palmyra in Syria and across the desert to Petra. She discovered the discomforts of desert travel – black beetles and muddy drinking water. As she chattered away to sheikhs and storekeepers in her now-fluent Arabic, she began to understand the complex and sometimes violent politics of these arid lands. This was also where she developed an interest in archaeology. She was never an excavator: she surveyed remote sites, photographed them and wrote about them.

After taking more than 600 photographs of ancient monuments, Gertrude Bell spent the next few years travelling in Egypt, Europe and Morocco, and studying archaeology in Rome and Paris. In 1902, she worked on excavations in western Turkey. Then in 1905 she went to survey and study monuments in Syria and Cilicia (Turkey) dating from the Byzantine Empire (the eastern continuation of the old Roman Empire; it finally fell to the Turks in 1453). Her travel book, *The Desert and the Sown*, was published in 1907, and her report on the churches in the Byzantine city of Birbinkilise – most of which no longer exist – established her as both a travel writer and a scholar.

Gertrude Bell was, above all, a desert archaeologist. Tough and fiercely independent, her primary interest was architecture and little-known but important sites from the time after the Roman Empire collapsed in the west (in AD 476). With Birbinkilise behind her, she now set off from Aleppo in Syria across the Syrian Desert to the Euphrates. She travelled through dangerous country with a small military escort. Her destination was the Abbasid castle of Ukhaidir, a huge rectangular fort built in AD 775. (The Abbasid Dynasty, descended from an uncle of the Prophet Muhammad, governed the Islamic Empire from AD 750 until about 1258.)

For four days, she photographed and surveyed the fort, which no one had described before. Her soldier guards insisted on clutching their rifles as they held her measuring tapes. 'I can't persuade them to put the damnable things down,' Bell complained. She did not excavate, but contented herself with a general description of

Ukhaidir's architecture. This was a major contribution, for Ukhaidir was virtually unknown. Her most famous book, *Amurath to Amurath*, which appeared in 1911, described the site for the general public and attracted much praise. Her academic report on Ukhaidir was published three years later and is still a principal source.

She was soon off again – to Baghdad and Babylon, and then on to Assur in the north, where German archaeologists Walter Andrae and Conrad Preusser were excavating the Assyrian capital. Expert archaeologists working on Greek sites had trained both men and she admired their careful excavations. They taught her how to use flashlights when photographing dark interiors.

On her way home, Bell stopped at the Carchemish excavations in northern Syria, where she found British archaeologists Reginald Campbell Thompson and T.E. Lawrence (later to become famous for his desert exploits in the First World War, which earned him the name 'Lawrence of Arabia' – see Chapter 20). With her usual bluntness, she told them that their excavations were 'prehistoric' compared with those of the Germans. Campbell Thompson and Lawrence were not best pleased and tried to impress her with their archaeological expertise. They failed. The Carchemish workers jeered as she left. Years later, she learned that Lawrence had told them she was too plain to marry.

By the outbreak of the First World War, Gertrude Bell had completed major survey work, but she also had vital knowledge of Arabia and the neighbouring regions. Her briefings for British Intelligence were so valuable that in 1915 she was posted to the Arab Intelligence Bureau in Cairo. A new chapter in her life began a year later when she was transferred to Basra, at the head of the Persian Gulf, to study local tribal politics. She was fascinated by Arab culture, became a champion of Arab independence and served as an expert adviser to local British officials.

Once the war ended, numerous foreign expeditions sought to return to Mesopotamia to investigate Eridu (said to be the earliest city in the world) and Ur (where the biblical Abraham, founder of Judaism, had lived). But times were changing and no longer could foreign archaeologists dig where they liked. Nor could they export all their finds. Governments were now also insisting on excavation permits, issued to qualified archaeologists.

The government of the new state known as Iraq was rightly concerned. Gertrude Bell was the only person in Baghdad with any knowledge of archaeological survey and excavation, and so she was appointed director of antiquities. No one expected her to excavate, but her experience of site surveys and her knowledge of archaeologists were invaluable. She also wrote laws governing the treatment of antiquities and organised the Iraq Museum.

The new laws required all excavation finds to be divided between the foreigners (usually a museum) and Iraq. Bell was a tough negotiator and the Iraq Museum collections grew rapidly. In March 1926, the government gave the museum a permanent home in Baghdad, where Bell displayed finds from all the major excavations, including the German digs at Babylon (see Chapter 20).

Gertrude Bell was rather a pushy woman, with strong opinions about local politics. She did not suffer fools gladly and she made numerous enemies. Government officials came to distrust her. Increasingly isolated, she buried herself ever deeper in archaeological matters. Overworked and in poor health, Bell committed suicide in July 1926. All Baghdad attended her funeral.

Though Bell's intelligence and archaeological learning were legendary, she does not enjoy a good reputation in Iraq today: many Iraqis believe she gave too much away to the foreign expeditions. There may be some truth in that, but Bell always tended to put the interests of archaeology and science above purely national goals; and at the time there were no facilities in Iraq to preserve the delicate objects. Nevertheless, the Iraq Museum stands as an enduring memorial to a unique and important figure in the history of archaeology.

The feisty Harriet Boyd Hawes (1871–1945), the first woman to excavate on Crete, was digging at the time Gertrude Bell was travelling. The daughter of a firefighting equipment manufacturer, Harriet Boyd's mother died early. With four older brothers, she learned to stand up for herself. She started attending Smith College in Massachusetts in 1881, just as Gertrude Bell entered Oxford. A lecture at the college about ancient Egypt by the English traveller, novelist and archaeological writer Amelia Edwards sparked in Harriet an interest in ancient civilisations. After graduating, she worked as a teacher, eventually saving enough money to visit Europe in 1895.

While in Greece, Harriet developed a keen interest in the ancient Greeks. She returned the following year to study at the British School of Archaeology in Athens. Between the balls, dinners and other social engagements, she found time to study ancient and modern Greek and to visit archaeological sites. She also caused a stir by cycling around Athens.

War between Greece and Turkey broke out in 1897. Harriet immediately volunteered for Red Cross duty in central Greece. Tending to the wounded under fire gave her first-hand experience of the horrors of war. Hospital conditions were dreadful: the men lay so close to one another that dressing their wounds was near impossible. After the war, she stayed on to nurse victims of a typhoid epidemic. The local people never forgot the debt they owed her.

Back in the United States, Harriet won a research fellowship to study inscriptions at ancient Eleusis, near Athens. She wanted to excavate, but the American School of Classical Studies in Athens was scandalised: it considered digging 'men's work'. Instead, a war refugee from Crete suggested she should dig on that island, where almost no one was working. So Harriet contacted Arthur Evans, who was about to start digging at Knossos, and the Oxford University archaeologist David Hogarth, who was already excavating on Crete. Sophia Schliemann, Heinrich's widow, also arranged for her to meet other important archaeologists passing through Athens.

Encouraged by these influential backers, and defying those who thought her adventure scandalous, Harriet arrived on Crete at a time when there were just 19 kilometres of paved roads on the island. Like everyone else, archaeologists travelled by mule. Evans and Hogarth advised her to talk to the local people as she explored a stretch of the north coast. Word of this unusual solitary female traveller spread through the local villages. A Cretan schoolmaster took Harriet to Mirampelou Bay. There she found a maze of partially exposed stone walls, numerous painted potsherds and traces of a narrow, stone-paved alleyway.

The next day, she returned with a crew of workers, who exposed blocks of houses. She displayed a remarkable flair for excavation. Soon she had a hundred men and unusually – perhaps a first – ten women uncovering what turned out to be the small Minoan town of Gournia.

Far smaller than Knossos, Gournia provided an unrivalled picture of a small Bronze Age community, with artefacts identical to those at Knossos. Harriet worked on the town in 1901, 1903 and 1904, focusing mainly on the highpoint of its existence, between about 1750 and 1490 BC. The excavations, sponsored in part by the University of Pennsylvania Museum, uncovered entire blocks of more than seventy houses, cobbled alleyways, a Minoan palace and a cemetery. Gournia was an astounding achievement for any archaeologist.

Four years after the excavation ended, Harriet published a large report in which she presented every detail of her excavations. No one could now accuse her of scandalous behaviour or challenge her archaeological credentials!

This was Harriet's last fieldwork, and it made her an admired pioneer of American archaeology in the Mediterranean. She became the first woman to lecture before the Archaeological Institute of America.

In 1906, she married British anthropologist Charles Hawes, and they had two children. In 1916 and 1917, during the First World War, she was heavily involved in nursing in Serbia and on the Western Front. Her involvement with archaeology continued, but strictly in the classroom: she taught ancient art at Wellesley College, Massachusetts, for many years.

Both Gertrude Bell and Harriet Boyd Hawes were the equals of any male archaeologists of their day. Bell, the desert traveller and expert government administrator, understood desert people better than almost any outsider. For her part, Harriet Boyd Hawes was a superb excavator. She returned to Crete once more, as a welcome guest, in 1926. Arthur Evans gave her a tour of Knossos, and she travelled to Gournia on a mule, arriving to a noisy welcome from the local people.

CHAPTER 20

Mud Bricks and a Flood

Babylon was one of the great cities of the ancient Mesopotamian world. From a small settlement founded around 2300 BC, it grew to become the centre of the Babylonian Empire between 609 and 539 BC. King Nebuchadnezzar II (r. 604–562 BC) turned it into a great city with eight gates, the northern one named after the goddess Ishtar. After its destruction in 612 BC, Babylon vanished from history as a confusion of dusty mounds.

The excavation of Babylon defeated several early archaeologists, including Henry Layard (see Chapter 4). They could make nothing of the decaying, unbaked bricks that remained. Then the Germans arrived and the great city came to life in the hands of a careful excavator. Robert Koldewey (1855–1925) was an architect and archaeologist. He was a precise excavator in the German tradition. Koldewey was certain that systematic excavation of the decayed brickwork would uncover Nebuchadnezzar's Babylon. His work there started in 1899 and continued for the next thirteen years.

German archaeologists, and Flinders Petrie in Egypt, had nailed the basic organisation of large-scale excavation. No longer did workers dig haphazardly into a city mound. Instead, they employed teams wielding picks and others using baskets. They worked closely together. Koldewey formalised the process, with light-rail wagons dumping soil away from the trenches. Then he trained labourers for specialised tasks.

He started with fired-brick structures that were easily identified. Unbaked mud brick was a huge challenge, for it tended to melt into the soil once abandoned and when exposed to rain and wind. So Koldewey trained skilled teams that did nothing but trace unbaked mud-brick walls. He and his colleague Walter Andrae (who was to excavate the Assyrian capital at Assur on the Tigris) found that the best excavation technique was to scrape the ground with hoes. The expert diggers looked out for changes in soil texture – or for actual walls. Once walls appeared, the workers traced them delicately until rooms were exposed. They left intact the fillings over the floors so that these could be dug later and the contents of each chamber recorded. The Koldewey system revolutionised city excavation.

Koldewey's greatest Babylon discovery was Nebuchadnezzar's Ishtar Gate on the north side of the city, dedicated to the mother goddess of fertility. He found that the king's architects had dug deep into the underlying sand for the foundations. The walls were still intact, allowing him to uncover huge reliefs of dragons and bulls made of glazed bricks. The actual gates and the archway were roofed with cedar.

In an inscription that stretches over ten columns, the king himself made a proud boast about his masterpiece, which was also described by the Greek author Herodotus. Patiently, Koldewey and others washed thousands of glazed brick fragments to free them of salt, then pieced them together. He reconstructed the gate brick by brick in the Pergamon Museum in Berlin. A paved Procession Street led through it to the temple of Marduk, Babylon's special god. The Ishtar Gate and its Procession Street stood over 13 metres above the surrounding plain.

Meanwhile, Walter Andrae ran parallel excavations far upstream at Assur from 1902 to 1914. He adopted the Babylon approach for an Assyrian capital that had stood on a cliff above the Tigris. His expert teams traced city walls, many houses and temple quarters. The major structure was the Temple of Ishtar, wife of the city's god, Assur. A deep trench uncovered six earlier temples on the same site. Andrae was the first excavator to dissect a Mesopotamian city layer by layer. Realising that excavation was destruction, both he and Koldewey recorded every single building before they removed it to access lower levels.

Andrae, Koldewey and others made possible the scientific excavations at Ur and other Mesopotamian cities after the First World War. Excavations were now sponsored by national museums, not individuals. In 1911, the British Museum decided to excavate the little-known Hittite city of Carchemish on the Euphrates River in northern Syria. The excavations began under David Hogarth (1862–1927), an experienced excavator who had worked with Arthur Evans at Knossos. Hogarth was notoriously bad tempered before breakfast, prompting his workers to call him the 'Angel of Death'. Hogarth's two seasons of excavation were so promising that the museum started a long-term project and chose thirty-three-year-old Leonard Woolley as the new director.

Charles Leonard Woolley (1880–1960) was a short man with a commanding personality. He went to New College, Oxford, to study to become a priest, but while still an undergraduate the warden of the college predicted that he would become an archaeologist. Woolley spent five years in the Sudan – from 1907 to 1911 – mainly working on cemeteries. There he gained expertise in dealing with labourers from other cultures, learning their languages and treating them firmly but fairly. He was an excellent choice for Carchemish.

Carchemish had guarded a major ford across the river until 717 BC, when the Assyrians captured the growing settlement. It later became a Hittite city, but almost nothing was known of these rivals to the Assyrians and Egyptians in the eastern Mediterranean world. More than 15 metres of occupation levels awaited excavation.

Woolley was an inspiring leader – one of those rare people who are never at a loss. He also had a lively sense of humour, essential when dealing with the shifting sands of local politics and a work-force that was given to violence if dissatisfied. Respect was his motto, but he could also be firm. When a local official refused to issue an excavation permit at once, Woolley just smiled. He produced a loaded revolver and held it to the man's head. The official raised his hands in terror and said there had been a mistake. Minutes later, Woolley left with the signed permit.

Woolley was a brilliant storyteller and a fluent writer, which sometimes makes it hard to decipher what really happened at Carchemish. The excavations were successful, largely because Woolley and T.E. Lawrence – who had been recruited from Oxford University because of his archaeological experience, and was travelling in Syria – got on well with each other and with the workers. The dig foreman, a Syrian named Hamoudi, whose two interests were archaeology and violence, was a genius at managing labourers. He became one of Woolley's closest friends, and they worked together on several digs from 1912 to 1946.

In 1912, little was known about the Hittites, except for what had been learned from the Amarna tablets found by Flinders Petrie in Egypt some years earlier (see Chapter 17). Woolley unravelled the layers of the citadel and uncovered two palaces. Stately figures of kings and marching soldiers adorned the palace walls.

The Carchemish excavations ended with the outbreak of the First World War. Like Gertrude Bell (see Chapter 19), Woolley became a valued intelligence officer, before being taken as a prisoner of war by the Turks.

After the war, in 1922, Woolley became director of an ambitious, long-term excavation at the biblical city of Ur (Ur of the Chaldees), sponsored by the British Museum and the University of Pennsylvania Museum. Quite apart from its location in a harsh desert landscape of extreme heat and cold, Ur was a complex and difficult site to excavate. A ruined temple pyramid, entire buried city quarters and many occupation layers all presented a tough challenge for even the most skilled excavator. But Woolley was ideal for the job, being energetic and full of ideas.

He was an exacting taskmaster, who ran the enormous dig with a handful of European assistants and the formidable Hamoudi. The excavations began at dawn and, for the European staff, rarely ended before midnight. Woolley's best colleague was Max Mallowan, who was later to become a first-rate archaeologist and the first to follow Layard's work at Nimrud. Mallowan married detective novelist Agatha Christie, and she is said to have based some of the characters in her novel *Murder in Mesopotamia* on people at Ur.

A trench in the 1922 excavation season yielded gold objects, possibly from a cemetery. Woolley suspected that he might be dealing with royal graves filled with great treasures, perhaps in fragile condition. He knew the task of clearing the burials would stretch his technical abilities to the limit, and his labourers would have to be trained for delicate work. So he waited four years before digging further there.

In the meantime, he dug trial trenches to establish the city's layout. Then he excavated a small village mound close to the site. It yielded very early painted pottery, but no metals. The inhabitants were perhaps the ancestors of the Sumerian builders of Ur.

Woolley had 400 labourers working under Hamoudi, who was strict, but sensitive to trouble and skilled at combating fatigue and boosting morale: on one occasion, he impersonated a Euphrates boatman, using his spade as a paddle as he sang lilting songs while the men cleared heavy soil.

Finally, once he had cleared the royal cemetery, Woolley dug a large trench down to the bottom of Ur. At the base, he unearthed a layer of flood deposits, but no artefacts. There was more evidence of occupation below, with pottery similar to that from the previously excavated small farming village.

Woolley's wife Katharine casually glanced into the pit and suggested that the mysterious layer could be from Noah's flood in the Book of Genesis. The suggestion was a public relations dream for a dig that was constantly short of money. Privately, Woolley doubted the idea, because the trench was a small one, and anyway, Ur lay in an area that was prone to flooding. But he made full use of Ur's flood in his popular writings, realising that the discovery of a possible biblical flood would have enormous popular appeal and would help raise funds.

By the time the Ur excavations ended, Woolley had cleared the great ziggurat (pyramid) of Ur-Nammu, which dominates the site today. He also uncovered dozens of small dwellings and hundreds of tablets which have thrown much light on Sumerian history. Excavating the royal cemetery was an enormous task. In fact, there were two cemeteries: one Assyrian and the other Sumerian. During four years of painstaking work, the excavators cleared the largely undecorated graves of no fewer than 2,000 commoners. Woolley also excavated sixteen lavish royal burials. Using seal inscriptions and clay tablets, he dated these to between 2500 and 2000 BC, the earliest period of written Iraqi history. These lay at the base of 9-metre shafts, accessed by sloping ramps. The royal corpses lay in stone-and-brick burial vaults and were surrounded by sacrificial victims. In one instance, ten women wearing elaborate headdresses were arranged in two rows. Recovering the delicate ceremonial objects took a lot of imagination and ingenuity. For example, by pouring liquid plaster into an inconspicuous hole, Woolley managed to make a cast of a decayed wooden lyre, decorated with a copper bull's head and shells.

After months of backbreaking work, Woolley wrote a popular account of a funeral ceremony. One of those rare archaeologists who can imagine himself in the past, he brilliantly re-created a royal burial: resplendent courtiers and soldiers filed into the mat-lined burial pit; royal ox wagons with grooms were steered by their drivers into the pit; everyone carried a small clay cup, took poison and lay down to die; and, finally, someone killed the oxen and the shaft was filled in.

Unfortunately, Woolley's field notes are incomplete, and so we cannot check his story. In fact, new research has shown that the royal attendants did not take poison, but were killed by blows to the head. The corpses were somehow treated to preserve them and were laid out in the burial pit. But you can forgive Woolley's use of drama and vivid re-creations, when you remember that he believed that archaeology was above all about people.

This excavation was the last of the huge digs run by a single archaeologist that defined early archaeology. Leonard Woolley rightly occupies a place among the greatest of all archaeologists.

But in 1922 Howard Carter discovered the tomb of the pharaoh Tutankhamun in Egypt (see Chapter 21). And in the end, Woolley's popular books were overtaken by the general obsession with golden pharaohs.

'Wonderful Things'

Valley of the Kings, Egypt, 25 November 1922. Howard Carter, Lord Carnarvon and Carnarvon's daughter Lady Evelyn Herbert waited in the hot, crowded passageway of the pharaoh Tutankhamun's tomb. Workers removed the last of the rubble fill in front of a sealed doorway. From another door that bore the king's seal, they already knew that this was Tutankhamun's burial place.

Tense with excitement, they sweated in the dense, humid air laden with dust. With trembling hands, Carter made a small hole in the plaster door and pushed an iron bar through. There was a rush of hot air from the space behind. He enlarged the hole and inserted a candle, the others crowding round behind. The candle flame flickered, then settled. 'Can you see anything?' asked Carnarvon impatiently. 'Yes, wonderful things,' Carter gasped.

He enlarged the hole and shone a flashlight into a crowded chamber, open for the first time in 3,000 years. Golden beds, a throne, collapsible chariots and a jumble of treasures swam before his eyes. After seven years of fruitless searching, they had found Tutankhamun's undisturbed tomb.

The road to the discovery began in 1881, with the sensational find of a cache of royal mummies and their burial goods in a rocky crevice in the hills on the west bank of the river opposite Luxor. By the 1880s, Egypt had become a fashionable winter tourist destination for both wealthy Europeans and travellers passing through the Suez Canal. The tomb robbers of Qurna on the Nile's west bank, opposite Luxor, were making good money. In 1881, rumours spread of exceptional antiquities for sale: lovely offering jars, magnificent jewels and fine statuettes. Some of the objects were unique and clearly from royal tombs.

Suspicion fell on two locals, Ahmed and Mohammed el-Rasul, known tomb robbers, who smuggled their loot into Luxor in bundles of clothing or baskets. They were arrested and tortured – but to no avail. Until, that is, Ahmed turned against his brother after they quarrelled over how to share out the loot. Mohammed confessed and led German-born archaeologist Émile Brugsch, a member of the Egyptian Antiquities Service, to a remote crevice on the west bank. Inside lay the mummies of some of Egypt's greatest pharaohs, including Thutmose II, Seti I and Rameses II.

Three thousand years earlier, the cemetery priests in charge of the Valley of the Kings had moved the royal mummies from one hiding place to another in a frantic race against ruthless ancient tomb robbers. They had worked in a hurry, and so the crevice was cluttered with priceless finds, the coffins of queens lying in heaps. Once Brugsch had recovered from his shock at the discovery, he employed 300 men to recover 40 pharaohs. Later, some of the mummies were unwrapped and archaeologists gazed on the faces of some of the ancient world's most powerful men. Seti I, whose tomb Belzoni had discovered, was the best preserved, and had a gentle smile on his face (see Chapter 2).

The royal mummies caused a sensation. Wealthy tourists flocked to the Nile, dreaming of finding a magnificent, gold-laden burial and hoping in vain to excavate in the Valley of the Kings. They spent lavishly on items found in less important tombs. Inevitably, the destruction and looting continued, with many officials looking the other way. Fortunately for science, a few archaeologists, notably

Flinders Petrie, trained up some younger excavators. He took young assistants into the field for years, among them a British draughtsman, Percy Newberry. During the 1890s, Newbury worked with a gifted artist named Howard Carter (1874–1939). He sent him to work with Petrie to learn excavation methods. Thus one of the two central characters in the Tutankhamun discovery was on the scene long before 1922.

Carter was of humble birth, the son of an artist. But he displayed exceptional talent, which brought him to the attention of William Tyssen-Amherst, a wealthy Englishman with a large Egyptian collection. In 1891, the Amherst family hired the seventeen-year-old Carter to draw items in their collection. And later that year, the Egypt Exploration Fund sent him to work as an assistant draughtsman to Percy Newberry, who was recording the decorated tombs of nobles at Beni Hasan in Middle Egypt that dated to about 2000 BC. Carter's copies of the Beni Hasan tomb murals were so exceptional that he was sent to work with Petrie at el-Amarna. The young artist took to excavation like a natural.

In 1899, French Egyptologist Gaspar Maspero, director of the Egyptian Antiquities Service, appointed Carter chief inspector of antiquities for Upper Egypt – one of only two such officials in the country. As inspector, Carter was a busy man. Much of his work centred on the Valley of the Kings, where he installed electric lights in some of the tombs.

A few wealthy visitors applied for permits to excavate in the valley, but they were turned down on the grounds that they were ill-prepared to search for a tomb. Carter was the archaeologist who judged applicants. The best prepared was Theodore Davis, a rich New York lawyer, who received a permit to work in the valley in 1902. Carter had excavated for Davis and helped him reveal the tombs of a noble named Userhet and Pharaoh Thutmose IV. Carter recovered part of the pharaoh's chariot and one of his riding gloves. Davis was a rough excavator, but he had the very good sense to employ archaeologists to carry out the excavations. Much of Carter's approach to Tutankhamun stemmed from his experience with Davis.

After Carter's brilliant success in the north, in 1904 Maspero transferred the chief inspector to Lower Egypt. There his work included preserving sites and dealing with sometimes difficult visitors. A stiff man, Carter barely tolerated tourists, and following a violent argument with some drunken French sightseers at Saqqara in 1905, he resigned in disgust. For the next couple of years, he scratched a living as an artist and guide in Luxor. In 1907, at a low point in his career, he met George Edward Stanhope Molyneux Herbert, Fifth Earl of Carnarvon (1866–1923). The other principal in the Tutankhamun discovery was now on the stage.

In complete contrast to Carter, Lord Carnarvon was a privileged nobleman, an art collector with fine judgement and exquisite taste, and a gambler on racehorses. As a boy, born Lord Porchester, he had been sickly and withdrawn, and was frequently bullied at Eton College in his teens. His education had been disastrous – perhaps he had learning disabilities. While at Eton, he struck up a lifelong friendship with an Indian maharajah's son, Victor Duleep Singh, who was a habitual gambler at the races. Lord Porchester went to Oxford and dropped out, considered a military career, and indulged his passions – horseracing, sailing, shooting and travelling. Meanwhile, he devoured books and educated himself in art and the humanities.

In 1890, Lord Porchester became the Fifth Earl of Carnarvon and inherited his father's estates. Five years later, he married aristocrat Almina Wombwell, who moved in the highest social circles. Carnarvon's weak lungs made the dry and warm Nile Valley a desirable place for him to spend the winter months. During his regular visits, he developed an interest in ancient art and photography. By 1905, he was bored with the endless round of balls and the usual tourist circuit. His mind turned to archaeology.

Carnarvon was one of many wealthy visitors who dabbled in excavation. Archaeology became an entertaining way to pass the time. Thanks to influential contacts, in 1907 he received an excavation permit for an already well-worked area of the Theban cemetery. He carried out his first six-week season with no expert assistance – and apparently thoroughly enjoyed it. His only significant finds were a mummified cat and an inscribed, plaster-coated tablet.

However, once deciphered, the tablet turned out to be a major find: it commemorated the victory of the pharaoh Khamose over the hated Hyksos kings, who had occupied the fertile Nile Delta in about 1640 BC. It is now known as the Carnarvon Tablet.

At this point, Antiquities Director Gaspar Maspero introduced Carnarvon to the unemployed Howard Carter. Carter was becoming increasingly obsessed with the Valley of the Kings, but to dig there required wealth and access to the highest levels of government. While Davis laboured in vain in the Valley of the Kings, Carter and Carnarvon became not only friends, but also an efficient team. Carter, with his long experience, was the leader. His standards of excavation were much higher than those of either Davis or Flinders Petrie. Meanwhile Carnarvon provided the funding and acted as a sounding board. He realised early on – when they were clearing tombs in the well-worked area of the cemetery – that Carter had an exceptional nose for discovery: he continued to make finds even when everyone else thought an area had been exhausted. The two men published a valuable account of five years' work as they waited for a chance to excavate in Theodore Davis's patch in the Valley of the Kings.

The meticulous Carter made a point of keeping in touch with Davis, although he disapproved of his methods. Unlike Carnarvon, who was almost always on site, Davis was the classic hands-off archaeologist. Rather than excavating, he preferred entertaining guests on his boat, which was moored on the Nile. But he was always present when a tomb was opened, and had been lucky in his assistants (not least Howard Carter).

Davis worked fast, with little attention to detail; but he was systematic in his search for tombs. He found several royal tombs, among them that of the XVIII Dynasty pharaoh Amenhotep II, who died in 1401 BC. The tomb of Yuya, a senior officer of chariotry around 1390 BC, and his wife Tuya contained a complete chariot, two beds and three gold-inlaid armchairs, as well as three coffins. Yuya and Tuya's tomb had been robbed, but it was the most complete tomb in the valley until the discovery of Tutankhamun's. Davis had the self-control and resources to dig for season after season, clearing rubble without success. He persisted until 1912, when he withdrew, proclaiming that the valley was exhausted. He had come within 2 metres of the entrance to Tutankhamun's undisturbed sepulchre. The excavation permit for the Valley of the Kings passed to Carnarvon in 1914, just as the First World War broke out. He and Carter started work in 1917.

Carter was a different kind of archaeologist from the casual Theodore Davis. He had walked every corner of the valley and was familiar with all the known graves. But one was missing: that of a little-known pharaoh, Tutankhamun, who had died in 1323 BC. Carter was convinced that Tutankhamun's tomb awaited discovery, probably in an area near the well-known sepulchre of Rameses VI. For seven years, the two men followed Carter's instincts and laboriously cleared rubble from the valley floor, looking for the tomb.

In 1922, Carnarvon was on the point of stopping – the hunt was costing him several thousand pounds a year. Carter offered to pay for one more season himself, but Carnarvon reluctantly agreed to support a dig close to workers' huts erected during the digging of Rameses VI's tomb.

On 4 November 1922, four days into the season, with Carnarvon still in England, the workers uncovered a rock-cut stairway leading to a sealed doorway. Carter waited for three weeks until Carnarvon and his daughter Lady Evelyn Herbert arrived. Then, on 24–25 November, they exposed the doorway, found Tutankhamun's seals on the plaster, and experienced that remarkable moment when Carter probed the barrier and saw 'wonderful things'.

Tutankhamun's tomb put a severe strain on Carter and Carnarvon's friendship. Carter insisted that the tomb be accurately and systematically cleared, whereas Carnarvon, a gambler since childhood, wanted to empty the tomb at once. After all the expense, he wanted to sell some objects and display the others. The pressure mounted and there were violent quarrels, especially after the formal opening of the burial chamber in February 1924. Tragically, a few weeks later Carnarvon died of an infected mosquito bite (as, curiously, had Tutankhamun), which put an end to the fourteen-year partnership.

Howard Carter took eight years to clear Tutankhamun's tomb. He completed the task with the aid of an expert team in 1929. His notes and records were meticulous and are still consulted by experts today. He worked on the clearance during a difficult time, when Egypt was claiming all the finds from the tomb. In 1930, Lady Carnarvon signed over to the Egyptian government all claims to the tomb and its contents; in exchange, she received the cost of the tomb's clearance. Howard Carter was exhausted from the stress and never completed the lavish report he had hoped to write. But his work on the tomb was a triumph, given the facilities available to him.

Tutankhamun's tomb was a landmark in archaeological research. The pharaoh's golden mask that rested on his shoulders is an iconic ancient Egyptian artefact that can be seen in the Egyptian Museum. The pharaoh wears a gold and blue headdress with a royal cobra ornament. He stares straight ahead. His carefully woven beard was recently broken off in an accident, but has been restored.

We owe the remarkable array of exquisite finds to Carter's skill. Despite his ferocious temper, the tomb clearance was a disciplined team effort. Other scholars now brought serious research to the Nile, among them University of Chicago Egyptologist Henry Breasted, who in 1929 commenced a long-term project of copying inscriptions that continues to this day.

Increasingly, Egyptian archaeologists came to assume an active role in excavation, survey and recording. In Egypt, as in other countries, the more international and professional archaeology became, the more the discoveries – both major and minor – became a matter of national pride. The discovery of the boy king and his treasures opened a new chapter in archaeology – one in which teamwork and slow, painstaking excavation became the norm.

CHAPTER 22

A Palace Fit for a Chief

I slipped through a narrow entrance in the high stone enclosure and found myself in a tight passageway between an outer and an inner wall. I had no idea what lay inside. A conical tower of carefully laid stone blocks stood in front of me – a solid structure, with no doorway and no obvious purpose.

As I wandered through the jigsaw of masonry (stonework) and hut foundations inside Great Zimbabwe's Great Enclosure, a feeling of confusion swept over me. I had spent much of the day visiting local African villages of thatched huts made of poles and clay. The contrast now was overwhelming. Why had farmers and herders living in such communities come together to build such a remarkable structure? It seemed a strangely alien and mysterious presence in the wooded landscape. There was no sign of great palaces or temples: only the imposing Great Enclosure stands high.

Great Zimbabwe occupies over 24 hectares. A large granite hill covered with enormous boulders overlooks a mishmash of stone structures, among them the Great Enclosure, the most prominent feature of the site. The hill, commonly known as the Acropolis

(Greek: 'high city'), is a maze of enclosures formed of boulders and stone walls. The largest of them – the Western Enclosure – was occupied for a long period of time.

The Great Enclosure is famous for its high, stone walls, built without mortar, and for its solid conical tower, which pokes just above the outer wall. The chief who ruled over Great Zimbabwe lived in this compound, probably isolated from his subjects. Several other smaller enclosures lie to the northwest.

But what exactly was Great Zimbabwe? Clearly, it was an important ritual centre. The Acropolis was a sacred hill isolated from the rest of the site. To judge from the various imported things like Indian glass beads, Chinese porcelain and seashells, the chiefs traded their gold, copper and elephant ivory with people from the East African coast.

We know that the men who lived here were chiefs because iron gongs – traditional symbols of African leadership – have been found in the Great Enclosure. Thanks to radiocarbon dating (see Chapter 27), we know that Great Zimbabwe flourished between about AD 950 and 1450. It was abandoned shortly before Portuguese ships arrived off the Indian Ocean coast in 1497.

The Portuguese sailed into coastal towns like Malindi and Mombasa in modern-day Kenya, which traded in ivory, gold and slaves from far inland. In 1505, they built a trading post at Sofala, a long-established Islamic trading station near the mouth of the Zambezi River. They found half-African merchants who would lead small parties upriver and into the highlands of the interior, carrying cheap Indian cloth, strings of colourful glass beads and seashells. In exchange, the traders obtained gold dust carried in porcupine quills, copper ingots and, above all, elephant tusks.

Some of the traded goods, such as Chinese porcelain and cloth, reached Great Zimbabwe. From their sporadic explorations inland, the Portuguese learned of a settlement built of stone, but never visited it. In 1531, Vicente Pegado, captain of the military force at Sofala, called it 'Symbaoe', a place built of 'stones of marvellous size'.

There matters rested until 1867, when a German-American hunter and prospector named Adam Render stumbled upon the ruins. Four years later, he showed them to Karl Mauch, a German explorer and geographer, who was astounded. Mauch claimed that Great Zimbabwe was the palace of the biblical Queen of Sheba, the remains of a great, gold-rich Mediterranean civilisation in southern Africa. He even claimed that a wooden door beam was carved from Lebanese cedar, brought to the site by travellers from the ancient Mediterranean world.

By this time, a stream of white settlers were moving north of the Limpopo River, now the boundary between South Africa and modern Zimbabwe. Some came to find gold and get rich; most were hungry for land and set about establishing farms. Many of the newcomers were poorly educated and looked down on Africans. A large number of them settled on the fertile land of what was called Mashonaland, where Great Zimbabwe stands. It was widely believed that a fabulously wealthy ancient kingdom created by white people from outside Africa lay in the north.

My wonderment when I visited Great Zimbabwe was probably nothing compared to that of the first Europeans to set eyes on the ruins after 1871. They stumbled through a maze of crumbling masonry masked by clinging vegetation. The conical tower was barely visible through the trees and undergrowth. Great Zimbabwe came as a profound shock. And it was an archaeological mystery. Who had built these unique stone structures? Were they the work of a long-vanished foreign civilisation? How long ago were they abandoned? When some gold beads turned up during casual digging in the Great Enclosure, excitement mounted.

The rumours reached the ears of British businessman Cecil John Rhodes and the British Association for the Advancement of Science in 1891. Together, they sponsored a season of excavations at Great Zimbabwe and other stone ruins north of the Limpopo. They chose British antiquarian J. Theodore Bent to undertake the excavations. Bent had no formal archaeological training, but had travelled widely in Arabia, Greece and Turkey (which seemed an admirable qualification). Fortunately, he took with him E. W.M. Swan, an expert surveyor.

Swan produced the first map of Great Zimbabwe. Meanwhile, Bent found gold objects, dug rough trenches and announced in *The*

Ruined Cities of Mashonaland, published in 1892, that the site was very ancient and the work of either people from the Mediterranean or Arabs. Local colonists loved a book that said a wealthy, non-African civilisation had built Great Zimbabwe! Academics and white settlers alike maintained that foreigners had built the site: no one believed that the ancestors of the local African farmers could have constructed the great buildings – such people were thought too primitive and lacking in expertise.

When gold and copper objects emerged from Bent's excavations, all the local settler talk was of long-vanished, fabulously rich civilisations from the Mediterranean world, and of great rulers who had colonised Mashonaland for its gold. This is hardly surprising, since many of the early colonists had themselves come to Africa to find gold and make their fortunes.

Moreover, if foreigners from the Mediterranean had built Great Zimbabwe, then it could be argued that their successors – the new arrivals who were displacing the local people and carving out farms for themselves – were merely repossessing land that had been seized by the Africans when they had overthrown this once-great kingdom.

The more ambitious among the settlers were so impressed by Bent's Zimbabwe gold finds that they established the Ancient Ruins Company in 1895 to exploit archaeological sites for their wealth. This was nothing more than an attempt to get rich quickly by digging out Great Zimbabwe and other archaeological sites. It was like Egyptian tomb robbing, but organised as a public company. Fortunately, it soon collapsed because of a lack of valuable finds.

Then Richard Hall, a local journalist, stepped in. His archaeological qualifications were non-existent, yet he was appointed curator of Great Zimbabwe. In 1901, he began some destructive excavations. In fact, all he did was to shovel out all the occupation levels from Great Zimbabwe's largest structure, the Great Enclosure. His trenches yielded fragments of gold sheet and beads, copper ingots and iron gongs, among other objects. He also found fragments of imported Chinese porcelain.

Hall was not aware of archaeological finds elsewhere and knew little history other than the popular, racist kind. First and foremost, he was a journalist and a creative storyteller out to make money from his writings. He wove the miscellaneous finds from his diggings into stirring tales of a long-vanished civilisation. A man of great energy and infectious enthusiasm (albeit with the colonial views typical of the day), Hall considered Great Zimbabwe the work of people from the kingdom of Saba in southern Arabia, in what is now Yemen. This was the land of the biblical Queen of Sheba who had visited King Solomon.

While Hall's excavations caused great excitement among local white settlers, the sober members of the British Association for the Advancement of Science were eager for disciplined excavations. In 1905, they organised an investigation of the ruins by archaeologist David Randall-MacIver (1873–1945). Randall-MacIver had extensive digging experience in Egypt, where he had learned the importance of artefacts for the creation of a timeline. Objective and well-practised, Randall-MacIver was struck by the absence of any artefacts of foreign origin that were earlier than medieval times. Nothing dated to the time of the ancient Mediterranean civilisations or the kingdom of Saba.

Fragments of Chinese porcelain vessels brought from the East African coast were found in his trenches. From their design, these could be dated accurately, and on the basis of these finds, Randall-MacIver stated firmly that Great Zimbabwe belonged to the sixteenth century AD or perhaps a little earlier.

Careful analysis of the datable, imported objects showed that Zimbabwe was built long after the Mediterranean civilisations alleged to have constructed it. All the porcelain found with the stone structures was medieval, imported along Indian Ocean trade routes. So local Africans, not foreigners, had built the structure. This was good, logically argued archaeology, but the settlers were furious and refused to believe him. So heated did passions in local white circles become that a quarter of a century would pass before anyone else excavated at Great Zimbabwe.

When the British Association for the Advancement of Science arranged for their annual meeting to be held in South Africa in 1929, to mark the occasion they decided to sponsor new Great

Zimbabwe excavations. They turned to English archaeologist Gertrude Caton-Thompson (1888–1985). A tough, no-nonsense woman, she had learned archaeology in Egypt with Flinders Petrie. But while Petrie looked for the tombs of nobles, Caton-Thompson laboured on much earlier Stone Age sites. She had mounted her own Egyptian expedition in 1924 with London geologist Elinor Gardner. They worked in the Faiyum depression, west of the Nile, and found small farming sites. Caton-Thompson estimated their date at about 4000 BC, the earliest farming settlements known at the time.

This up-and-coming archaeologist was an ideal candidate for the excavation of Great Zimbabwe. Her training with Petrie had included both small artefacts and the importance of cross-dating, using objects of known age to date prehistoric settlements.

Caton-Thompson arrived at Great Zimbabwe by ox cart in 1928. She placed her trenches with meticulous care and dug a deep cutting into the Western Enclosure on the Acropolis. Using fragments of imported Chinese porcelain and Islamic glass found in her trenches, she showed how Great Zimbabwe had begun as a small farming village before expanding dramatically to become a major centre, with masonry and enclosures. Her conclusions confirmed that Randall-MacIver had been correct: Great Zimbabwe had been at the height of its glory in the centuries before the Portuguese arrived off the East African coast in 1497. This most remarkable of archaeological sites was entirely of African inspiration and construction.

Caton-Thompson presented her conclusions to the 1929 British Association meeting. Once again, there was uproar from settler interests. But archaeologists everywhere accepted her carefully argued conclusions, which have stood the test of time. Her work ignited such fury among white settlers that no one returned to dig at Great Zimbabwe until the 1950s, when radiocarbon dating confirmed her chronology. Caton-Thompson stood firm despite the abuse. She put away the numerous crank letters she received in a file marked 'Insane'. After the Second World War, her brilliant 1928 excavations laid the foundations for the study of black African history.

Gertrude Caton-Thompson never worked in Africa again, but her research led to a powerful conclusion: racist interpretations of the past do not hold up against carefully argued and well-excavated archaeological data. And her Great Zimbabwe excavations came at an important moment, when archaeology was taking hold in places far from Europe and the Mediterranean.

CHAPTER 23

East and West

Archaeology took different paths of development in Asia and Europe – in East and West. Some 2,000 years ago, Chinese historians worked to trace historical events back to at least 3000 BC and the three major dynasties of rulers in the north: Xia, Shang and Zhou. They charted the various conflicts and the rise and fall of small kingdoms, until finally, in 221 BC, the country was unified under the first Chinese emperor, Qin Shihuangdi (see Chapter 31).

The Chinese realised that their history was complex and constantly evolving; that dynasties came and went, but that civilisation endured. In this they were helped by the distinctive Chinese writing system, which dates back to around 1500 BC. It had originated in picture symbols, but gradually developed into a script that was widely used by government officials after 500 BC.

For the most part, Europe had a different experience of history. Written records there began with the Romans and with the conquest of Gaul (France) by Julius Caesar in 54 BC. Anything earlier can only be studied using archaeological methods. For example, the Three-Age System and the research of Oscar Montelius and others documented prehistoric times after the Ice Age (see Chapter 11). Instead of relying on written records, European archaeologists refined their excavation and survey methods, paying close attention to such small objects as brooches and pins.

China's scholars were curious about their remote history well over 2,000 years ago, and there was enduring interest in the history of the ancient civilisations. Archaeology in China began with a passion for collecting – with the prestige that came from owning fine objects from the past. Antiquarians were active as early as the Song Dynasty (AD 960–1279). From then on, Chinese emperors habitually collected fine antiquities.

For centuries, farmers in northern China unearthed ancient animal bones of all kinds in their fields, calling them 'dragon bones'. They ground up the fossil fragments to make medicines. In 1899, some inscribed bones came into the hands of Wang Yirong, chancellor of the Imperial Academy in Beijing. Wang collected ancient bronzes and realised that the script used on the bones was identical to that on some Zhou Dynasty vessels, among the earliest in China. In 1908, Lu Zhenyu, an antiquarian and language expert, translated some of the bone inscriptions and traced them to Anyang in the Yellow River valley, capital of the ancient Shang Dynasty, one of the earliest Chinese civilisations.

Excavations at Anyang by archaeologist Li Ji from 1928 to 1937 recovered 20,000 inscribed bone fragments – ox shoulder blades. These were oracle bones that had been heated then cracked with hot metal pointers. Priests interpreted the cracks as divine messages and added the inscriptions. When translated, the inscriptions turned out to be prophecies performed for, or by, the Shang royal household. They covered everything from health to agriculture and prospects of victory in war. Li Ji also excavated eleven Shang royal tombs and discovered numerous priceless bronzes.

Except for the excavations at Zhoukoudian, near Beijing, which yielded bones of *Homo erectus* (see Chapter 8), in the early days of modern archaeology, most excavations were in the hands of non-Chinese explorers (or a few local private archaeologists who worked on their own). Most of them operated in northwestern

China, Mongolia and Tibet. The most famous of these scholars was Aurel Stein (1862–1943).

An explorer, obsessive traveller and archaeologist, Stein was one of the last true archaeological adventurers. Born in Budapest, as a teenager he displayed considerable intellectual talent. His Hungarian military training also gave him an eye for landscape and expertise in surveying. Like other archaeologists working in remote lands, Stein had an exceptional flair for languages, which enabled him to travel widely in little-known Central Asia. Except for the ancient Silk Road and other trade routes, this was virtually a geographical blank in the Western world. (The Silk Road was a network of trade routes across Central Asia that linked China and the West.)

Stein joined the Indian Education Service in 1887, but transferred to the Indian Archaeological Survey in 1910. By then, he had already penetrated deep into remote country on the Chinese and Indian borders. There he investigated the mysterious Khotan Empire, an early centre for the spread of Buddhism from India to China. Khotan had grown rich on the Silk Road trade during the eighth century AD. Stein's major interest was in artefacts and sacred books that were being sold to European collectors.

Between 1906 and 1913, Stein vanished into the least accessible parts of China. He visited the Caves of the Thousand Buddhas, where painted sculptures had been carved into sandstone at Dunhuang in the far west of China. Chinese monks had established the earliest shrine in the caves in AD 306. Eventually, there were 492 temples at what had become an important junction of the Silk Road. Some 45,000 square metres of wall art adorn the caves, some of the earliest Chinese art known.

Stein heard rumours of a collection of ancient manuscripts, and a monk showed him a sealed chamber crammed with documents of all kinds. These were Chinese versions of Buddhist texts, written between the third and the fourth centuries AD. Many were designed to be hung in shrines.

Stein bought the entire collection, plus another seven cases of manuscripts and more than 300 paintings, for four silver horse-shoes. He discreetly packed everything onto his camels and ponies and spirited the collection away to the British Museum. Though Stein has been criticised for his dishonest looting, he did manage to save numerous priceless artefacts of early Buddhism and ancient Central Asian culture from being sold on the open market.

Quite apart from Stein's collecting activities, the Indian Archaeological Survey supported his expeditions and long absences as a way of gathering vital geographical and political information. Between 1913 and 1916, he penetrated deep into Mongolia and traced long stretches of the Silk Road. By now, though, he faced competition from other archaeologists and suspicion from officials. Despite these difficulties, Stein returned with another rich haul of manuscripts, jade artefacts and fine pottery, all purchased at the lowest possible price or collected from the surface of deserted sites.

Stein stayed constantly on the move in remote parts of Central Asia until he was well into his seventies. During the 1920s, he scoured little-known regions of Persia and Iraq for cultural links to the Indus cities of Harappa and Mohenjodaro (see Chapter 25). As late as the 1940s, he was mapping the remote eastern frontiers of the Roman Empire. Almost single-handedly, this remarkable traveller linked the ancient East and West. To the Chinese, who regard him as a thief, his methods were questionable; but he opened the eyes of Western archaeologists and historians to the huge blank that had been Central Asia.

What influence did the Middle East and China have on ancient Europe? Vere Gordon Childe (1892–1957), an Australian-born archaeologist and philologist (a specialist in language), provided some answers. The son of a Church of England clergyman, he rebelled against his respectable upbringing and became a political activist while still at the University of Sydney. Childe then went to study the archaeology of Greece and Rome at Oxford University. After a brief involvement in Australian Labour Party politics, he returned to Britain and then spent five years travelling through Europe, studying its past.

Gordon Childe always thought of prehistory as a form of history. His sources were not documents, but the artefacts, sites and behaviour of prehistoric societies. Unlike many earlier archaeologists, he took a very broad view of the past, which contrasted dramatically with the narrow, artefact-based obsessions of other archaeologists. His extensive experience of sites and tools throughout Europe allowed him to build up a portrait of the development of later European societies, starting with farming and ending with the arrival of the Romans. For inspiration, he looked to the ancient societies of the Middle East, whose innovations and ideas had spread into Europe.

This idea was nothing new. Childe's archaeological predecessors had long believed that civilisation had developed in Egypt and Mesopotamia. But Childe thought differently from those who assumed that Europe had imported everything new from outside. Whereas Middle Eastern societies had formed larger political units, and eventually civilisations, their European contemporaries had fragmented into numerous smaller political units. Childe argued that this fragmentation allowed craftspeople and traders to move and spread their ideas and innovations over wide areas. Then, when iron became freely available to all, the first truly democratic states came into being.

A fluent writer with an easy-going style, Childe wrote a series of widely read books. Most famous was *The Dawn of European Civilization*, published in 1925, which became a bible for generations of students right into the 1960s. *The Dawn* was narrative history, based on archaeology. Childe talked not of kings and statesmen, but of human cultures, identified by groupings of artefacts (such as clay vessels, bronze brooches and swords), and also by architecture and art.

He believed that the Danube Basin in Eastern Europe, with its fertile soils and ample rainfall, was the region where many European farming and metal-using societies developed ideas and technologies before these spread westwards towards the distant Atlantic.

Childe also used artefacts and ornaments to trace changes in human societies through time. This approach is called 'culture history' and has become a basic tool of archaeologists everywhere. His dates for developments such as early farming were, for the most part, closely argued estimates and are now known to be inaccurate (see Chapter 27).

In 1927, Childe was appointed professor of prehistoric archaeology at Edinburgh University. But he was not a good teacher, and instead spent his time travelling and writing. He has relatively few excavations to his name – at around fifteen sites in Scotland and Ireland. His most famous dig was that of Skara Brae, a Stone Age village in the Orkney Islands off northern Scotland, where he found still-intact stone furnishings, now dated to about 3000 BC. These he interpreted by comparing them to the stone furnishings of nineteenth-century rural dwellings in the Scottish Highlands.

From artefacts, Childe's interests shifted to economic developments in the past, especially agriculture and the origins of civilisation. He argued that widespread droughts at the end of the Ice Age had driven human societies into oases. There they came into contact with wild grasses and wild animals that could be tamed. They turned to farming and animal herding, in what he called the Agricultural Revolution (see also Chapter 30). In 1934, he spoke of an Urban Revolution, which led to the emergence of cities and civilisations.

These two revolutions, Childe concluded, encouraged major technological advances, produced more food supplies and large population increases, and then ultimately craft specialisation, writing and civilisation. He argued that the Agricultural and the Urban Revolutions had as great an impact on human history as did the eighteenth-century Industrial Revolution, with its steam engines, factories and cities.

In 1946, Childe left Edinburgh to become professor of European archaeology at the Institute of Archaeology in London. By the 1950s, though, his ideas were coming under attack. The advent of radiocarbon dating overturned many of his European chronologies (see Chapter 27). Partly on these grounds, a new generation of archaeologists downplayed the influence of the Middle East. New research emphasised internal change in societies, rather than external influences. Childe became depressed and began to regard his life's work as a failure. Nor did his well-written stories of the past influence the direction of contemporary society. Childe retired in 1956, returned to Australia and committed suicide a year later.

To the vigorous and outspoken Gordon Childe we owe some of the first grand narratives of human prehistory, which embraced areas far larger than a single country or region. He, Aurel Stein and the Chinese archaeologists who worked at Anyang brought together East and West. They turned archaeology into a global study of the past.

CHAPTER 24

Shell Heaps, Pueblos and Tree Rings

There is a motorway exit at Emeryville, across the bay from San Francisco in California, that is named Shell Mound Street. And with good reason, for it was with this enormous shell heap that Max Uhle (1856–1944), a German-born archaeologist, boldly challenged the widespread assumption that California Indian societies had not changed over thousands of years. The situation was similar to that of Great Zimbabwe: simply, no one believed that Native Americans in California were capable of innovation.

The huge prehistoric shell mound that Uhle excavated has long since vanished under modern buildings. But back in 1902, Uhle, who had worked for years on archaeological sites in Peru, was employed to excavate shell mounds in the San Francisco Bay area. He started work on the one at Emeryville, which was one of the largest. The site was 30 metres long, more than 9 metres high, and towered over the surrounding flat land. His trench went down to the water level and below.

Uhle drew detailed cross-sections of ten major layers and counted the number of artefacts found in each. At a time when few California excavators thought about long sequences of occupation layers, this was a major step forward. Hitherto, people had dug shell heaps quickly and untidily, mainly in a hasty search for burials and arte-facts. These were unspectacular sites, monotonous to excavate and haphazardly accumulated by shellfish collectors. Earlier prejudices persisted that such people were at the bottom of the human ladder.

In the end, Uhle reduced the ten strata to two major compo-nents. The people of the lower one had lived mainly off oysters, had buried their dead in the mound and had made tools from local stone. The later inhabitants had used cremation, had consumed enormous numbers of clams rather than oysters, and had imported fine-grained stone for toolmaking. Uhle estimated that the Emeryville mound was in use for more than 1,000 years.

Uhle was an unsophisticated excavator by today's standards, but his methods were far better than the crude digging that was commonplace at other sites. Furthermore, he had enormous prac-tical experience of both excavating and analysing artefacts and occupation levels in different environments. He had worked at the pre-Inca ceremonial centre at Tiwanaku in highland Bolivia in 1894 (when he had stopped local soldiers from using the carvings there for target practice). And after 1896, he had worked on the arid Peruvian coast, where he paid close attention to pottery and textile styles, the latter preserved by the dry environment, as they changed through time. Everywhere he worked in Peru, he devel-oped chronological sequences, using graves in cemeteries for the purpose. In a way, he was another Flinders Petrie in a different desert landscape. His harsh criticisms of local archaeologists offended both his Bolivian and his Peruvian colleagues, who accused him of selling artefacts for profit. He left South America and became involved with California's shell mounds.

Uhle was both efficient and very experienced. He published his excavations promptly and in detail. It might have been expected that other archaeologists would welcome his thorough assessment of changes in the lives of the Emeryville shellfish gatherers. His conclusions were clear, well documented and based on his long years of studying evolving Native American cultures in Peru.

But instead, the wrath of local archaeologists descended on his head. They had long assumed that California Indian cultures had remained static throughout the past, and they saw no reason to change their minds. A powerful anthropologist named Alfred Kroeber dismissed Uhle's conclusions out of hand. Knowing he was right, Uhle just kept working. Later generations of shell mound researchers have proved him correct.

Max Uhle was not alone in showing that ancient American societies did change profoundly over thousands of years. He worked with unspectacular shell heaps, stone tools and mollusc shells. But in the American Southwest, there were much more impressive archaeological sites and multi-storey pueblos. The dry climate there preserved far more than stone tools and pottery – baskets, textiles, sandals and even burials. There were few archaeologists in the Southwest in Uhle's time, but some of them tried to date pottery styles and pueblos. One such was Alfred Kidder (1885–1963).

Kidder introduced to the Southwest the practice of excavating in layers, and later became a major force in Maya archaeology. Born in Marquette, Michigan, he was the son of a mining engineer. Admitted to Harvard University as a pre-medical student, he soon shifted his focus to anthropology. At the time, Harvard was the country's foremost centre for anthropology.

In 1907, Kidder's Harvard mentors, including a distinguished Maya expert, Alfred Tozzer, sent him on an archaeological survey to the Four Corners region of the Southwest, where four US states meet. Kidder had never been west of Michigan, but he immediately fell in love with the area and became fascinated by its archaeology. He graduated in 1908, visited Greece and Egypt with his family, and then entered graduate school in 1909. Early on, he took a course in archaeological field methods run by George Reisner, a well-known Egyptologist. Kidder visited Reisner's excavations in Egypt and the Sudan and learned his methods for stratigraphic (layer) analysis and for excavating large cemeteries, a major part of Sudanese archaeology.

Kidder's doctoral dissertation was a study of Southwestern pottery styles. He found the work near impossible, because excavators of the day ignored stratified layers. For his fieldwork in New Mexico's Pajarito Plateau, where modern-day Los Alamos lies, he used both ancient and modern pottery to develop a cultural sequence. This he published in an influential paper in 1915.

That same year, the Robert S. Peabody Foundation for Archaeology in Andover, Massachusetts, appointed Kidder director of a long-term excavation project at Pecos, New Mexico, where deep, undisturbed refuse heaps marked an abandoned pueblo. However, the First World War intervened. Kidder served with distinction on the Western Front, being promoted to the rank of captain in 1918. The Pecos research resumed in 1920 and continued until 1929. The project was a brilliant success. Kidder was an enthusiastic and dynamic leader with a personality that attracted young students. Many of them went on to enjoy distinguished careers elsewhere.

Like other Southwestern archaeologists, Kidder cleared pueblo rooms, but with a difference. He looked closely at changing pottery styles and asked what the changes meant. He dug into the Pecos refuse heaps on a massive scale. But instead of digging in arbitrary levels, he took careful note of features, such as heaps of discarded bones and broken utensils. He followed Reisner's practice of recording every find in three dimensions, so that he could document even the smallest stratigraphic differences. His detailed pottery logs followed Reisner's practice.

Within a few seasons, Kidder had put together a remarkable chronicle of changing Pecos pottery styles, marked especially by surface decoration, such as black painted designs. He had also excavated hundreds of human burials. Harvard anthropologist E.A. Hooton, an authority on ancient human skeletons, visited the excavations, observing the bones and determining their sex and age. Valuable and unique information on both life expectancy and the effects of hard work on the human skeleton emerged from this research. Hooton showed that most ancient Pecos people died in their twenties.

Actual excavation virtually ceased at the Pecos site after 1922, whereupon Kidder changed his strategy. He had acquired information on the architecture and expansion of the pueblo and had excavated its earliest levels. Now he extended his research to surveys and excavations at other sites while analysing the enormous quantities of finds. His studies ranged much further than archaeology, delving into modern Pueblo Indian agriculture and even public health. The Pecos project was a remarkable example of team research at a time when most North American archaeology was very unsophisticated. Pecos foreshadowed the close-knit field projects of today's archaeology.

In 1927, Kidder had enough information to compile a detailed sequence of Pueblo and pre-Pueblo cultures in the Southwest. His long sequence began with Basket Maker cultures that were at least 2,000 years old. These people made no pottery and had no permanent homes. They were followed by pre-Pueblo and Pueblo cultures. At Pecos, Kidder found no fewer than six settlements, one above the other. There was enough information for him to argue for eight major cultural stages between 1500 BC (the Basket Makers) and AD 750. Then there were five Pueblo stages after 750, ending in the period of written history (which began in 1600). The Pecos sequence showed that Southwestern people developed their cultures and institutions quite independently of other areas. Kidder's sequence for the Southwest has been the basis for all subsequent research. There have, of course, been numerous modifications, but that is only to be expected.

Kidder took his ideas further. He arranged an informal conference in his excavation camp at Pecos in August 1927. Forty archaeologists attended to review progress and to lay the foundations for a basic cultural framework, which was essential as more archaeologists began work in the Southwest. The conference established three stages of Basket Makers and five stages of Pueblo inhabitants as a provisional chronological sequence. Like the Three Ages in nineteenth-century Europe, the Pecos scheme reduced the chaos that surrounded earlier excavations. The Pecos conference is still an annual event in the Southwest and is attended by several hundred people.

The Pecos sequence had one major disadvantage. There was no means of dating the sequence in calendar years. Fortunately, a

University of Arizona astronomer, A.E. Douglass (1867–1962), had been studying climate change since 1901. He was interested in the effect on the climate of astronomical events like sunspots. With brilliant insight, he argued that the annual growth rings in Southwestern trees could document major and minor climatic shifts. Douglass found that there was a direct relationship between the thickness of growth rings and the amount of annual rainfall. Thin rings marked drought years, thicker growth wetter years.

Douglass's initial experiments took him back about 200 years. From the oldest living firs and pines, he extended the technique to dead trees, using beams from Spanish churches of the colonial period. Then he turned to prehistoric ruins. In 1918, he devised a wood borer that enabled him to take tree-ring samples from ancient beams without disturbing the structures they supported.

Douglass's first borings came from ancient pueblo beams, made from trees that were felled long ago. Because they were so old, they could not be linked to rings from living trees of known age. There was a sequence of eighty years from the Aztec ruins in northern New Mexico and another from the great semi-circular Pueblo Bonito in Chaco Canyon. But Douglass could not pin down the dates accurately – the tree-ring sequences 'floated' about in time.

It took him ten years to link up known tree-ring history and his earlier floating chronologies. In 1928, the Indians allowed him to bore into the beams of Hopi villages in northern Arizona; that took him back to AD 1400. A year later, a charred beam from a ruin at Show Low, Arizona, had a tree-ring sequence that overlapped with the floating chronologies of earlier sites. Now he could link tree-ring sequences from Pecos to his master timescale. The new science of dendrochronology (tree-ring dating) finally dated the Pecos sequence and provided a chronology for the great flowering of Pueblo culture from the tenth to the twelfth centuries AD.

Alfred Kidder's methods of artefact analysis and excavation spread gradually across North America. All subsequent research in the Southwest, and much of the Americas, stems ultimately from the Pecos project. Thanks to his field training, his gifted students took the latest field methods with them when they worked elsewhere. Kidder himself moved on to an important position supervising Maya research at the Carnegie Institution in Washington, DC in 1929.

In 1950, he retired to Cambridge, Massachusetts, where his house became a gathering place for archaeologists and students until his death in 1963. By then, American archaeology had built on Kidder's foundations and was ready for more detailed research. He made accuracy, careful observation and team research the basis of American archaeology.

CHAPTER 25

A Fire-Breathing Giant

Mohenjodaro, Pakistan, 1947. A small group of young archaeologists and students gathered in front of a confusion of mud bricks and sand high above the ancient city on the banks of the Indus River. Silence fell as an upright, middle-aged archaeologist with a bristling moustache strode up to them.

Mortimer Wheeler was a formidable man, and the students were terrified of him. With few words, but commanding gestures, he set them to supervising teams of local labourers who attacked the sand. A few weathered bricks became many. The stark walls of a huge platform emerged from the hillside. A fort, he announced in a loud voice. 'It towers grim and forbidding above the plain.' The archaeologists and students nodded their heads timidly in agreement. The bold announcement was typical of an archaeologist once described by a disgruntled colleague as a 'fire-breathing giant'.

Many early archaeologists had strong personalities. They had to have, as they often worked almost alone and often in remote lands. Many of their digs were on a large scale, using small armies of labourers. Mortimer Wheeler was a born leader, but those skills were developed while he was an artillery officer in the First World War. At Mohenjodaro, he directed an excavation that trained young Indian archaeologists in his rigorous methods. Wheeler managed them with a firm hand and left no one in any doubt about who was boss. If he told his students that a mass of bricks was a fort, it was a fort. There was no argument.

The 'fire-breathing giant' was not the first archaeologist to work at Mohenjodaro. Archaeology was new to India, where written history began with Alexander the Great's invasion in 326 BC. The first professional archaeologist to dig there was an Englishman, John Marshall, who became director-general of India's newly founded Archaeological Survey in 1921.

Marshall moved into Mohenjodaro in strength: during the 1925–26 field season, he used a workforce of 1,200. He also trained young Indian archaeologists in excavation. The digs uncovered entire blocks of brick houses, networks of streets and elaborate drainage systems. A huge stone-lined water tank that served as a ceremonial bath came to light among buildings high above the city. When archaeologists working in Mesopotamia found artefacts identical to those from Mohenjodaro that dated to the third millennium BC (the period between 3000 and 2000 BC), Marshall had a rough chronology to work with. His report on Mohenjodaro and the Indus civilisation was the standard reference work on the subject – until Mortimer Wheeler came along.

Robert Eric Mortimer Wheeler (1890–1976) burst onto Indian archaeology like a thunderclap, becoming director of the Archaeological Survey in 1944. He inherited a dying institution, but the decisive and flamboyant Wheeler was the ideal man to breathe new life into it.

The son of a journalist, he was born in Edinburgh. He studied classics at University College London. After graduating, he went to Germany's Rhineland to research Roman pottery. His artillery experience during the First World War convinced him that he had a gift for logistics and organisation, essential qualities in an excavator. In 1920, Wheeler became keeper of archaeology at the National Museum of Wales in Cardiff, and then, four years later, its director.

While in Wales, Wheeler and his wife Tessa undertook a series of major excavations of Roman frontier forts. They had studied the almost forgotten excavation methods of General Pitt Rivers (see Chapter 16). Like him, they paid careful attention to even shallow layers in the soil, recovered the smallest of artefacts and published their work promptly. Wheeler's fine drawings served as illustrations. Nothing like this had been seen before in Roman archaeology. Wheeler went even further. Convinced that the public had the right to know about his work, he encouraged visitors to the site and gave numerous popular lectures.

Prehistoric and Roman Wales, published in 1925, the same year as Gordon Childe's *Dawn of European Civilization* (see Chapter 23), established Wheeler's reputation. He turned down a professorship at Edinburgh (which Gordon Childe subsequently accepted) and in 1926 became keeper of the neglected London Museum. With his boundless energy, Wheeler rapidly transformed the place. Meanwhile, he and Tessa excavated more sites, carefully chosen to study the relationship between native British people and the Roman settlers. He also trained a new generation of young archaeologists on his hectic excavations.

In 1928 and 1929, Wheeler excavated a Roman sanctuary at Lydney, Gloucestershire. Then he turned his attention to the Roman city of Verulamium, just north of London, in open country where large-scale excavation was possible. Between 1930 and 1933, he and Tessa exposed nearly 4.5 hectares of the city. They unravelled the complicated history of its earthworks and of earlier settlements.

Still full of energy, having set the London Museum in order, he went on to found the London Institute of Archaeology in 1937, becoming its first director. Under his leadership, the institute became famous both for its fieldwork and for its excellent training in excavation and scientific methods, such as pottery analysis.

Tired of the Romans, the Wheelers undertook their most ambitious British excavation, the huge 2,000-year-old Maiden Castle hillfort in southern England, with its massive earthworks. From 1934 to 1937, the husband-and-wife team dissected the complex fortifications with deep, vertical trenches. They also investigated parts of the interior with shallow trenches laid out in a series of boxes. Such a horizontal layout enabled them to trace different layers over a wide area. With the trenches carefully labelled and recorded, stratigraphy allowed them to build a chronology of the site from one side to the other.

The Maiden Castle excavations achieved a level of sophistication that was unheard of at the time. Wheeler actively encouraged visitors and wrote vivid accounts of the site. His most famous tale describes a Roman attack on the fort in AD 43, with survivors creeping back in the night to bury their dead (whom Wheeler had found in his trenches). This is Wheeler at his most enjoyable and flamboyant best.

Wheeler was a formidable personality, with flashing eyes and flowing hair. He disliked criticism and did not suffer fools gladly. He drove both his paid workers and his volunteers hard, and cared little for their feelings. He made enemies with his abrupt ways and his ambition, as well as his love of publicity. But with their disciplined planning and carefully laid-out trenches – dug to get information, not goodies – he and Tessa brought British excavation into the modern world.

The outbreak of the Second World War found Wheeler back in the Royal Artillery. He fought at the Battle of El Alamein in North Africa, distinguishing himself under fire. Then, out of the blue, in 1944 the viceroy of India invited him to become director general of the Archaeological Survey of India.

Wheeler shook up that lazy organisation almost overnight. In a rigorous six-month training programme at Taxila, sixty-one students learned a standard of excavation previously unheard of in India. Wheeler's first Indian excavation was at Arikamedu, a trading station on the southeast coast. He found Roman pot fragments, which showed that Roman goods had been traded as far afield as there.

But his greatest challenge came at Harappa and Mohenjodaro. Wheeler had excavated towns and forts before, but he had never tackled sites as large and complex as these two ancient cities. For five years, his trained staffers joined him in probing the two sites.

Wheeler divided Mohenjodaro into two sections: the higher buildings, the citadel, on the west side; and the predominantly residential lower town. His excavators uncovered a grid layout of narrow streets lined with brick dwellings. These ran from north to south and from east to west. Covered drains linked the streets and alleyways. The sophistication of the drainage and sewerage systems was unparalleled in the ancient world. Both Wheeler and Stuart Piggott, another very competent British archaeologist who also spent part of the war in India, were struck by the technological achievements of what appeared to have been a modest civilisation: there were no godlike rulers boasting of their conquests on palace and temple walls, as was the case in Egypt and Mesopotamia.

When Wheeler excavated the Mohenjodaro and Harappa citadels, he interpreted the structures on top as public buildings. One jumble of bricks he proclaimed to be a granary. We now know that Wheeler was wrong: it was a columned hall. A careful excavator, though at times aggressive, he was keenly aware of the public relations value of an important discovery. He often immersed himself totally in the past during his excavations, a characteristic that could lead him to exaggerate the importance of his finds. Flashes of inspiration – like the Mohenjodaro granary – were typical of much of his research. Like Leonard Woolley, he was also a vivid writer and would use even small finds to paint a picture of ancient behaviour that appealed to a wide audience.

For all its cities and citadels, the ancient Indus civilisation was very different from others. There were no palaces or royal sepulchres. Few portraits of Indus people survive, but one well-known sculpture shows an apparently calm man, who gives the impression of a priest rather than a powerful ruler.

Wheeler and Piggott described a civilisation that was distinct from those of Egypt or Mesopotamia. Its cities lay within walls with imposing gateways. At first they were compact. Then, as their populations grew, suburbs developed outside the walls, where archaeologists uncovered barrack-like buildings. Wheeler argued that workers had lived there. But again, later research suggests that they were probably workshops for the manufacture of metal tools and pottery; those who worked in them likely dwelt in the cities.

It should be remembered that Wheeler arrived in India straight from a battlefield and that he was an expert on Rome, a society in which armies played a leading role. He thought of the Indus city walls as defensive. When he discovered the skeletons of thirty-seven men, women and children lying in Mohenjodaro streets that dated to the closing period of occupation, he immediately jumped to the conclusion that there had been a last-ditch massacre of people defending their homes. But he was just plain wrong: the 'victims' came from different groups in the lower town, not from the citadel, which would have been defended to the last. None of the burials shows any sign of violence. Biological anthropologists believe they perished from disease rather than war. In fact, the massive platforms and walls were erected to defend not against invaders, but against unpredictable and sometimes catastrophic Indus River floods.

Wheeler never published the full details of his Indus excavations. He wrote a preliminary report and a general book on the Indus civilisation for a broader audience. This is one reason why his interpretation of the Indus cities has endured. Today, we know that the Indus civilisation flourished in a fertile (if unpredictable) environment, where farming land, grazing grass and all kinds of resources were scattered over an enormous, diverse landscape. This was a civilisation that arose because people and communities needed one another to supply the necessities of life. Apparently they thrived without conflict.

After leaving India in 1948, following its independence, Wheeler spent five years as professor of the Roman provinces at the London institute he had founded. Then he became administrator of the declining British Academy, revitalising it. He carefully directed funds to young archaeologists working overseas.

To Wheeler, archaeology was a global happening, far wider than Gordon Childe's vision of Europe and the Middle East. In Wheeler's later years, he became a TV celebrity, thanks to his appearances on the BBC's *Animal, Vegetable, Mineral?* programme, in which experts identified objects from the past. He also continued to write for the public and to lecture widely, for he believed that archaeologists had to share their work with general audiences.

Wheeler may have been a vivid personality, but his brilliant excavations set new standards. He may have been outspoken, but his achievements were enormous. Mortimer Wheeler was an international figure who helped lay the foundations of world prehistory.

CHAPTER 26

Around the River Bend

Most people have never heard of the Shoshone Indians of the Great Basin in western North America. More's the pity, for their way of life had a profound influence on how a whole generation of American archaeologists thought about the past.

Unlikely heroes, the Shoshone people lived in small bands in one of the driest landscapes in the United States. They ate small game and plant foods of many kinds, used only the simplest of digging sticks, grinders and bows and arrows, yet thrived in a very harsh, arid environment for thousands of years. Why were they so successful?

Anthropologist Julian Steward (1902–72), who was very aware of archaeology, spent many months with the Shoshone. He attributed their success to their constant mobility, and to their remarkable knowledge of the available foods in what he called an edible, if very dry, landscape. The Shoshone moved across the Great Basin landscape constantly, their movements dictated by food and water supplies. In a classic anthropological study, Steward mapped how their patterns of settlement changed from one season to the next. But he was no narrowly focused anthropologist: he realised that changing settlement patterns across different landscapes were key to understanding ancient societies. His approach became known as cultural ecology, the study of the relationship between people and their environments.

Much of Steward's career brought him in touch with archaeologists through a huge archaeology project on the Missouri River, known as the River Basin Surveys programme, which began after the Second World War.

During the 1950s and early 1960s, a surge in dam construction began to transform the United States – and archaeology. The large-scale water works provided hydroelectric power, stored water for agriculture, controlled floods and expanded navigation on major rivers. But they also destroyed thousands of archaeological sites. The most ambitious project involved harnessing the Missouri River. This would drown 1,600 kilometres of valley land and destroy over 90 per cent of the historical and archaeological sites along the river.

The River Basin Surveys developed as archaeologists fought to salvage the past. Such surveys transformed American archaeology beyond recognition. Previously, most research had unfolded in limited areas like the Southwest. By the time the programme ended, we had the first portrait of an ancient North America, far more diverse than merely burial mounds and pueblos.

The scale of the Missouri River dam building and survey operations alone was enormous. There were still only very few qualified archaeologists available to do the survey work. Twelve universities, four museums and various other organisations joined in at once. By 1968, when the River Basin Surveys ended, hardworking field-workers had surveyed about 500 reservoir basins big and small. They had tested more than 20,000 archaeological sites. Many of them filled in blanks on the archaeological maps, for the surveys examined hitherto unknown areas. Nearly 2,000 significant reports came from the surveys.

An avalanche of new data in the form of artefacts and other finds descended on archaeological laboratories around the country. Perhaps most important of all, many archaeologists became aware of the threat to the fragile archives they relied upon. Excavation destroyed sites, and so they also came to believe that digging was a last resort. Ever since the surveys ended, most archaeology in the United States has been devoted to conserving the record of the past that remains.

Many young American archaeologists served their apprenticeships on the River Basin Surveys and on projects in the Southeast funded by the Works Project Administration. They surveyed threatened landscapes and digging sites before they vanished under water. The sheer number of artefacts, many of them from sites occupied over long periods, was overwhelming. Bag after bag of stone tools and pot fragments had to be washed, labelled and classified.

The people who undertook this work confronted a problem similar to that of Christian Jürgensen Thomsen in Copenhagen 150 years earlier (see Chapter 9). How did you create a chronological framework for America's remote past? There was no Three-Age System in North America.

Some River Basin Surveys archaeologists devoted their entire careers to this past. One of them was James A. Ford, an artefact expert, who assembled hundreds of collections from thousands of sites into long, elaborate charts that extended over thousands of years. I recall sitting through one of his presentations, complete with graphs and flip charts. Ford was not an interesting lecturer – this was long before computers – and his endless stream of data was unintelligible and boring. I must confess that I dozed off.

Much archaeology of the day was obscure, bogged down in minute changes in artefacts, and nothing more than a framework of changing technologies. Fortunately, a few scholars approached their work with a broader perspective, a determination to move away from pure data to the study of ancient people. Gordon Randolph Willey (1913–2002) was one such visionary. He was destined to become one of the best-known archaeologists of the twentieth century.

Willey worked on the River Basin Surveys and on another survey in northwestern Florida while still a student. The experience gave him not only a grounding in artefacts of many kinds, but also an understanding of how people adapted to changing landscapes over thousands of years.

Willey served as an anthropologist at the Bureau of American Ethnology at the Smithsonian Institution from 1943 to 1950. While there he worked on the River Basin Surveys in the southeastern United States. He collaborated with Ford and others on a series of reports that raised the study of culture history (see Chapter 23) to new levels. This work was far more sophisticated than Kidder's work at Pecos in the Southwest thirty years earlier (see Chapter 24). During his survey years, he worked closely with Julian Steward, who told Willey and others that they should stop examining single sites and look at people and their settlements in the context of their landscapes.

When he finished with the surveys, Willey had almost unrivalled experience of archaeological survey work in the field. But as well as being an archaeologist, he was also an anthropologist. His training had combined the two, for his teachers made it clear that you could not study ancient North Americans without taking account of living Indian societies as well. In North America, archaeology was not only excavation and survey, but also anthropology.

Steward strongly encouraged Willey to carry out an archaeo-logical survey in one of the river valleys of the arid north coast of Peru. He helped him set up a project to study the varied landscape and changing prehistoric settlement patterns in the little-known Viru Valley. Willey looked at the entire valley with the help of aerial photographs (images taken from the air). He surveyed the most promising areas on foot, and carried out limited excavations. In his report on the project, published in 1953, he told the story of the valley as a series of ever-changing complex economic, political and social landscapes. Stratigraphic sequences and artefacts were but a small part of the story. Willey's Viru research founded what is now called settlement archaeology, an important strand in today's archaeological world.

The Viru research earned Willey the prestigious Bowditch Professorship of Central American and Mexican Archaeology at

Harvard University in 1950. He worked there for the rest of his career, carrying out important fieldwork on the Maya civilisation. He also worked on settlement surveys at important sites in Belize and Guatemala. The emphasis of his research was not on major cities, but on the lesser settlements that flourished in their shadows.

Gordon Willey was a charming, learned archaeologist and a superb mentor of young students. Above all, he stressed that good archaeology is based on data, not just on high-flown ideas. As we shall see in later chapters, this was an important point.

Willey was not, of course, alone. There were other larger-than-life figures who worked in North America during this time. Jesse David Jennings (1909–97) was a major figure in the archaeology of the American West. Jennings joined the University of Utah in 1948. His first field research in the Great Basin involved excavating several dry cave sites, especially Danger Cave (so named because a falling rock nearly killed two archaeologists). Here he excavated 4 metres of occupation levels with painstaking care. They revealed an estimated 11,000 years of occasional visitations.

Preservation conditions in the dry levels were near perfect, allowing Jennings to study the small adjustments the inhabitants had made to changing climatic conditions in the area. At the time the cave was occupied, there had been nearby marshes, where fish, edible plants and waterfowl abounded. Jennings found cords made from plant fibres, leather clothing fragments, basketry and stones used for grinding nuts. He even excavated well-preserved beetle remains and human faeces, which revealed much about the predominantly plant diet of the inhabitants. He wrote of a long-lived cultural tradition, which endured until AD 500. Like Willey and Ford in the Southeast, he laid sound foundations for all later Great Basin work. Witty and sometimes sarcastic, Jennings preferred data and digging to theories. His excavations set standards for a generation.

Meanwhile, in eastern North America, Kansas-born James B. Griffin (1905–97) of the University of Michigan also helped transform North American archaeology. Griffin was, above all, an artefact man. He spent a great deal of time studying the enormous collections assembled by the River Basin Surveys. Like Ford and Willey, Griffin tried to bring order to storage rooms full of unsorted artefacts. His knowledge of archaeological finds in eastern North America was legendary. He founded a Ceramic Repository at the University of Michigan. This vast pottery collection is a fundamental archive for today's researchers.

By the early 1960s, a general framework for the North American past before Columbus was in widespread use. It was based on excavations, surveys and artefacts. Like Gordon Childe in Europe, those who developed it assumed, quite reasonably, that the distribution of human cultures over wide areas meant that they flourished at much the same time. Griffin, Jennings and Willey were, above all, data experts. However, as Willey with his Viru research well knew, change was afoot.

A new generation of archaeologists was aware of research into ancient environments, pioneered in the Southwest by, among others, A.E. Douglass of tree-ring fame (see Chapter 24). They began to ask new questions, some of them arising from the River Basin Surveys. How had environments and landscapes changed through time? How had human societies living in them adapted to such changes? What impacts did the need for such adjustments have on society as a whole?

North American archaeology from the 1930s to the early 1960s was mostly a matter of describing the past, classifying minor details of different tools, and defining changing societies on the basis of their technologies. Few people thought about why these cultures had changed. Why, for example, had people taken up agriculture instead of hunting, fishing and collecting plant foods? Why were some hunting and gathering societies, like those in the Pacific Northwest, more complex than those in, say, the Great Basin or central Alaska?

The new generation wanted to move beyond classification to more sophisticated approaches to the past. They were also looking for new ways of dating ancient societies. It was one thing to say that one culture was older than another. But how old were they both in calendar years? How much older in years was one than another? As we shall see, the development of radiocarbon dating (Chapter 27) was part of a major revolution in archaeology that was about to take place.

Until the 1950s, the centre of gravity of archaeology had rested in Europe and the Mediterranean, and also in southwestern Asia. Gradually, archaeological research expanded far from European shores. The process had long been under way, in part because of the global distribution of British and French colonies. Both archaeology and anthropology had been activities associated with colonial rule, whether in India, Africa or the Pacific. The roots of what came to be called world prehistory had been put down in the nineteenth century. Now world prehistory was to blossom.

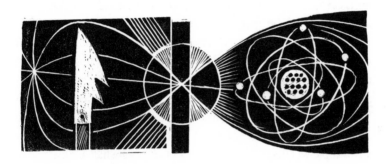

CHAPTER 27

Dating the Ages

How old is it? This is one of the basic questions that archaeologists ask whenever they excavate a site or examine an artefact. As we have seen, any dating – in years before the present, or in AD/BC – used to be generally little more than a 'guesstimate'. Only tree-rings and objects of known age, such as Roman coins, could date prehistoric sites (see Chapters 11, 24 and 26). Then, in 1949, Willard Libby came up with the radiocarbon dating method, which made it possible to date sites and artefacts as far back as 50,000 years.

Willard Libby (1908–80) was an American chemist, not an archaeologist. Yet he did more than almost anyone else to revolutionise archaeological research. A farmer's son, Libby became an expert on radioactivity and nuclear science. During the Second World War, he worked as part of the Manhattan Project, which developed the atomic bomb. After the war, he moved to the University of Chicago, where he started work on radiocarbon dating. This, he believed, could offer a way of dating archaeological sites in calendar years. He won a Nobel Prize for his efforts.

Libby's research assumed that radiocarbon (radioactive carbon, known as carbon-14) is constantly being created in the atmosphere by the interaction of cosmic rays with atmospheric nitrogen. Along with normal (non-radioactive) carbon, some of the carbon-14 in the air is absorbed and stored by plants. Animals then acquire the radio-active carbon by eating the vegetation. When an animal or plant dies, it stops exchanging carbon with the environment. From that moment on, the carbon-14 content decreases as it undergoes radioactive decay. Libby realised that measuring the amount of carbon-14 left in a dead plant, wood fragment or bone provides a way of calculating how old it is. The older the sample, the less carbon-14 it contains. He also determined the rate of decay: half of the radioactive carbon in any sample will decay after about 5,730 years (the half-life).

His experiments took many years to refine. Libby and his colleague, James Arnold, tried dating samples of known age, using wood from the tombs of Egyptian pharaohs Djoser and Sneferu, which, according to historical sources, dated to about 2625 ± 75 BC. The radiocarbon dates came out at 2800 ± 280 BC. Libby and Arnold published their research in 1949. By 1955, Libby had processed almost 1,000 dates both from objects of known age and from hitherto undated prehistoric sites.

Initially archaeologists wondered just how accurate radiocarbon dating was. For various reasons, some of them were reluctant to provide samples of known age. Many were sceptical about Libby's experimental dates. Others were afraid that radiocarbon dating would disprove their cherished theories. As research progressed, so more and more collaborators provided samples. There were, of course, uncertainties, as was only to be expected with a new dating method. But by the early 1960s, archaeologists had embraced radiocarbon dating with enthusiasm, for it had the potential to revolutionise knowledge of the past 50,000 years of human exis-tence. Anything older than 50,000 years contains traces of radio-active carbon too minute to be useful.

If radiocarbon dating was accurate, the potential was enormous. Archaeologists drooled at the thought of being able to date the first Americans, or the origins of agriculture in different parts of the world. Theoretically, too, it would be possible to measure the rate of cultural change, like the transition from hunting to farming, or the spread of different prehistoric peoples into Europe or across the Pacific thousands of years ago. The prospects were tantalising.

There were, however, serious technical obstacles to surmount. The results with some types of samples seemed to be more accurate than with others. At first, wood and charcoal set the standard, while bone and shell were regarded as less accurate. It soon became clear, too, that samples had to be collected meticulously to avoid contamination. Their exact position in a site was also important. Results could be skewed by whether a sample had come from a hearth, from the contents of a cooking pot, or simply from charcoal scattered through an occupation level – to mention only a few possibilities. These difficulties were gradually overcome, as radiocarbon dating became increasingly sophisticated.

Another fundamental problem was that radiocarbon dates were ages in radiocarbon years, not calendar years. Libby had originally assumed that the concentration of radiocarbon in the atmosphere remained constant through time. But this is wrong: changes in the strength of the earth's magnetic field and fluctuations in solar activity alter the concentration of radiocarbon both in the atmosphere and in living things. For instance, samples from 6,000 years ago were exposed to much higher radiocarbon concentrations than are samples from today.

The solution came by comparing radiocarbon dates against tree-rings. By the time radiocarbon dating was developed, tree-rings provided accurate calendar dates in the American Southwest and elsewhere to as far back as 12,500 years. This was just before the end of the Ice Age. In recent years, comparisons using fossil corals from the Caribbean and ice cores from Greenland and elsewhere have allowed scientists to date even older objects in calendar years.

Environmental fluctuations through the ages mean that the dates calculated solely from the carbon-14 samples and the dates obtained with the assistance of such sources as tree-rings, ice cores or historical documents can vary – sometimes by as much as 2,000 years. Intensive research using ice cores and other sources has resulted in tables that allow researchers to convert carbon-14 dates into accurate calendar chronologies.

The first radiocarbon dates for developments such as the origins of farming and the spread of agriculture into Europe caused both amazement and confusion. Gordon Childe's widely used dates for major events in Europe were far too late: the origins of farming, for example, jumped from about 4000 BC back to 9000 BC. Today, thanks to even more accurate dating, farming is thought to have originated around 12,000 years ago. With thousands of radiocarbon dates to work with, researchers can analyse the past in ways that were unimaginable in Willard Libby's time.

By the time radiocarbon dating was developed, archaeologists were working in many parts of the world. The new technique raised basic questions. How long ago did farming take hold in Egypt and Syria, in Turkey and across Europe? How old was Stonehenge and what were the dates for its different architectural stages, carefully dissected by excavation? For the first time, it was possible to date the arrival of farmers in Scandinavia, the first human settlement of the Americas, and the arrival of iron-using farmers in southern Africa.

By the early 1960s, rough outlines of a global prehistory had been assembled from a small patchwork of radiocarbon dates. Samples poured into radiocarbon laboratories from all over the world – Australia, Iceland, Peru and remote Pacific islands. For the first time, scholars could compare the dates in calendar years for the beginnings of farming in different parts of the world. They established, for example, that agriculture began at about the same time in the Middle East and in northern China.

Above all, one could seriously contemplate writing a history of humankind before literate civilisation within a well-established chronological framework. Such an advance was of great importance, especially in regions like Africa south of the Sahara, many parts of India, and the Americas, where the first written records dated to recent centuries. In some parts of Central Africa, the first historical archives date to the 1890s.

As radiocarbon dating became more refined, researchers turned to accelerator mass spectrometry (AMS) for more accurate readings. AMS was a huge advance. It allows samples to be dated on the basis of a single tree ring or an individual wheat seed (or even fragments of a seed). It also allows for the dating of many more samples, so that scientists can statistically analyse dozens – or even hundreds – from a single occupation level. Until recently, timescales in prehistory were still somewhat loose. But the introduction of sophisticated new statistical methods is now producing startlingly accurate chronologies.

One famous archaeological site, the West Kennet Long Barrow in southern England, is a case in point. It held the remains of around forty men, women and children, and had long been dated to about 3650 BC. It was a communal burial place, but for how long was it in use? Highly accurate radiocarbon dates were the only way to find out.

Sophisticated analysis of dozens of samples from the dead showed that the sequence of the burials unfolded over a mere thirty years, beginning in about 3640 BC. Other burial mounds nearby were actively used for three or four generations at most. The West Kennet Long Barrow was a communal burial site used for a short time – almost a family history of some Stone Age farmers. Because it was in use for such a brief period, those buried in the barrow's chambers were not just remote, anonymous ancestors: some of them had been known personally to the people still going about their business.

Looking slightly further afield, we now know that the use of long burial mounds was brief and ceased around 3625 BC. All this raises some fascinating questions. Were people buried in the long barrows in order to claim territory in a place and at a time where competition for land was increasing? Or were the communities that buried their dead in them short-lived because they were unstable and did not endure during times of political stress? The new chronology revealed a time of occasional rapid change and sudden events.

Radiocarbon is not the only means of dating the past. The earliest chapters of the past date back more than 3 million years – far beyond the scope of radiocarbon dating. And so we rely on a geological dating method, potassium–argon dating.

The potassium–argon method dates rocks by measuring the ratio of radioactive argon to radioactive potassium contained in them. Radioactive potassium-40 decays to radioactive argon-40 in both minerals and rocks. The ratio of argon-40 to potassium-40 in a mineral or rock provides an age for the sample. Argon is an inactive gas that escapes when rock material, such as volcanic lava, is in a molten state. When it cools, and crystallises into volcanic rock, the argon can no longer escape. A spectrometer can measure the concentration of argon in the rock. Researchers can then use the known rate of decay to calculate the rock's age.

Fortunately, many early human sites, like those at Olduvai Gorge in Tanzania and near Hadar in Ethiopia, lie in areas of volcanic activity, where potassium–argon dating is useful. Some are buried between layers of volcanic ash. At Olduvai, Louis and Mary Leakey used the potassium–argon method, developed in the late 1950s, to date human fossils to more than 2.5 million years (see Chapter 29). Humanlike footprints in volcanic ash at Laetoli, also in Tanzania, date to about 3.5 million years. Potassium–argon dating has extended the timescale of human evolution to dates that are unimaginably earlier than the few hundred thousand years of previous estimates.

People are constantly experimenting with new dating methods, but none rivals the radiocarbon and potassium–argon methods, which span the entire human past. The accuracy improves every year, so soon we will routinely date individual generations.

We have come a long way since the 1950s. When, for example, did people settle the offshore islands of the South Pacific? Over 1,500 radiocarbon dates provide a fascinating answer. The settlement of all the islands in the central and eastern Pacific, including Hawai'i and Rapa Nui (Easter Island), took place within a mere century after AD 1000. These were long voyages that unfolded over a remarkably short time. Now we must find out why people made them.

Above all, the new dating methods have allowed archaeologists to think of a truly world prehistory – of a human past that linked continents long before the European Age of Discovery in the fifteenth century. Now we have a sense of human history, where events like the development of farming and urban civilisation unfolded in a world that was as diverse as it is today.

CHAPTER 28

Ecology and World Prehistory

The skipper of the English trawler *Colinda* cursed when his nets brought up a lump of peat from the North Sea's Leman and Ower Banks in 1931. But as his crew bent down to throw the dark mass overboard, the peat split open. A brown, barbed object fell out onto the deck, some peat still clinging to it.

The skipper was intrigued and – fortunately for science – he brought the find back to port. Eventually it reached Norwich Museum, where experts identified it as a classic bone harpoon of a type made by Stone Age hunters in Scandinavia. It was exhibited at a meeting of the Prehistoric Society of East Anglia in 1932. Among those in the audience was a young archaeologist from Cambridge named John Grahame Douglas Clark (1907–95).

As a teenager at Marlborough College, Clark had been nick-named 'Stones and Bones' for his fascination with stone tools and animal bones. His first exposure to archaeology was in the narrow world of flint tool collecting. Most archaeology was still in the hands of amateurs, who haunted quarries and river gravel exposures looking for stone tools and pottery. These were people with limited interests, but Clark learned a great deal by associating with them.

The world of archaeology was still focused on local sites. Only a few scholars like Gordon Childe had a broader vision. Childe thought of the European past as a form of history, in which artefacts, rather than people, were the main players. Clark found this far more interesting than merely describing stone tools.

In the 1920s, Cambridge University did not offer a three-year degree course in archaeology alone. And so when Clark went there in 1926, he spent his first two years studying history – an invaluable experience, for it exposed him to some remarkable scholars, among them world historian George Trevelyan. Economic historian Michael Postan also introduced Clark to the latest research on medieval economies, which would play an important part in his thinking in later years.

When the time came for Clark to embark on the two-year archaeology honours curriculum, he had knowledge not only of prehistory, but also of biological and social anthropology. Logically, he looked at the past by calling on a range of academic disciplines. This was an unusual approach.

At the time, Cambridge archaeology was concerned almost entirely with Europe. But Clark did sit in on lectures by Leonard Woolley about the Ur burials (see Chapter 20), by Gertrude Caton-Thompson on her findings at early farming villages in Egypt's Faiyum (see Chapter 22), and by Gordon Childe about Bronze Age Europe. At the time many archaeologists assumed that prehistoric cultures developed in the same way everywhere, and so what was found in Europe would be repeated elsewhere. In 1928, Clark heard another British archaeologist, Dorothy Garrod, boldly inform the Prehistoric Society of East Anglia that this was not so. Their cherished European cultures were quite different from those of the Middle East. This was not a popular idea at a time when Stone Age archaeology centred on Europe. Clark absorbed all of this eagerly. He also spent long hours in Louis Leakey's laboratory, examining stone tools from Africa (see Chapter 29). The lectures and laboratory experience exposed him to archaeology far from home – to what was slowly becoming a global subject. Clark's Cambridge mentors encouraged him to study the Stone Age cultures of Britain from the end of the Ice Age to the arrival of farming. These were termed 'Mesolithic' (Greek: *mesos*, middle, and *lithos*, stone), a 'Middle Stone Age' that was thought of as a transitional period before agriculture. Clark found himself looking at thousands of small flint arrowheads and razor-sharp stone barbs in museums and private collections. His dissertation was, inevitably, a dull study of tiny stone tools, most of them collected casually from the surface and not from occupation levels. However, his book *The Mesolithic Age in Britain* appeared in 1932 and established him as an authority on this obscure subject.

As part of his research, Clark travelled extensively in Scandinavia, realising that he needed to know what had happened on the other side of the North Sea. There, the record of Mesolithic cultures was much richer, thanks to sites preserved in waterlogged marshes. They yielded perishable finds, such as antler and bone spear points. There were even the remains of fish traps and nets from camps covered by shallow water.

Clark also walked along beaches situated above the modern sea level, left by an earlier version of the Baltic Sea that had been far more extensive than it is today. This was a wake-up call, for it made him realise the magnitude of the changes that had affected Northern Europe immediately after the Ice Age. To understand human societies of the time, you often had to relate them to dramatic environmental change.

The dissertation years were busy ones for Clark, who became increasingly impatient with amateur collectors obsessed with artefact trivia. Grahame Clark did not hesitate to criticise the status quo. He and Stuart Piggott, another future great who was working at Avebury, were among a group of young rebels who engaged in animated discussions in college rooms. They became increasingly influential voices, despite their youth. In a closing appendix to *The Mesolithic Age in Britain*, Clark pointed out the huge potential for environmental archaeology in the Fens, the marshy terrain close to Cambridge. This research would have to include botanists, geologists and others, not just archaeologists. The finding of the Leman and Ower Banks harpoon was one of the events that sent Clark's research in a new and exciting direction.

The North Sea discovery inspired Clark and others to look for stratified Mesolithic sites in the peat levels of the East Anglian fenlands. While working on his doctorate, Clark had become friends with botanists Harry and Margaret Godwin. The Godwins were students of Arthur Tansley, the founding figure of British ecology. Tansley recommended that they learn palynology, the science of pollen analysis. This method uses minute pollen grains in peat bogs to study major changes in vegetation since the Ice Age. It had been pioneered by Swedish botanist Lennart von Post during the First World War. The Godwins studied the peat attached to the Leman and Ower Banks harpoon and showed that it was of the same period as identical weapons found in Denmark. They were ideal partners in Clark's new projects.

The Godwins, Clark and others formed a multidisciplinary research group, the Fenland Research Committee, in 1932. Clark was its most active member, starting work at a site buried under peat at Plantation Farm, 11 kilometres east-northeast of Ely. He found flints on a sandy ridge, then dug down to uncover a scattering of stone tools on what had once been a sandy island in a swamp. The excavation revealed a sequence of two peats, separated by fine sand formed by a higher sea level. The site extended from the Stone Age to the Bronze Age.

In 1934, Clark and the Godwins excavated Peacock's Farm, another location close by. They sank a trench into peat and this time struck archaeological gold. A handful of Mesolithic flints lay below a layer with Stone Age pot fragments. Above this Neolithic layer was Early Bronze Age pottery. They had unearthed a rare stratified sequence that covered much of prehistoric times. With pollen samples and molluscs, the small group of researchers documented major environmental changes over time. This was the first effort at multidisciplinary, environmental archaeology in Britain.

In 1932, Clark became a fellow of Peterhouse College at Cambridge University, and soon afterwards an assistant lecturer in archaeology. He would remain at Cambridge for the rest of his life. From 1932 to 1935, his fellowship freed him from teaching. He used this time to travel extensively in Northern Europe, mostly by bicycle. There he learned to appreciate the great range of perishable artefacts made from wooden and other organic materials. He developed a major interest in waterlogged sites, believing that it was only a matter of time before one came to light in Britain.

Clark's northern travels, during which he explored folk cultures, ethnography, archaeology and environmental change, resulted in his second book, *The Mesolithic Settlement of Northern Europe*, published in 1936. In this brilliant volume, he pointed out that ancient societies had interacted with their environments. They could be thought of as part of much larger ecological systems, the elements of which interacted with one another. This was a radical idea at the time. The dominant themes of this superb book were ecological and environmental.

If ever an archaeologist was single-minded, it was Grahame Clark. He devoted himself totally to environmental archaeology, the study of people and their changing environments. He was also convinced that archaeology had a major role to play in society. Clark argued that the most important function of archaeology is to explain how ancient peoples lived.

During the war years, Clark (who could not serve for medical reasons) wrote a series of articles on economic archaeology, the study of how people made their living in the past. In *Prehistoric Europe: The Economic Basis*, published in 1952, he brought these articles together into a series of essays on everything from ancient beekeeping to whale hunting.

He combined archaeological evidence with traditional folk culture that still survived in Scandinavia, collected during his trips to Northern Europe. His economic and ecological perspectives became highly influential, even in the United States, where he himself was virtually unknown. Just as this important book was

published, Clark was elected Disney Professor of Prehistoric
Archaeology at Cambridge, at the time the leading professorship in
prehistoric archaeology in the world.

Clark had never abandoned his hope that a waterlogged
Mesolithic site would come to light. In 1948, an amateur archaeologist reported a likely site at Star Carr, near the North Sea in northeastern Yorkshire. Clark realised at once that the stone axes found
on the surface resembled those from Scandinavia, and there was a
strong likelihood that they came from waterlogged peat deposits.
He excavated Star Carr on a shoestring budget over three seasons
between 1949 and 1951. The site, on the shores of a long dried-up
glacial lake, lay on a birch platform, among reeds. A radiocarbon
date of about 7500 BC provided a basic chronology.

In his excavation report, Clark painted a picture of a tiny
encampment set in a landscape of birch forest, where the inhabitants hunted red and roe deer. He described Star Carr not just from
tools and animal bones, but in the context of its surrounding environment, a first for Britain. Fifty years later, teams of researchers
with the latest high-technology methods re-excavated Star Carr
and found that it was actually a larger settlement than Clark had
reported. AMS radiocarbon tests now date the site to between 9000
and 8500 BC.

As Disney Professor, Clark followed Dorothy Garrod, who had
taught the first world prehistory course at Cambridge. He created
a department that treated prehistory as a global subject, and he
travelled widely – as far afield as Australia. Clark and his colleagues
trained a generation of young archaeologists, whom he encouraged
to work overseas, often in little-known archaeological areas. (I was
one of them and went to Africa.)

His travels and the radiocarbon revolution resulted in one of his
best-known works, *World Prehistory*. The book was unique in 1961.
Other authors – such as Gordon Childe – had written summaries
of ancient Europe, of Maya civilisation and North America's prehistoric past. But no one before had attempted a work that explored
early human history in every corner of the world. *World Prehistory*
ran to three editions and was widely read.

Grahame Clark was a shy, retiring figure, who was nevertheless capable of harsh criticism of his fellow archaeologists. But his authoritative writings and his insistence on the importance of economic archaeology endured long after his death. Not only did he make this a central part of twentieth-century archaeology, but he also helped turn archaeology into the global discipline that it is today. Clark, like others who emerged later, rebelled against an obsessive concern with artefacts and chronological sequences. His writings influenced a generation, while his students worked – and some still do work – all over the world.

CHAPTER 29

'Dear Boy!'

Olduvai Gorge, Tanzania, East Africa, 17 July 1959. Louis Leakey was in bed in camp with a slight fever when his wife Mary left to re-examine a location where they had found stone tools eight years earlier. At the site, Mary brushed away fine soil from two large teeth that were set in what appeared to be a human jaw. Her heart stopped. Leaping into her Land Rover, she raced back to camp. 'I've got him!' she cried. Fever forgotten in all the excitement, Louis and Mary examined the teeth together.

But what form of hominin (a species related to, or an ancestor of, humans) lay in the soil? When all the pieces were recovered, Mary assembled the skull of a robust-looking ape-human. They named the find *Zinjanthropus boisei*, 'Southern ape-human of Boise', after a Mr Boise who had sponsored the research. *Zinjanthropus boisei* was a strongly built hominin, the first discovered outside South Africa. The Leakeys called him 'Dear Boy'.

The modern search for human origins had begun many years earlier. In 1924, South African anatomist Raymond Dart (1893–1988) identified a tiny hominin skull found in a lime quarry at

Taung in South Africa's Cape Province. The teeth looked quite modern, the face jutted forward and the head was somewhat rounded – a mix of modern and ancient features. Dart called it *Australopithecus africanus*, 'Southern ape from Africa'. He proclaimed that *Australopithecus* was the link between living apes and humans. But Dart was prone to jumping to conclusions.

As we saw in Chapter 8, the scientists of the day had rejected Dutchman Eugène Dubois's find of *Pithecanthropus erectus* from Java in 1889 as a potential missing link. Mesmerised by the Neanderthals, they were also obsessed by the forged Piltdown skull, with its large brain and small teeth, found in England in 1912. Dart was laughed to scorn. He joined Dubois on the list of discredited fossil hunters.

Even by the mid-twentieth century, we still did not know much about early human evolution. More Neanderthals had come to light in Europe, and now in the Middle East. The *Homo erectus* fossils at Zhoukoudian in China had proved Dubois correct (see Chapter 8). The *Australopithecus* finds from South Africa were now accepted as possible human ancestors. Otherwise, the African slate was virtually blank. Then Louis and Mary Leakey came along and changed everything.

Born to Church of England missionaries in Kenya, Louis Seymour Bazett Leakey (1903–72) became one of the most remarkable archaeologists of the twentieth century. Brash, driven and opinionated, Leakey studied archaeology at Cambridge University, where he caused controversy by wearing shorts on a tennis court!

Leakey had always wanted to dig in Africa, where he was convinced that human origins lay. After graduating in 1926, he organised a shoestring expedition to Kenya and excavated Gamble's Cave in the Great Rift Valley. He found stratified layers of human occupation dating back at least 20,000 years. The earliest visitors were probably contemporaries of Neanderthal cultures in Europe. The later levels yielded finely made spear points, knives and other tools. These much more sophisticated people were the African equivalents of the Upper Palaeolithic folk found in French caves (see Chapter 10). The stone tools showed conclusively that prehistoric African societies were very different from those of Europe. There were also hints of much earlier Africans from crude artefacts found at other sites. Louis Leakey became convinced that East Africa was where humans originated.

In 1931, Leakey accompanied German palaeontologist Hans Reck to Olduvai Gorge. Some 40 kilometres long, Olduvai is a jagged slash in the Serengeti plains of northern Tanzania, where violent earth movements exposed deep, stratified layers of ancient lake beds. Reck was looking for fossil animals. Meanwhile Leakey was convinced that there would be evidence of early human settlement in the gorge. Reck bet Leakey £10 that he would not find stone tools at Olduvai. Leakey collected on the bet on the very first day.

Leakey was a fluent Kikuyu speaker from boyhood. He was therefore a natural candidate for a year-long anthropological study of the tribe, which began in 1936. That same year, he married his second wife, Mary. London-born Mary Leakey (1913–96) was the opposite of Louis. Quiet, modest and methodical, she was a superb technical artist, a meticulous excavator and an expert on stone-tool technology. She kept many of her husband's more hare-brained schemes in check and completed many of his excavations.

Neither of them let the Second World War stand in their way. In 1943, they excavated a series of sites at Olorgesailie in the Rift Valley, near Nairobi, where ancient hunters had butchered big game. These sites date to about 300,000 years ago. Olorgesailie is a fascinating place to visit. You can see dozens of large stone butchery tools lying just where their users dropped them hundreds of thousands of years ago. The Leakeys also found dense concentrations of stone tools and fragmentary animal bones, as well as places where the hunters had camped, eaten and slept. No more than a few metres across, these sites are priceless archives of ancient human behaviour. With careful excavation, you can find everything from tiny tools to mouse bones or even snake fangs.

After the war, and operating on a virtually non-existent budget, the pair worked at Olduvai, excavating thousands of stone tools from stratified lake beds. In 1951, the Leakeys published a report on the long stone-tool sequence at the gorge, starting with crude chopping tools that were little more than simple flaked lava cobbles.

Once the stone-tool sequence provided a framework, the couple switched their focus from stone tools to the fine clays and sands exposed in the gorge. As you look up at what were once lake beds, it's hard to imagine that animals large and small drank from their shallow waters. This time, the Leakeys searched for lakeside camps where people had butchered their prey with crude stone choppers and sharp-edged flakes of stone. Except for a few fragmentary teeth, there were no traces of hominin fossils. Then, in July 1959, Mary Leakey found *Zinjanthropus boisei*, or 'Dear Boy'.

'Dear Boy' made the Leakeys international celebrities. The National Geographic Society funded the complete excavation of the *Zinjanthropus* site. Mary excavated the scatter of bone fragments and stone debris with meticulous care. She recorded every artefact and bone where it lay before lifting it. For the first time, archaeologists could reconstruct very early human life.

I once visited Mary's excavation. She crouched under an umbrella, her Dalmatian dogs lying nearby. With brush and dental pick, she gently eased lake sand away from a small antelope bone. Her patience was remarkable. Mary's slow-moving excavation methods are now common practice for excavating sites this old.

How old was *Zinjanthropus boisei*? Louis had dated the fossil by guesswork to about 600,000 years. When two geophysicists from the University of California, Berkeley used the new potassium–argon method to date it to 1.75 million years (see Chapter 27), the Leakeys and the international scientific community were stunned. From one day to the next, human origins had nearly trebled in age.

The search for human ancestors now widened. Large-scale excavations at other Olduvai locations yielded more hominins. Skull fragments and an almost complete foot from a slightly earlier site belonged to a slender, more slightly built hominin, quite different from *Zinjanthropus*. South African biological anthropologist Phillip Tobias studied the remains and identified *Homo habilis*, 'Handy person'. With characteristic boldness, Louis Leakey called *habilis* the earliest toolmaker of all, dated to 2 million years before the present day.

Mary Leakey undertook the massive task of writing up the early sites. Her report was a detailed study of a simple technology of stone choppers and flakes. She named this technology 'Oldowan' after the gorge. Meanwhile, Louis travelled widely, lecturing and forever proposing new theories of human origins. He also encouraged young researchers to investigate the behaviour of living primates such as chimpanzees, orangutans and gorillas. Such studies might provide insights into early human behaviour. Louis was an important mentor for Britain's Jane Goodall, who became a world authority on chimpanzees, and American Dian Fossey, who specialised in gorillas.

Louis died in 1972. In 1977, Mary opened excavations at another promising location at Laetoli in Tanzania. She amazed her colleagues by uncovering in hardened volcanic ash two trails of hominin footprints that were made 3.59 million years ago. The Laetoli footprints came from the bed of a seasonal river. Thin layers of fine volcanic ash had formed a pathway for animals travelling to nearby waterholes. The hardened volcanic ash also preserved the footprints of elephants, rhinoceroses, giraffes, a sabre-toothed tiger and many antelope species.

The two trails of hominin footprints, about 24 centimetres apart, were probably made at different times. The distinctive heel and toe prints were left by two individuals under 1.5 metres tall. Mary described their gait as rolling and slow-moving. Their hips swivelled as they walked, unlike the free-striding gait of modern people. Most likely, the footprints were made by individuals like 'Lucy', the diminutive *Australopithecus afarensis* found in Ethiopia by Don Johanson in 1973, one of many such finds. The Laetoli hominins walked upright, bipedally (on two feet). Since coming down from the trees was a distinctive human characteristic, bipedalism was key to successful hunting and foraging in open country.

For years, those scientists who studied human origins, working with few fossils, tended to think of early human evolution as linear (proceeding in a straight line). But by the 1970s, it was clear that there was a far greater diversity of hominins in East Africa and perhaps elsewhere, and that most of them were still unknown. This diversity became clear as more researchers began work in East Africa, among them Don Johanson and the Leakeys' son, Richard.

Palaeoanthropology (the study of human fossils) itself now relied on field teams of different specialists as interested in the local environment and human behaviour as they were in fossils. The Leakeys tended to work alone. They did their own geology, and only little by little began to call on experts in other fields, such as botany, dating and zoology. But this limited use of specialist colleagues changed the research. New chronologies based on molecular biology showed that chimpanzees, our closest living relatives, and humans split from one another some 7–8 million years ago.

The search for human origins now included fossils far earlier than *Homo habilis* and *Zinjanthropus boisei*. Richard Leakey investigated fossil-bearing beds on the east side of remote Lake Turkana in northern Kenya. His team found a range of well-preserved *Australopithecus* fossils and the remains of a human ancestor that displayed a mixture of both primitive and more advanced features. Now that there are more fossils to study, *Homo habilis* is today called early *Homo*, our earliest direct ancestor.

During the 1990s, another American palaeoanthropologist, Tim White, found at least seventeen small hominins at Aramis in the arid Awash region of Ethiopia. They come from *Ardipithecus ramidus*, a hominin who probably lived between 4.5 million and 4.3 million years ago. 'Ardi' seems closer to chimpanzees than to humans, and may have lived in more wooded environments than did his successors. This little-known creature, which stood on two feet, was close to the first hominins to diverge from African apes. Its bones have been found in layers at Aramis underlying later Australopithecines. By the standards of *Ardipithecus*, Don Johanson's 'Lucy', at 3 million years old, is much younger.

Today, we know that a great array of hominins flourished in eastern Africa between 7 million and 2 million years ago. Many of them are still unknown, but it appears that Australopithecines were among the most common. And among them were hominins with more rounded heads, as well as other distinctive features in the hips and limbs that justify them being called early *Homo*, our earliest ancestors. Quite when they appeared remains a mystery, but they apparently made stone tools and may have evolved around 3 million years ago.

Like other archaeologists of the earlier twentieth century, the Leakeys spent much of their careers working alone and with minimal funds. Their discoveries helped put the study of human origins on a modern footing. Today, with many more fossils to work with, we think of human evolution as a tree with numerous branches, most of which led to dead ends. A few, however, led to early *Homo*, *Homo erectus* and ultimately to modern humans.

CHAPTER 30

The First Farmers

During the 1930s, Gordon Childe wrote of an Agricultural Revolution that supposedly began during Middle Eastern droughts (see Chapter 23). He estimated that the changeover from hunting and gathering to farming and animal herding began around 4000 BC, or perhaps somewhat earlier. Childe was guessing, and had very little information to support his ideas. What had happened to change human life fundamentally in this region? Three-quarters of a century later, numerous excavations, radiocarbon dating and new climatic data are providing some clues.

Childe wrote of a revolution that changed history. Agriculture did indeed alter the course of human life; but it was a changeover, not an invention, as Childe well understood. Everyone who collected edible grasses knew that they germinated, grew and then shed their seed. But why go to the effort if there were wild grasses for the taking? People began planting wild cereal grasses as a survival strategy, when natural harvests dwindled. The changeover from hunting and gathering plant foods to farming was one of the major turning points in human history. Where and when did it first occur, and why?

These questions have fascinated archaeologists for more than a century. But, unfortunately, early farming sites are few and far between. It is hard for archaeologists to distinguish between wild and domesticated (cultivated) grains, and the bones of wild goats and sheep are almost identical to those of tamed animals. This is archaeology that requires good preservation conditions, slow-moving excavation, and the use of very fine sieves to recover tiny seeds. It also needs teamwork, as one man in particular understood.

Robert John Braidwood (1907–2003) was the son of a pharmacist. He enrolled at the University of Michigan to study architecture, and eventually graduated with degrees in architecture, anthropology and history. Braidwood then worked for the Oriental Institute of the University of Chicago, where he became an expert on chronology, building timescales from deep, stratified trenches. He married his wife Linda in 1937, and they worked together for sixty-six years in one of the most enduring partnerships in archaeology. They died in their nineties within just a few hours of one another.

Braidwood asked a fundamental question: where had people found wild grasses that could be cultivated? He talked to biologists and botanists, who directed him to mountain country in the northern Middle East. Braidwood accordingly headed for northern Iraq. His research took him to Jarmo, a village mound in the foothills of Iraq's Zagros Mountains in the late 1940s and early 1950s.

This was a project with a difference. For generations, archaeologists had asked specialists to identify the occasional animal bone sample or carbonised seed found in their digs. But Braidwood realised that he needed more than part-time specialists. He insisted on close partnerships with expert scholars, and on carefully planned research work. He took along a geologist to study the interactions between the inhabitants and their environment. Other team members included a zoologist, a botanist, a pottery specialist and a radiocarbon-dating expert.

Jarmo had twelve occupation levels. It consisted of some twenty-five houses with mud-brick walls and clay roofs, laid out on stone foundations. Perhaps 150 people had lived at Jarmo. Braidwood's teamwork paid off, as his specialists pieced things together. The inhabitants had cultivated two forms of wheat, also lentils, and had herded goats and sheep. Being an expert in chronology, Braidwood was naturally fascinated by radiocarbon dating. To his surprise, the earliest Jarmo dates came in at about 7000 BC, far earlier than the generally assumed date for early farming of 4000 BC.

Jarmo was remarkably old, and yet farming was already well established there. Clearly there was a significant time gap between these farmers and the earlier hunting societies. Braidwood assumed that the very earliest farmers had lived in simpler villages than Jarmo, and so he set out to find them.

He moved to Çayönü mound in southeastern Turkey. To his astonishment, he unearthed another well-planned village, now known to date to between 9400 and 7200 BC. Braidwood realised that the changeover to farming was a much more complex process than people had thought. But he was unprepared for the extraordinary discoveries made around the same time at Jericho.

Kathleen Kenyon (1906–78) was a British archaeologist famous for her love of excavating, fox terriers and gin. She had studied history at Oxford, and then in 1929 had accompanied Gertrude Caton-Thompson to Great Zimbabwe, where she developed a passion for excavation (see Chapter 22). Kenyon's training was impeccable. Her remarkable digging skills came from four seasons under Mortimer and Tessa Wheeler at Roman Verulamium from 1930 to 1934 (see Chapter 25).

Kenyon built such a formidable reputation as an excavator that she was invited to dig in Palestine, at Samaria, the capital of ancient Israel. The rest of her career was spent in the Middle East. While Braidwood was digging Jarmo, Kenyon was funded to excavate the ancient city mound at Jericho, now in Jordan. Her expertise in deciphering complex, stratified layers filled with pot fragments was unique. No better person could have been chosen for the work.

Jericho was, of course, a biblical location, and also a major Bronze Age walled city. Kenyon was concerned with the entire history of the place. She dug down to the base of what is called Tell es-Sultan, close to the modern city, and collected numerous radiocarbon samples from the early levels. At the base, by a spring, lay a tiny settlement that had been occupied before 9500 BC. Jericho had soon become a compact settlement of small, circular dwellings built of clay and sun-dried brick. After a century, there were about seventy houses. Between about 8350 and 7300 BC, it became a small town, perhaps with several hundred inhabitants, surrounded by a massive stone wall over 3.6 metres high. A stone tower with an internal staircase stood inside the wall. It is not known if the tower and wall were a defence against the River Jordan's floods or against people.

The inhabitants of the town were certainly farmers, as were their successors, who lived in rectangular houses built on stone foundations. By 6900 BC, the inhabitants were burying the heads and the (sometimes headless) skeletons of their ancestors under the floors of their houses. Some skulls had the facial features reconstructed with plaster to create crude 'portraits', with seashells used as eyes. Under a house floor, Kenyon found one pit containing ten tightly packed plastered skulls.

Kenyon's Jericho excavations were a classic example of what is commonly known as vertical excavation. Deep, usually narrow trenches provide details of who lived in, say, a city and when. They show changes in ancient societies through time. In fact, vertical excavation was Kenyon's only option, as Jericho's city deposits were very deep: to expose more area of the earliest levels would have been prohibitively expensive. But her vertical excavation provided the basic history of the city through many centuries.

Kenyon's Jericho excavations confirmed what Braidwood suspected: the beginnings of farming had been a long process that had taken hold in many places. Today, we know of a scattering of small villages running from southeastern Turkey into Syria and farther south that were farming at least 11,000 years ago. Few of them have been extensively excavated, except for Abu Hureyra, a small village on the edge of woodland and more open country in Syria's Euphrates Valley. British archaeologist Andrew Moore excavated the settlement's mound in 1972–73, knowing that a hydroelectric dam would shortly flood it. Abu Hureyra provided a remarkable portrait of an early farming village of 10,000 BC, reconstructed by expert digging and team research.

The climate of the whole region was somewhat warmer and damper than it is today. A few families dwelt in small houses that were partially dug into the ground and roofed with reeds. The inhabitants lived off a wide variety of wild animals and edible grasses and nuts. They hunted the gazelle (desert antelope) herds that migrated from the south each spring: more than 80 per cent of the animal bones from the tiny settlement came from these small animals, the meat dried for later consumption. The villagers also consumed half a dozen staple wild plants and used more than 200 other species as mind-altering drugs, dye pigments and medicines. The Abu Hureyra people carefully managed and tended their environment, and some 300–400 people dwelt in this successful village. Then, abruptly, they abandoned the settlement in the face of persistent drought.

We know this from profound changes in the different edible grasses and nuts in the occupation layers. One of Moore's experts, botanist Gordon Hillman, collected plant remains from the occupation levels. He floated seed-rich soil samples through water and fine screens, and this provided him with large plant collections. He showed that as conditions became drier after 10,000 BC, the nut-bearing forests and wild grasslands retreated ever farther from Abu Hureyra. As the drought intensified, so plant foods became scarcer and scarcer.

One can imagine the growing catastrophe. Day after day, the sun shone from a cloudless, pale-blue sky. The horizon never darkened with rain. Clouds of dust swirled across the usually green plains by the Euphrates River. The open, now brown grasslands receded with every month of the drought. And each year, the villagers had to walk longer distances to the forests to gather nuts and edible grasses. The harvests were far poorer than before, so that by winter the villagers were hungry. By spring, they were starving. Hillman and Moore believe that a combination of drought and deforestation (caused by a growing demand for firewood – a result of the cooling temperatures and rising number of people) eventually forced the inhabitants to leave.

In about 9000 BC, an entirely different, larger settlement arose on the original village mound. At first, the inhabitants continued to hunt gazelle. Then, within the space of a couple of generations, the people switched to herding goats and sheep. Over the next ten centuries, goats and sheep became ever more important as gazelle hunting declined. The village came to cover 12 hectares. Visitors would have found themselves wandering through a community of rectangular, single-storey mud-brick houses joined by narrow lanes and courtyards.

Experts estimate that it must have taken between 1,000 and 2,000 years to domesticate and control wild grasses for human harvest. The need to safeguard the supply of food in the face of prolonged drought may well have been the trigger that led people to cultivate crops. At first, the inhabitants of Abu Hureyra (and elsewhere) probably planted wild grasses to increase seed harvests – first rye, then wheat and barley. After a while, they became full-time farmers, tied to their fields and the grazing lands of their animals. Their agriculture depended entirely on rainfall, and the first planting required careful timing lest the crops wither before it rained. This was high-risk farming in an environment with unpredictable rainfall.

Whether it was the thousand-year drought in the eastern Mediterranean region from about 10,000 BC that triggered agriculture is still open to debate. But it probably was one of the major factors that turned hunters and foragers into farmers.

Abu Hureyra is just one of the many early farming villages dating to around 10,000 BC that are now known across a wide area of the Middle East. All of them share the general characteristics of the changeover seen at the Syrian site. The origins of farming were much more drawn out – and far earlier – than anyone thought even a generation ago. And the shift was not a unique development confined to the Middle East. Farming began at much the same time on the other side of the world, in China; and a little later in the Americas.

From this changeover came an explosion in population growth, far more complex human societies and, within a few thousand years, the world's earliest civilisations in Egypt and Mesopotamia.

CHAPTER 31

Defending the Emperor

Chinese emperor Qin Shihuangdi wanted to be remembered for all eternity. In 221 BC, this brutal, violent ruler turned China from a patchwork of states into a single kingdom, only to die eleven years later at the age of just thirty-nine. There was an ancient Chinese belief that mercury brought everlasting life, and so Shihuangdi had swallowed countless mercury pills. Instead of making him immortal, they probably killed him.

The emperor died at the coast, but he was to be buried some way inland. As his coffin travelled slowly by carriage, accompanied by trusted royal officials, rotting fish was used to mask the smell of the decomposing body.

Shihuangdi had started building his burial mound about 40 kilometres east of Xian, in northwestern China, long before he became emperor. But work intensified during his reign. Some 700,000 men dug and shaped his burial place at the foot of the prominent Mount Li. Then a small army of craftspeople created an entire underground kingdom.

The workers dug down until they came to a series of freshwater springs. Then they filled the sepulchre with replicas of palaces and other buildings in special caverns. A bronze outer coffin was fashioned for the emperor. The ceilings mimicked the night sky, with pearls as stars. According to a guide to Chinese civilisation written in 94 BC, mercury was used to model the ocean and major rivers, which even appeared to flow. Once again, mercury – the substance that probably killed Shihuangdi – was being used as a symbol of immortality. This makes the burial mound a dangerous place: soil samples taken around the tomb display high levels of contamination.

Written sources tell us that craftsmen set up mechanical crossbows primed to shoot any intruders. Immediately after Shihuangdi's funeral, those who had worked on the tomb were sealed inside, to prevent them from passing on any information.

Shihuangdi's burial mound rises 43 metres above the surrounding countryside. The builders planted trees and bushes so that it blended into the landscape. The emperor's burial place was part of a huge death park, surrounded by a 5 kilometre-long outer wall.

What else lay within the enclosure remained a secret until 1974, when some workers were digging a well 2.5 kilometres east of the unexcavated burial mound. There they found a full-sized terracotta (clay) soldier. Then another. And another. A team of archaeologists and conservation experts found themselves digging up an entire royal regiment. These are the famed terracotta warriors. The team excavation was so large that no one person can take overall credit for the work.

Unfortunately, I was unable to visit the excavations up close, and could only see the warriors at a distance, as a tourist. And so my description must be a general one. But I was astounded at the sight. The figures are incredibly realistic. They stood in eleven parallel corridors, each about 200 metres long. A roof of woven matting, strengthened with clay, covered the passageways. I could easily imagine a real military force. The men parade in forty ranks, mostly four abreast. Alert and disciplined, every figure stands up straight, ready for battle. The troops wear replica coats of mail originally made of stone slates joined by copper wires that opened and closed on the right side. They are without helmets, looking forward. Each man has a different face, as if they were all modelled from actual people. But they are expressionless and apparently without emotion. The figures now are all light brown in colour, with only a few traces of paint; but when the regiment was buried, they all had brightly painted uniforms – the effect must have been dazzling.

Almost 200 bowmen and crossbowmen stand in three rows in front. They wear cotton garments (modelled in terracotta) but no armour, as those using bows and crossbows shot from a distance rather than fighting in close quarters. The ranks took turns to fire volleys so that there would be a continuous stream of arrows or crossbow bolts in the air. Modern experiments show that the crossbows of the time had a range of about 200 metres.

Six chariots and three unarmoured infantry squads parade behind the archers. Four terracotta horses pull the chariots, each with a charioteer. Two or three soldiers would have accompanied each one into battle. Two of the chariots were command vehicles for officers, from where drums would be beaten or bells struck to signal an advance or a retreat. Some of the officers have flowing moustaches and wear a slight smile.

I found the scene overwhelming. These were attack soldiers, who went into battle without shields. We know from historical records that soldiers of the Qin Dynasty were ferocious. Their commanders believed that attack was the best form of defence. Their close-range fighting would have been bloody and vicious. Everyone fought with bronze swords and spears, or with halberds – combined spears and battle axes that could kill a man with a single blow.

Shihuangdi protected himself with a powerful, well-trained regiment. But they guarded him in terracotta, perhaps because such elite soldiers were too valuable to sacrifice.

There was more. A second pit contained just over 1,500 soldiers and horses, divided into four groups. In one corner, ranks of unarmoured spearmen surrounded kneeling archers. The rest of the pit held chariots, with sixty-four in one unit alone. It was all meant to send out a message of vigilance, of soldiers on guard against a surprise attack.

A third pit, dug in 1977 after five years of arduous excavation and conservation work, held the chariot of the commander and his guards. They were exceptionally tall men at over 1.9 metres, some 10 centimetres taller than the average soldier in Pit 1.

Just uncovering the fragile figures was a delicate exercise in teamwork. The local clay was heavy enough to allow the sculpting of full-size figures. Each figure had been modelled in parts and then assembled, the head made separately from the body. This allowed the artists to produce more or less standardised figures, while the heads were sculpted as individual portraits.

The conservation work has been extremely demanding. Quite apart from reassembling many of the figures, the conservators have also tried to discover what colour uniforms they wore from tiny paint fragments. The slow-moving conservation work has been completed with an eye to the tourist trade. Emperor Shihuangdi's terracotta regiment has become a major international attraction, visited by tens of thousands of people every year. This is archaeology carried out on the public stage, where archaeologists face problems such as overcrowding and air pollution affecting the figures.

The discoveries keep on coming. A pit found in 1998, southwest of the burial mound, held thousands of armour fragments and helmets, and was perhaps the site of an armoury. But there is far more appearing from the soil.

A year later, another pit, just to the south, yielded eleven clay figures and a bronze cauldron. Judging by the gestures of the exquisite figures, these were acrobats, perhaps intended to entertain the emperor in the afterlife. Other pits contained fifteen musicians who had once held instruments (long decayed), perhaps to divert the emperor as he walked in his garden.

Forty-six bronze birds from yet another pit stood on a platform by a water channel. One even had a (bronze) worm in its beak. It is chance finds like these that instantly transport you back into the past. The bird with its worm reminds you that the ancients also appreciated beauty, quiet ponds and wildlife.

Shihuangdi's park is awe-inspiring in its size and complexity. For instance, the emperor's stables lay outside the central area – a place where real horses were buried with kneeling terracotta grooms. Why they had to be living horses, we do not know. Perhaps they were some of the emperor's favourites, in a land where horses had high prestige. There are unconfirmed reports of a pit full of terracotta models of the emperor's women. A nearby series of mass graves reminds us of the enormous human cost of the emperor's quest for a happy immortality.

As recently as 2012, a huge palace complex 90 metres long and 250 metres wide came to light, complete with central courtyard and a main building overlooking it. There will be archaeologists working on Shihuangdi's memorials for generations.

And there remains the burial mound. Chinese archaeologists have paused, for they doubt that they yet have the technical expertise – or the funds – to excavate and conserve the burial chamber. And of course, there is the danger posed by mercury contamination.

So far, they have relied on magnetometers – devices that measure the different levels of magnetism deep inside the mound. Such instruments react to iron, brick, burned soil, and even decayed wood and other organic materials. The magnetometers have revealed that an underground palace lies at the centre of the mound, surrounded by a wall. Experts also know that there is an abundance of metal within the burial chamber, and an excellent drainage system. Unusually high levels of mercury are present, perhaps confirming the description of the interior from 94 BC (see above).

Intense controversy surrounds the potential excavation of Shihuangdi's tomb. Archaeologists argue that the methods they currently have at their disposal are not adequate (as the damage caused to some of the terracotta soldiers during excavation shows). Nevertheless, some people push for immediate excavation, claiming that it will deter looters; others point to the huge tourist potential and the economic benefits offered by the royal tomb.

All of this raises an important question for archaeologists everywhere. Should the needs of the tourist industry take priority over pure archaeology? The hordes of visitors who swarm over sites such as the Pyramids of Giza in Egypt or Angkor Wat in Cambodia raise real fears about wear and tear at important sites. Chinese archaeologists know that the excavation of Shihuangdi's burial mound will be the most important excavation of the century, if not of all time. Quite rightly they want to wait until they have the necessary tools and knowledge to conduct what will be a unique research project.

As the debate rumbles on, the Chinese are gaining experience by digging other royal burials. In 74 BC, the Han clan overthrew Emperor Liu He (92–59 BC) after a mere twenty-seven days in power. He was dethroned because he was a playboy with an 'inclination to pleasures' and loose morals. He also had no talent as a leader. Instead, high officials made him the Marquis of Haihun, a small kingdom in the north of Jiangxi, near Nanchang. Despite his disgrace, Liu was honoured with a lavish walled cemetery containing ten tombs, including one for his wife.

A research team under archaeologist Xin Lixiang has been excavating the cemetery since 2011. Liu's burial included gold ingots and plates, amassing 78 kilograms of gold alone. Ten tonnes of bronze coins and ten cauldrons accompanied the marquis. There were lamps in the form of wild geese, and chariots with real horses that had been sacrificed.

Liu's coffin was raised in 2015 when the entire inner section of the tomb was removed using hydraulic lifts and taken to a nearby research centre for detailed analysis. A seal inside the coffin bears his name, and his identity has been confirmed from writing on some of the accompanying bronze items. The tomb is unique, having been totally undisturbed. The marquis's body has been tested for DNA to establish his relationship to other Han nobles. As was the custom, jade ornaments covered his eyes, nose, ears and mouth. Liu's burial is proof of the astonishing wealth of Han China 2,000 years ago.

Shihuangdi's tomb is an example of the huge challenges that Chinese archaeologists of the future will face, especially with rich burials. Their task will be made somewhat easier by increasingly sophisticated scientific methods, such as remote sensing, DNA and studies of the isotopic (radioactive) content of human bones that can reveal changes in diet through life. They know that long-term team projects will be the rule, and that discovery must be balanced with conservation and with the demands of the enormous domestic tourist industry.

We can be sure that some of the best archaeology of the future will come from China. And we can be certain that spectacular discoveries await us.

CHAPTER 32

Underwater Archaeology

Archaeologist George Bass (born 1932) is an expert on the Mycenaean civilisation of mainland Greece. He is also one of the world's leading experts on underwater archaeology. Bass became an underwater archaeologist by chance, as a graduate student at the University of Pennsylvania. The university museum needed someone to direct the excavation of a shipwreck on the seabed off Cape Gelidonya in southwestern Turkey. They chose Bass. He knew nothing of diving, and so the museum sent him to a local youth club for some scuba training. It was an inspired choice.

In 1954, Kemal Aras, a Turkish sponge diver, had spotted a pile of bronze objects off the cape. Apparently, a ship's bottom had been ripped open on a rock. As she sank, the vessel spilled artefacts in an irregular line at a depth of almost 27 metres. Enter Peter Throckmorton, an American journalist and amateur archaeologist, who in 1959 was cataloguing ancient wrecks along the coast. He realised that the shipwreck was unusually old and suggested that the museum organise a scientific excavation to investigate it, the first such deep-water enterprise ever undertaken. Underwater archaeology was born.

George Bass is, above all, an archaeologist. As soon as he saw the wreck, he insisted that the same standards of excavation and recording had to be upheld under the water as on land. He pointed out that the merchant ship had been carrying a cargo of goods from one place to another. This could provide vital information on ancient trade routes. It had sunk, taking its cargo to the bottom of the sea, and until its discovery many centuries later, no human had disturbed the wreck. It thus differed from archaeological sites on land, such as a hunting camp or a city, which are constantly moved or rebuilt, and are disturbed by all kinds of later human activity. They are never 'sealed' in the same way as underwater wrecks, which often lie in deep water accessible only by divers.

The Cape Gelidonya wreck lay on a bare, rocky seabed. First, Bass and his divers photographed it. They couldn't use paper to record measurements and the position of artefacts, and so they relied on sheets of frosted plastic and graphite pencils that write underwater. The cargo itself consisted mainly of solid masses of copper, bronze and artefacts that had fused together on the bottom. All Bass could do was lift the lumps using a heavy-duty car jack. Then the excavators took them apart ashore.

The cargo proved a valuable one. Much of it consisted of copper ingots that could be traced back to Cyprus. And then there was tin, used to make bronze weapons. Metal was so precious that the crew had even packed bronze scrap in wicker baskets. Many of the artefacts from the wreck had come from Syria and Palestine. Bass reckoned that the ship had travelled to Cyprus to load copper and scrap metal on its way to the Aegean Sea. But when had it gone down? Painted pots and radiocarbon samples from the cargo gave a date of 1200 BC. The vessel had sunk during the late Bronze Age.

Bass moved on in 1967 from the relatively straightforward Cape Gelidonya wreck to a Byzantine ship near Yassiada, an island off western Turkey. The wreck was essentially a pile of amphorae (large clay storage jars). He built two underwater towers over the ship for taking photographs. The archaeologists set up a grid over the site, just as they would at an excavation on land. Divers hovering over the grid recorded the position of every artefact before carrying it to the surface. Big hoses sucked seabed mud and shell away to be examined.

This time, coins dated the shipwreck to the first half of the seventh century AD. Enough survived of the hull for the excavators to be able to study the tile-roofed galley (ship's kitchen) that sat midway between the bow (front) and the stern (back) of the ship, deep in the hull (the body of the ship). There was a tiled stove, and tableware and cooking utensils were still in place.

Some iron objects had decayed inside lumps of sand and shell that littered the site. One member of the research team, Michael Katzev, sawed through the lumps, then filled them with an artificial rubber compound. When the mould was broken, he was left with a cast of the original tools – double-bladed axes, woodworking tools, files and even a device for caulking the hull of the ship (making the joins watertight).

Underwater archaeology is more time consuming than excavation ashore. It took 3,575 dives to investigate the Yassiada ship. Its timbers were so light that divers had to clear them of sand, then pin each one to the seabed with bicycle spokes in order to measure and record it, otherwise the fragile wood would have floated away before being brought to the surface. One team member, Frederick van Doorninck, studied records of every wood fragment, even of joints and bolt holes, to draw the hull of the 21-metre vessel. He succeeded, but both bow and stern were very incomplete.

The Yassiada excavation resulted in the basic methods used to study all shipwrecks. The technology became more refined with Katzev's 1967–69 excavation of a humble Greek vessel of the fourth century BC off Kyrenia in northern Cyprus. The almost 15-metre merchant vessel had settled on its port (left) side and had later split open. Fortunately, three-quarters of the hull timbers survived.

The ship had had a hard life. It was well worn and had been repaired several times. The cargo was far from glamorous: 35 tonnes of almonds and amphorae filled with olive oil and wine, as well as millstones. Ships like this were the anonymous traders that spent their lives sailing from port to port between the Aegean Sea and Cyprus in the eastern Mediterranean. The Kyrenia ship was an important find because it documented not wealthy royal cargoes, but humble folk going about their daily business at sea.

The Kyrenia excavation was of a modest ship carrying basic goods. But there were others at sea with far more valuable cargoes, such as the heavily laden vessel that crashed onto the vicious rocks of the Uluburun cliffs in southern Turkey in 1305 BC. We do not know why it sank: perhaps a sudden storm hurled it onto the rocks. As the crew jumped overboard to perish in the waves, the cargo ship sank in 45 metres of water.

Some 3,300 years later, sponge diver Mehmet Çakir reported to his captain that he had spotted metal objects 'with ears' on the bottom, close to the Uluburun cliffs. For several years, underwater archaeologists had been giving talks in local ports, showing pictures of what ancient shipwrecks looked like. They hoped that local sponge divers might report any ships they came across. Fortunately, the skipper had been to one of the lectures and knew that the eared objects could be copper ingots. He reported the find and expert divers visited the wreck in 1982, confirming that it was a Bronze Age ship.

Archaeologists Cemal Pulak and Don Frey from Texas A&M University, a leading centre of underwater research, inspected the site in 1996. They found undisturbed rows of copper ingots and huge storage jars from Cyprus stretching more than 9 metres down a steep slope. Bass called the Uluburun ship an archaeologist's dream – not for its rich cargo, but because it was a priceless sealed time capsule of exotic goods from several lands. Tree-rings from the ship's timbers dated the wreck to about 1305 BC. Even more important, it was from a period when little-known trade routes linked Egypt with Syria, Cyprus, Turkey, Crete and the Greek mainland.

The ship had gone to the bottom at a time of intense competition for the very profitable eastern Mediterranean trade. Egypt to the south was a brilliant civilisation at the height of its power. To the north were the Hittites, who were expert traders and warriors. In the west, the palaces of Crete and the kings of Mycenae on the mainland traded olive oil, wine and other commodities throughout the Aegean islands. Hundreds of merchant ships plied the coasts and ports of the eastern Mediterranean.

The 15-metre Uluburun ship was not unusual, and its short mast and square sail would not have stood out at a crowded quay. Only a close observer would have noticed the dozens of ingots being loaded. The vessel carried a shipment so exceptional that Bass and Pulak wondered if it could have been a royal cargo.

They faced an underwater investigation of extraordinary complexity that would take years. The depth at which the wreck lay created serious problems: divers could only spend a limited time on the bottom and had to receive doses of pure oxygen on their way back up to the surface to avoid becoming ill. Between 1984 and 1992, 18,686 dives resulted in 6,000 hours of excavation, followed by more in the last two seasons.

The Uluburun excavation required exceptional teamwork – far closer than during land-based digs. Bass estimated that the laboratory analysis resulting from a month's underwater investigation was the equivalent of that generated by a year's work on land. The excavation began with teams of divers making cross-sections of the wreck and the rows of ingots. The measurements from each ingot were essential in order to reconstruct the curvature of the ship's hull. A hand-held ranging and positioning system recorded the location of large objects such as stone anchors.

The Uluburun ship held enough copper and tin to make 300 bronze helmets and corsets. More than 6,000 weapons lay in the holds, enough for an infantry regiment. Chemists and metal experts from Harvard and Oxford identified the distinctive elements in the copper to tie the ingots to northern Cyprus, a major copper source 3,500 years ago. The tin, essential for fabricating bronze, was much harder to pin down, but probably originated in central Turkey or Afghanistan. The lead came from Greece and Turkey.

Uluburun's metals were mainly from east of the wreck site. The large storage jars aboard carried pottery from Cyprus. The amphorae came from the Syrian and Palestinian coast, farther east. Some of the cargo was transported in large Minoan and Mycenaean jars from the Aegean region. Egypt provided scarabs (sacred beetle ornaments) and a stone plaque inscribed with hieroglyphs. Cylinder seals (small clay or stone cylinders bearing cuneiform inscriptions) may have come from the trading city of Ugarit in northern Syria.

Most likely, the Uluburun ship sailed westward from a Canaanite port in Syria to Cyprus, following a circular route travelled many times before: a ship would sail as far west as Sardinia before crossing the open Mediterranean to the North African coast and back to the Nile. Egypt would have supplied some of the exotic items on board, including short logs of ebony – the same precious black wood that was used for a bed, chair and stool found in Tutankhamun's tomb.

Gold objects, including a scarab inscribed with the name of Egyptian Queen Nefertiti, Pharaoh Tutankhamun's mother; amber beads from the Baltic coast; even a writing tablet – all this came from the wreck. Judging from the artefacts, the heavily constructed ship carried an international crew. It was a clumsy vessel, but it had a large sail which allowed it to lumber along in following winds. It carried twenty-four stone anchors and would have spent days at rest, waiting for favourable winds. Densely woven fibre fencing protected the deck cargo and the crew.

The Uluburun ship excavation is a classic example of the kind of carefully organised teamwork that underwater archaeology requires. The vessel carried a cargo from at least eight locations. High-technology analysis and meticulous conservation and excavation have provided a unique glimpse of an international trade route that existed more than 3,000 years ago. The same methods applied on land have provided unexpected snapshots of America's first colonists.

CHAPTER 33

Meeting the Colonists

'The past is a foreign country: they do things differently there.'
To understand the people of the past, what is needed is a time
detective. Ivor Noël Hume (1927–2017) was just such a man. He
was one of the first archaeologists to blend history and archaeology
into what is now known as historical archaeology. Apart from
being a superb excavator, he was untiring in his search for small
historical clues to throw light on his finds. And he was an entertaining writer, who made archaeology (and history) accessible
to all.

Born in England, Noël Hume first worked at London's Guildhall
Museum (now the Museum of London) from 1949. He learned his
archaeology the hard way, working on bomb-damaged London's
building sites. Radiocarbon techniques were useless for dating the
different levels in a crowded historical city rebuilt time and time
again. So instead, Noël Hume taught himself to identify seventeenth-
and eighteenth-century pottery and glass wine bottles. So expert did
he become that in 1957 historians at the living-history museum of
Colonial Williamsburg in Virginia invited him to study their glass

and pottery. For thirty years he was director of Williamsburg's archaeology programme.

The incomplete historical records tell us relatively little about the pioneer settlers in Virginia who arrived by ship from 1607. Their settlements were often temporary, and their houses were built of wood and thatch, which rapidly vanished once they were abandoned. Jamestown on Chesapeake Bay was the first settlement. It served as Virginia's capital until 1698, when a nearby plantation, soon named Williamsburg, became the centre of government for eighty-one years. The state government moved to Richmond in 1780, and Williamsburg became isolated and fell into decay. The eighteenth-century town had practically vanished by 1926, when the restoration of what is now called Colonial Williamsburg began. The work continues today, but now the architects rely heavily on archaeology as well as historical records for their work. They realise that valuable, invisible data lies below the ground.

Colonial Williamsburg was the perfect place for Noël Hume. Previous work had focused entirely on architecture, but he had a different perspective – the lives of the ordinary people who had lived there, out of the historical spotlight. Outspoken and something of a perfectionist, Noël Hume's approach to historical archaeology combined the skills of a detective and master storyteller with an encyclopaedic knowledge of china and glass. The result was archaeological magic.

One of his first excavations was Wetherburn's Tavern, where he refined his already state-of-the-art methods. The architects knew the layout of the building, but only archaeology could reveal what life had been like inside the tavern. Some 200,000 artefacts were uncovered, including forty-seven buried wine bottles filled with cherries. Coins and other finds emerged from a 12-metre well. Life in the pub came alive.

Noël Hume also excavated a cabinet shop and several houses, with equal success. One of his largest digs was the Eastern State Hospital, which housed the mentally ill and had burned down in 1885. He excavated the foundations before it was rebuilt in 1985. It is now a museum.

Wolstenholme Towne, part of the Martin's Hundred plantation along the James River, presented a different problem. (A 'hundred' is a subdivision of an American county.) Founded in 1619, this was a tiny colonial village, just over 11 kilometres from Williamsburg. The settlers had built a fort with a low watchtower and wooden palisade (fence) to protect themselves against Indians and Spanish pirates. On 22 March 1622, local Powhatan Indians attacked and set fire to the village. The survivors fled as their houses burned. No one returned to the settlement, and it was soon forgotten.

When the investigations began, only the basic facts were known from historical documents. There were just a few references to the unimportant settlement in court books and in the records of the Virginia Company of London. Only archaeology could reconstruct the buildings and lives of the inhabitants. Wolstenholme was like a shipwreck on the seabed – a snapshot of a moment in the past. After his excavations at Colonial Williamsburg, Noël Hume was a master at chasing down historical clues from tiny objects. He excelled himself at Wolstenholme.

Noël Hume and his wife Audrey spent five years digging Wolstenholme. They started in 1976 and revealed a jigsaw puzzle of graves, postholes and rubbish pits. The site was shallow, and so it was relatively easy to uncover almost all the settlement. Postholes in the subsoil traced the outline of the fort with its two gates. A square marked the base of a watchtower. A gun platform protected the southwestern corner.

Inside, the settlers had dug a well. There was a store and a dwelling. To the south stood a Virginia Company compound with a pond, sheds and a wooden longhouse, lying behind another wooden fence. In one spot, Noël Hume excavated an earth-filled pit. It looked like a cellar, but there were no signs of a dwelling above it. At first, he was baffled. Then he learnt of a description of early settler houses in New England that had been written in New Amsterdam (now New York). They were pit-houses, the roofs resting on the ground. Once the owners could afford it, they moved above ground and built a more conventional house. He had found such a dwelling.

Who had lived in the pit-house? The excavators had unearthed a short length of twisted, woven gold near the foundations – a form of decoration worn by gentlemen and military officers. In 1621, a law was passed that forbade anyone in Virginia to wear gold on their clothing except members of the governing council and 'heads of hundreds'. The head of Martin's Hundred was Martin Harwood, one of those who had passed the law. Could this have come from his clothing? Another find on the site – a cannon ball – bolstered the idea. Again, the archives provided a clue: Harwood was the only person at Martin's Hundred allowed to own a cannon.

Noël Hume also found burials, among them casualties of the attack. A pathologist who had investigated a gruesome murder in England identified the marks on one of the Martin's Hundred skulls as identical to those on the modern victim, a man killed by his wife with a garden shovel.

Archaeologist William Kelso (born 1941) learned his excavation from Noël Hume. He became well known for his work on the slave quarters at Thomas Jefferson's plantation at Monticello. In 1994, Preservation Virginia asked him to excavate at Jamestown Island, the earliest European settlement in Virginia. Kelso was to find the original James Fort, used from about 1607 to 1624.

Three Virginia Company ships landed the first English settlers in Chesapeake Bay in April 1607. The colonists built a fort on a marshy peninsula about 80 kilometres upstream. Every historian believed that the original settlers had died out from fever, hostile Indians and starvation. They had come in search of gold and had failed in their quest. The original fort was a triangular structure, which everyone assumed had been swallowed up by the river. Kelso proved them wrong.

By 2003, his excavators had uncovered the perimeter of the fort. Only one corner had been lost to the river. Since then, Kelso has excavated several dwellings within the fort, recovered thousands of artefacts, and the skeletons of some of the residents. The Indians attacked the fort in 1608. Two casualties – one an adult and the other a fifteen-year-old boy – lay in shallow graves just outside the palisade.

Kelso filled in many details of what had been a disastrous start for the settlement. Historians had always assumed that the settlers were poorly equipped. But the archaeologists have shown that this was not so. They have found fishhooks and weapons, woodwork tools and traces of glassmaking – apparently German craftsmen were brought to Jamestown to make glassware for sale back in London.

A cellar from one building had been filled with junk in 1610 on the orders of the newly appointed governor. It contained a surprising amount of Native American arrowheads and pottery. This may be an indication of peaceful contact between the local Powhatan Indians and the settlers – peaceful contact that did not last.

By 1608, Jamestown was in trouble: the settlers were starving, even after three growing seasons. But was the hunger their fault? Kelso and his colleagues believe that it was not. They learned of a 1998 tree-ring study based on local cypress trees which shows that tree growth slowed dramatically between 1606 and 1612, just when the settlers arrived. The previously unsuspected drought was the worst for 800 years. It dried up water supplies and destroyed the crops on which both Indians and colonists relied. Food shortages may have triggered war between the two sides. Certainly, relations improved when the drought eased.

William Kelso's Jamestown findings have rewritten Jamestown's history. What were once seen as lazy settlers were, in fact, hard-working folk confronted by a savage drought which almost killed the settlement. There may have been some idle gentlemen at Jamestown, but they must have been in the minority. Not that life was easy for anyone, of course. Seventy-two poor settlers lie in humble, unadorned graves west of the fort.

In 2010, Kelso struck archaeological gold when he found a series of large postholes, marking the site of the colony's first church. There were four graves at the east end of the rectangular building, the most sacred part of the church, near the altar. The bones were in poor condition, making it hard to establish what the four people had died of, though it was most likely fever or starvation.

One grave held a fine silver-decorated silk sash; another a military staff and a small silver box, too fragile to open. The investigators used an X-ray machine to reveal a tiny lead capsule and some bone fragments inside the box: it was a religious reliquary, a container for holy relics, used by Catholics, but not by Protestants. Few Catholics had lived at Jamestown, which was very much a Protestant settlement.

Douglas Owsley, a biological anthropologist at the Smithsonian Institution, examined the bones. He found that they had a high lead content, probably a consequence of the fact that people at the time ate and drank from lead-glazed or pewter vessels. (In those days, pewter was an alloy of tin and lead, which is toxic to humans.) The bones were also high in nitrogen, suggesting that the deceased had had a better diet than most settlers. Burial records and archaeology identified them. One grave was that of the Reverend Robert Hunt, the first pastor to the colony. Sir Ferdinando Wainman was a horseman, with exceptionally strong thighbones. He had supervised cannons and horses. Captain William West was a gentleman, who had died aged twenty-four, fighting Indians. He was the owner of the silvered silk sash. Finally, Captain Gabriel Archer was a Roman Catholic, which accounted for the reliquary in his grave.

Archaeological and biological research is allowing us to get to know the first English settlers in North America. Kelso and Noël Hume's detective work has led the Virginia settlers out of the shadows by combining historical records from both America and Europe with the data acquired in the trench and the laboratory. The breadth of knowledge needed for such research is much wider than is usually required on a dig. For instance, some of the buildings inside the fort used architectural styles found in eastern England. Why? Because one of the first Jamestown settlers was William Laxton, a carpenter from Lincolnshire. It is as if we are looking over the shoulders of the colonists, as archaeology, history and science tell their story. A magnificent site museum now takes visitors through the archaeology and the finds, and weaves them into a fascinating narrative.

At both Jamestown and Wolstenholme Towne, Virginia's colonial past has come vividly to life. Here, archaeologists study people as individual players in their history in unique ways. The timescale is short by archaeological standards, which allows us to use historical sources to fill in the picture.

The challenges of studying individuals from much earlier times are very different, especially if they are humbler folk. Only rarely does a combination of archaeology and modern medical science allow us to study the life of someone who lived over 3,000 years ago. But that is what happened when a Bronze Age man was discovered high in the Alps.

CHAPTER 34

The Ice Man and Others

In September 1991, German climbers Helmut and Erika Simon spotted something brown protruding from ice and meltwater at the base of a gully some 3,210 metres up in the Alps, near Hauslabjoch, on the border between Italy and Austria. They realised it was the skull, back and shoulders of a man who had his face in water.

At first, police assumed he was the victim of a climbing accident, and he became simply corpse 91/619 on the local coroner's dissection table (coroners are the officials who certify deaths). But the official soon realised that the body was very old and called in the archaeologists. An excavation was organised at the site, now buried under fresh snow. Diggers used a steam blower and a hair dryer to recover a grass cloak, leaves, tufts of grass and wood fragments. By the end of the quick excavation, the recovery team had named the victim Ötzi the Ice Man. He had put down his axe, bow and backpack on a sheltered ledge. Then he had lain down on his left side, his head resting on a boulder. His relaxed limbs suggested that the exhausted man had gone to sleep and frozen to death within a few hours. Ötzi was preserved undisturbed in cold storage, just like a side of beef.

A complex detective story now unfolded. Experts radiocarbon dated the body to between 3350 and 3150 BC, the early European Bronze Age. They calculated that he stood 1.6 metres tall, and was forty-seven years old when he died some 5,000 years ago. Ötzi was a self-sufficient man and had spent his last day on the move. He was carrying a leather backpack on a wooden frame, a flint dagger and a copper-bladed axe with a wooden handle. He also had a long bow made of yew wood and a roe deer-skin quiver with fourteen arrows. He had spare arrowheads on him, together with dry fungus and iron pyrite – equipment for lighting fires.

His clothing was well suited to the mountains. He wore a sheep-skin loincloth fastened with a leather belt. Suspenders from the belt held up a pair of goatskin leggings. His outer coat was a sturdy garment made from alternating strips of black and brown skin from several different animals. Over his coat he wore a cape of twisted grass – just like those worn in the Alps as recently as the nineteenth century. A bearskin cap fastened below his chin kept his head warm. Bearskin and deerskin shoes stuffed with grass protected his feet, the grass kept in place by string 'socks'.

Height and age calculations were routine stuff. But where had Ötzi lived? A research team used his bones, intestines and teeth to answer that question. Dental enamel is fixed when a tooth is first formed, and so the teeth the researchers examined contained traces of chemical elements from whatever foods Ötzi had eaten when he was three to five years old. Bone re-mineralises (regenerates) every ten to twenty years, and so the researchers also had information on where the Ice Man had lived as an adult.

He was born in one of the many river valleys of the southern Tyrol (the most likely candidate being the Eisack Valley, south of the mountains). Ötzi's bone chemistry showed that he had lived at a higher altitude as an adult. The scientists zeroed in on the tiny fragments of mica in Ötzi's intestine. They believed that this mineral came from grindstones used to prepare his food. Potassium–argon dating (see Chapter 27) of the specks identified them as belonging to mica formations in the lower Vinschgau area, west of the Eisack Valley. Ötzi's biography was complete. He had spent his early years in the lowlands, and then lived in the nearby mountains. He never moved more than about 60 kilometres from his birthplace.

The Ice Man's corpse also provided a wealth of medical information. His bones revealed that he had experienced malnutrition in his ninth, fifteenth and sixteenth years. He suffered from an irritating intestinal parasite caused by whipworms, the eggs of which were in his intestines. Two fleas came from his clothing. The smoke he had inhaled from indoor fires had made Ötzi's lungs as black as those of a heavy tobacco smoker today. His hands and fingernails were battered, scarred and chipped from constant manual labour. Ötzi's stomach was empty, and so he was probably weak and hungry at the time of his death.

It is almost as if we are meeting Ötzi face to face. But what was he doing in the mountains and how did he die? Originally, the researchers thought that Ötzi had died a peaceful death, perhaps caught out in bad weather. But they changed their minds when they discovered an arrowhead buried deep in his left shoulder. There is also a dagger wound on one of his hands, as if he had defended himself against a close-quarters attack. DNA came into play again. Samples revealed that he had fought with at least four people. In the end, it was the arrow wound that proved fatal, causing him to bleed to death. Perhaps Ötzi had fled into the mountains and died of his wounds at high altitude.

The Ice Man has a surprisingly complete biography, pieced together at enormous expense by teams of scientists from many countries. Hundreds of scientific papers describe his body and his medical conditions. It was the deep-freeze of the high Alps that allowed us to study him: the cold preserved his clothing, equipment and weapons. We know far more about Ötzi than we do about millions of other prehistoric hunters and fisherfolk, farmers and cattle herders, Roman soldiers and medieval craftspeople. He gives us a vivid impression of the difficult conditions in which he and others of the time lived. We're lucky to know what we do from this single humble individual. The find reminds us that archaeology is about people, not things.

Archaeologists have always been fascinated by human skeletons. We have long relied on biological anthropologists to get at the details of the lives as they were lived. They can determine the sex of a skeleton and its age, identify lower backs ruined by hard labour or leg bones bowed by constant horse-riding.

Recently, we have moved beyond bones and can look at the once-living human being behind them. Thanks to cutting-edge medical technology, even skeletons can be made flesh-and-blood bodies from the tiniest of clues. Biological anthropologists use DNA to trace human migrations. And they use medical imaging technology to study mummies without unwrapping them. Analysis of bone chemistry tells us where people lived their early lives and what diets they preferred. Thanks to medical science, we know more about the Ice Man than he knew himself. Ancient bodies, whether well preserved or mere bones, are a hot topic in today's archaeology.

Thousands of individuals have come down to us, most of them skeletons, but also a few well-preserved bodies found in swamps. Ancient Egyptian and Peruvian mummies are mines of information about both noble and common folk. Medical imaging has peered through their bandages and revealed the painful dental abscesses (swellings) suffered by Egyptians of 3,000 years ago. They must have been in agony for months, or even years.

Occasionally, a sacrificial victim is found, and so we learn of violent death. In Peru, some 6,210 metres up in the southern Andes, American anthropologist Johan Reinhard and his Peruvian assistant Miguel Zarate came across the mummy bundle of a fourteen-year-old girl who was sacrificed five centuries ago. She wore a finely woven dress and leather moccasins. Scans of her skull showed that she had died from a swift blow to the head: blood from the head wound had pushed her brain to one side.

The wounds inflicted in hand-to-hand medieval battles could be horrendous. I once examined the bones of some of those who had died during one such encounter. At Towton Hall in northern England, a burial pit containing thirty-eight individuals left a shocking impression of the savagery of medieval warfare. The victims had died in a bloody conflict fought during a snowstorm on

29 March 1461, during a series of conflicts known as the Wars of the Roses. All the skeletons were of men aged between sixteen and fifty. They were active, healthy individuals, whose bodies displayed signs of hard toil from an early age, as one might expect of peasant farmers. Some also displayed elbow injuries resulting from pulling longbows.

Most of the dead perished from savage blows to the head, but there was one whose face had been cut in half by a sword. Another man had suffered at least eight blade wounds from close combat, before being killed by being struck on the head. Crossbow bolts, arrowheads and war hammers inflicted terrible injuries, many of them fatal. The forearms of several men carried wounds caused by fending off blows from attackers. The men had perished in a bloodbath. Not that life at that time was easy for anyone: scurvy and rickets, both diseases resulting from vitamin deficiencies, were common.

Apart from Ötzi, the most thorough research on individuals has examined well-known figures from history. Pharaoh Rameses II (1304–1212 BC) is the best known of all Egyptian kings. He saw military service when young and had more than a hundred sons and (literally) countless daughters. Rameses lived a very long time: he died at the age of ninety-two at a time when most people could only expect to live into their twenties or thirties.

The pharaoh was mummified and buried in the Valley of the Kings. French experts used the latest medical technology on his mummy. They admired the king's fine nose, its shape maintained by peppercorns that had been stuffed into it by his embalmers (the people who had preserved his body). The pharaoh had suffered from arthritis, painful dental abscesses and poor circulation – hardly surprising, given his age.

As pharaoh, Rameses had lived off the fat of the land. But Egyptian commoners certainly did not: theirs were lives of ceaseless toil. A recent study looked at workers' burials in a cemetery at el-Amarna, capital of the pharaoh Akhenaten in the fourteenth century BC (see Chapter 17). Almost all of them died in their twenties and thirties. Their bones display tell-tale signs of malnutrition, while years of backbreaking labour had crushed spines, broken limbs and caused chronic arthritis in arms and legs.

There are more recent rulers whose bodies have been recovered by historical research and the spade. King Richard III of England (1452–85) died fighting his rival, the future King Henry VII, in the final battle of the Wars of the Roses in Leicestershire, central England. Little was known about Richard. Historical records stated that he was deformed, though that was not known for sure – it could perhaps have been a metaphor for his bad character.

Richard's body had been stripped naked and taken to Leicester, where it was put on display. He was then buried without ceremony in a Franciscan friary (a type of monastery). The site of his grave was known long after the friary was demolished, but it came to be forgotten in the nineteenth century. Prolonged historical detective work located the friary site under a city-centre car park, where excavations began in 2012. On the very first day, two leg bones were uncovered. The skeleton had been crammed into a grave that was slightly too small. The backbone was curved in an S-shape and the hands were behind the body, as if they had been tied. Everything pointed to a hasty burial.

The skeleton was that of an adult male who suffered from severe curvature of the spine, which made one shoulder higher than the other. There were major injuries to the skull. Was this King Richard's body? The researchers turned to DNA for the answer. Samples from the bones were compared with the DNA of living descendants of the monarch, and it was confirmed that the skeleton was indeed that of a deformed Richard III. His body was reburied in Leicester Cathedral.

Today's medical technology is helping archaeologists write history in the kind of detail that was unimaginable even just a generation ago. Some physicians were X-raying Egyptian mummies in the early 1900s. But nowadays we can tell where someone spent his youth and where he travelled. We are becoming biographers, writing people's life stories.

CHAPTER 35

The painted scene on the revolving pot tells the whole story. It is around AD 400. A Moche lord sits under a shelter on top of a pyramid on the north coast of Peru. He is in the shade, but the late afternoon sun causes his golden headdress to blaze. In his right hand, he holds a clay vessel filled with human blood. Calm and austere, covered in gold and turquoise ornaments, he gazes down on a row of naked prisoners, stripped of their armour and weapons.

A priest in a bird costume quickly slits the prisoners' throats, catching their spilling blood in a pot. The bodies are dragged away, to be cut into pieces by other waiting priests. The lord drinks more blood, displaying no emotion. His cup is immediately refilled. One day, he will be buried exactly where he sits, as another warrior-priest takes his place.

This scene is one of many on Moche pots of all kinds that were once burial offerings – or were possibly used in daily life, to be displayed at feasts. Some were symbols of social status. Narrative scenes show warriors running in line, hunting deer and seal, and in processions. Moche potters were sculptors as well as painters. Their portrait vases of prominent men are famous, but they also modelled birds, fish, llamas, deer – even spiders. Nor did they forget corn, squash and other plants. Or supernatural beings. Much of what we know about the Moche and their rulers comes from their superb pottery – as well as from richly decorated burials.

The Moche state came into being about 2,000 years ago along Peru's northern coast. The coastal plain is one of the driest landscapes on earth, and so the Moche lived off the abundance of anchovies to be fished from the Pacific. Fertile river valley soils, fed by mountain water from the Andes, allowed them to grow maize, beans and other crops in carefully irrigated field systems.

As food supplies improved, thanks to more efficient farming, small numbers of wealthy families rose to prominence. The rulers and their families were the elite of Moche society, which increasingly became divided between the nobles and the common folk. The rulers built ever larger mud-brick pyramids and temples. These provided the stage for elaborate ceremonies that had but one purpose: to show commoners that their leaders had close links with the supernatural world.

Over the centuries, hundreds of ordinary people toiled on the great temples that rose above the Moche River. They paid their taxes in labour – a common practice in early Peruvian states. The great mud-brick platform of Huaca del Sol rises more than 40 metres above the river, inland from the Pacific. When in use and before floods and looters ravaged it, this enormous huaca (a sacred place) was cross-shaped and faced north. It was built in four sections to give it a stepped effect. The façade was once painted in red and other bright colours. The pyramid that stands there today is but a shadow of the vast structure that was both the royal palace and the burial place of the Moche rulers who lived there.

A second pyramid, Huaca de Luna, stands about 500 metres away. This was a smaller monument with three platforms, connected and enclosed by three high adobe walls. Brightly coloured murals showed divine beings that were part animal, part human. Experts believe that this was a place where the rulers worshipped the major gods that presided over the Moche state.

In one secluded courtyard, archaeologist Steve Bourget unearthed the skeletons of about seventy warriors who had been sacrificed. In many cases, their bodies had then been separated limb from limb, just as shown in the pottery frieze. Clay statuettes depicting naked men with bodies covered in intricate symbols lay alongside some of the remains. At least two of these sacrificial rituals took place during periods of heavy rainfall, a rarity in the arid Moche landscape. They occurred during irregular El Niño events, which are caused by complex climatic shifts in the western Pacific. El Niño brought warmer water to the coast, disrupting the anchovy fisheries. The rains it produced could wipe out entire field systems in hours.

Who were the Moche leaders? We know from the painted pots that their political power depended on success in war. It also depended on carefully staged public ceremonies. This was where the temples and courtyards came in. You can imagine the scene. As the sun sinks in the west, a large crowd of commoners in their best cotton clothing gather in the great plaza below Huaca del Sol. Drums beat and the smell of incense rises from sacred fires as loud chanting resounds in the still air. Brilliant sunshine bathes the entrance to the pyramid on the huaca's summit. Silence falls as a figure appears in the small doorway, his brightly polished golden headdress reflecting the setting sun with hypnotic brilliance. As the sun finally sets, he vanishes into the dark space, as if returning to the supernatural world.

Moche pots display human sacrifice and prisoners being killed, but reveal little about the lords themselves. We know nothing of the rituals that surrounded them. We do not even know their names. They were not literate. We can only guess at the powerful beliefs that guided Moche society. But we can gaze on some of their features, thanks to the skill of the potters. The ceremonial portrait vessels may well depict once-living individuals. That they were important people is certain, for the vessels appear in richly decorated graves. Some lords smile, or even laugh; but most are serious and severe. You get the impression that Moche lords had absolute confidence in their own authority.

All these clues give only a vague impression of the Moche lords. Few of their burials have survived the attention of looters and Spanish soldiers. The Spaniards even diverted the waters of the Moche River to wash away parts of the Huaca del Sol in a ruthless search for gold. They are said to have found some, which encouraged them to wash away even more of the huaca. This loss makes the magnificent tombs of the so-called Lords of Sipán an archaeological find of exceptional importance – one of the major discoveries of late twentieth-century archaeology.

In 1987, tomb robbers broke into the undisturbed, gold-laden sepulchre of a Moche lord, deep in the pyramids of Sipán in the Lambayeque Valley, a major centre of Moche power. Fortunately, Peruvian archaeologist Walter Alva, a Moche expert, visited the site almost immediately. His subsequent excavations, carried out by a team of archaeologists and conservators, filled in a picture of the mysterious rulers of the Moche kingdom.

By 2004, fourteen tombs had been identified in this major huaca, which was built sometime before AD 300. Known as the Huaca Rajada, its burial chambers consist of two small adobe pyramids and a small platform. The graves of three Sipán lords emerged from Alva's excavations, each wearing rich ornaments and accompanied by grave offerings.

The first lord to be excavated was only about 1.5 metres tall and was aged between thirty-five and forty-five. He lay in ceremonial dress in an adobe chamber, with solid benches along the sides and at the head end. The mourners set hundreds of fine clay pots into small niches in the benches. Then they placed the lord in a plank coffin in the centre of the chamber, the lid secured with copper bands. Spouted vessels stood at the head and the foot. He lay in his full regalia (distinctive clothing), complete with headdress, golden mask and chest ornament, earrings and other jewellery of the highest quality. He wore two necklaces of gold and silver beads in the shape of peanuts, an important Moche food crop.

He was not alone. Five cane coffins held the bodies of adults. Three were women, perhaps wives or concubines (women who share a bed with a man but are not married to him), who had died somewhat earlier. Two males, one accompanied by a war club, may have been warriors. A third male with crossed legs sat in a niche overlooking the burial. The feet of the warriors had been amputated, presumably to prevent them from escaping. A dog and two llamas also lay in the sepulchre. Once the coffin was in place, a low beam roof had been set close above it. Then everything had been filled in.

A second tomb was uncovered in 1988, near that of the first lord. The man in this sepulchre was his contemporary. His regalia included a sacrificial bowl and artefacts associated with worship of the moon. He may have been a priest.

A third chamber was slightly older, but the ornaments and clothing showed that the occupant was a person of the same high rank as the first lord. DNA tests revealed that the two were related through their mothers. A young woman and a warrior with amputated feet, presumably the lord's bodyguard, also lay in the tomb.

Three lords in elaborate, very similar attire, went to eternity accompanied by ritual objects. Who exactly were these individuals? The ceremonial rattles, exquisite nose and ear ornaments, copper sandals and fine bracelets indicate clearly that they were powerful men.

Only one possible source of information is available – the paintings on Moche vessels. Archaeologist Christopher Donnan photographed the painted pots as they revolved on a turntable, thus 'unrolling' complete friezes of the scenes. There are hundreds of scenes that depict two men engaged in combat, one defeating and capturing the other. In each, the victor strips off his enemy's clothing, bundles up his weapons and puts a rope around his neck. Then the tethered prisoner is forced to walk in front of his captor. Other scenes show rows of captives being displayed before an important individual, who is sometimes sitting atop a pyramid. Then the captives' throats are cut. Priests, attendants and the individual presiding over the ceremony drink the fresh blood.

The most important participants in these ceremonies wear a conical helmet with a crescent-shaped headdress, circular ear ornaments and a crescent nose ornament – as do the Lords of Sipán.

Donnan calls these lords warrior-priests – men who supervised the most important ceremonies in Moche society. He points out that the regalia of the lords changed little from one generation to the next. Nearly every artefact buried with them had meaning. For example, they wore gold on the right and silver on the left, representing the opposites of sun and moon, day and night. Judging from the grave offerings, the Sipán lords were believed to have supernatural powers. They must have been aggressive, competitive warriors, who organised raids and wars of conquest in the constant pursuit of victims.

The graves of the Moche lords were so rich in gold that few have survived the ravages of looters. This means that we know little about warrior-priests other than those at Sipán. Three noble burials have come from the 32-metre-high Dos Cabezas pyramid close to the mouth of the Jequetepeque River. They date to between AD 450 and 550. The three lords were remarkable for their height: each stood nearly 2 metres tall. Biological anthropologists suspect that they may have suffered from a genetic disorder known as Marfan syndrome, which causes thin, long limbs.

The most important individual wore a headdress decorated with gilded copper bats. He wore a nose ornament fashioned in similar form. Bats were apparently prominent in Moche ritual: they appear on painted pots, in scenes of human sacrifice and ritual blood-drinking. The man may not have been a warrior-priest, but perhaps a metalworker – a respected occupation in Moche society.

Leaders like the Moche warrior-priests knew that their rule depended on their ability to convince people that they had a special relationship with powerful supernatural forces. Their elaborate clothing and ornaments, carefully staged public ceremonies and rituals, and the endless chants were ways in which they did so. A little human sacrifice along the way reinforced the message.

The archaeological unravelling of the relationship between ruler and ruled involved slow-moving fieldwork, a passion for minute detective work and painstaking conservation of the finds. Even small ornaments like decorated earrings revealed the spiritual opposition between the sun and the moon, between night and day, that was a central part of Moche belief. The warrior-priests thought they had a special relationship with the supernatural which gave them power. To understand their complex world, archaeologists had to assemble a jigsaw puzzle from dozens of tiny clues. Thanks to Alva and his colleagues, we now have a fascinating picture of long-forgotten Moche rulers – men whose wealth rivalled that of the Egyptian pharaoh Tutankhamun.

CHAPTER 36

Tunnelling for the Cosmos

Some 48 kilometres north of Mexico City, in the Basin of Mexico, towers the Pyramid of the Sun at Teotihuacán. This massive 71-metre high structure makes you feel like a speck of dust in the presence of the gods. And that is exactly what the builders intended. Those who dwelt at Teotihuacán lived at the heart of a vast sacred landscape. The city itself covered more than 21 square kilometres, and it dominated the basin and the surrounding highlands. By AD 100, at least 80,000 people lived there. And between AD 200 and 750, Teotihuacán's population swelled to more than 150,000. At the time, it was as big as all but the largest cities of China and the Middle East.

Archaeologists have worked there for nearly a century. They've learned that Teotihuacán was a vast symbolic landscape of artificial mountains, foothills, caves and open spaces that replicated the spiritual world. Over a period of more than eight centuries, the Teotihuacános built 600 pyramids, 500 workshop areas, a huge marketplace, 2,000 apartment complexes and several squares or plazas.

At some point, the city's rulers decided to rebuild much of the city. They constructed standardised, walled residential compounds, probably to replace crowded urban areas. Some of these housed artisans and their workshops. Others were military quarters. Foreigners from the Valley of Oaxaca and lowland Veracruz on the coast of the Gulf of Mexico lived in their own neighbourhoods, which are identified by distinctive pottery styles.

Everything followed a grid plan, with the streets all running at right angles to one another. Dividing the city in a north–south direction was a wide avenue, known ever since the Spanish Conquest as the Avenue of the Dead.

The great Pyramids of the Sun and the Moon dominate the avenue's north end. Between AD 150 and 325, the city's rulers remodelled the Pyramid of the Sun into its present form, enlarged the Pyramid of the Moon and extended the Avenue of the Dead more than a mile southwards to include the Ciudadela – the city's new political and religious centre. Until recently, not much was known about this impressive structure, but in 2003, the National Institute of Anthropology and History in Mexico City embarked on an ambitious long-term programme to investigate and preserve the Ciudadela temples. In recent years the project has made some spectacular discoveries.

The Ciudadela complex is enormous, with high walls and a large courtyard. As many as 100,000 people could gather within the enclosed space for major public ceremonies. The Temple of Quetzalcoatl, the ancient feathered serpent god of Central American civilisation, lies within the enclosure, facing the open space. This is a six-level stepped pyramid with a huge stairway running up it, the steps of which form small terraces. Heads of feathered serpents and a snake-like creature, perhaps a war serpent, decorate the faces of these terraces. Reliefs of the feathered serpent also appear under each row of heads, together with a depiction of water. The entire temple was painted blue and carved seashells provided decoration. What the colour and the heads and other decorations signified is unknown, but it seems possible that they represented the cosmos (the universe) at the time of creation – a calm ocean.

The excavators started from scratch, working on a temple that had been badly damaged, partly by rain and high groundwater levels, and partly by large numbers of tourists. In 2004, the World Monuments Fund provided money and technical assistance for the conservation of this unique structure.

Excavations by Mexican archaeologists in the large plaza beside the Temple of the Feathered Serpent uncovered the remains of several structures that by AD 200 had been built on what was originally farmland. These had formed the first religious complex. One of the structures was more than 120 metres long and may have served as a court for ceremonial ball games (an ancient ritual that could include the sacrifice of the losers). The architects of Quetzalcoatl's temple destroyed these buildings when they erected the Ciudadela in its present form.

The open space in front of the temple in the Ciudadela was designed to be flooded with water to form a reflective surface. It was a kind of water mirror, a symbolic reflection of the calm sea that existed before the creation of the world and humans. According to ancient origin myths, a Sacred Mountain is said to have risen from this watery mass at the beginning of time. All this suggests that the Ciudadela was the setting for rituals in which myths about the creation of the world were re-enacted.

Heavy rains in 2003 revealed a depression and a deep hole in the ground in front of the steps of the Quetzalcoatl temple platform. Now, after years of work, archaeologists have explored under the temple for the first time. One – Sergio Gómez Chávez – was lowered by rope through the small opening. He reached solid ground almost 14 metres down and found an underground tunnel leading east towards the Temple of the Feathered Serpent and west towards the centre of the great plaza. The tunnel was mostly filled with earth and carved stone blocks, put there by the Teotihuacános.

To clear and explore the underground passageway required careful planning. In 2004, 2005 and 2010, before they went underground, Chávez and his colleagues used ground-penetrating radar to plot the passage from the surface. This suggested that the tunnel was between 100 and 120 metres long, with the eastern end at the centre of the Temple of the Feathered Serpent. The radar plots hinted at a large chamber in the middle of the tunnel and an even larger one at the eastern end. They also provided a way of planning the underground exploration.

The investigation was based on a series of carefully thought-out assumptions. First, the researchers assumed that Teotihuacán was a replica of its inhabitants' vision of the universe, with three levels formed by the gods – the heavens, the earth and the underworld. The horizontal plane represented north, east, south and west. And the corners of the plane were the corners of the world.

Second, the excavators assumed that the Temple of the Feathered Serpent symbolised the Sacred Mountain of the creation, thought to have emerged from the calm sea at the beginning of time. The temple stood on a sacred spot, the centre of the world. Here you could communicate with the different layers of the cosmos.

Third, they assumed that a sacred cave, thought to lie below the Sacred Mountain, was the place of entry into the underworld. This was inhabited by the gods and by the creative forces that maintained the cosmos. The tunnel, which was partly explored by Chávez with radar, was a symbolic representation of this underworld. According to ancient cosmology (beliefs or myths about the origin of the universe), the underworld had its own sacred geography.

Finally, they assumed that the underground passage was visited frequently, but only by those individuals involved in rituals that bolstered their influence. This was where such people acquired spiritual powers by performing ritual acts. Some objects from the rituals, perhaps even the remains of those who gave and received gifts, might be present in the tunnel.

The underground excavations started in 2006 and continue to this day. Chávez began in an area of about 100 square metres, where he thought the main entrance to the tunnel once lay. A pit covering 5 square metres lay about 2 metres below the surface. This provided access to a tunnel leading towards the pyramid.

Artefacts and stone blocks filled the narrow passageway, making it hard to plan the excavation. Chávez turned once again to remote sensing, this time underground. Then he used a laser scanner – a highly accurate measuring device – to plan the next stage of the work. A first attempt recorded 37 metres of the tunnel. Another scan in 2011 reached 73 metres. These measurements confirmed that there was indeed a long tunnel leading towards the pyramid, but its precise overall length was still uncertain.

Next, Chávez used a small remote-controlled robot equipped with video cameras. This penetrated 37 metres into the tunnel to test for stability and potential working conditions, and aided the excavation of the previously laser-scanned segment of the passageway. In 2013, a more sophisticated robot with an infrared camera and a miniature laser scanner managed to get through the final previously inaccessible 30 metres of the tunnel. This was no easy task. Ancient Aztecs had visited the tunnel on many occasions to leave offerings there. To do so, they had to make their way through, and often partially demolish, more than twenty thick walls that had blocked the tunnel. In the end, the entire space was filled with offerings. Chávez and his colleagues were the first people to enter the tunnel for 1,800 years.

By 2013, the excavation extended 65 metres into the tunnel. Two side chambers were revealed. Their walls and roofs had been finished using a powder created from a metallic mineral, and they shone like a starry night or sparkling running water. One of the chambers contained more than 400 mineral metal balls. These objects remain a complete mystery. After the two side chambers, the tunnel's depth gradually increased by a further 2 metres and it continued for 35 metres to the east. At the end were three chambers, facing north, south and east.

More than 75,000 objects have emerged from the excavation, which now extends over 103 metres of the tunnel and to a depth of 17 metres below the surface. Thousands of offerings have come from the dig, among them minerals such as jade, serpentine and turquoise; obsidian (volcanic glass); and liquid mercury. Hundreds of clay vessels and mirrors made from polished pyrite (a shiny mineral often confused with gold) lay alongside seashells. Dozens of unusual clay vessels have come to light, as well as rubber balls, necklaces, wooden objects and fragments of human skin.

What do all these finds mean? Chávez and his teammates argue that the Ciudadela re-created the sacred geography of the cosmos and the work of the gods. The Pyramid of the Feathered Serpent symbolised the Sacred Mountain, which served as a link between the various layers and regions of the cosmos. The underground tunnel and caves beneath the temple transformed space on earth into a wet, cold, dark underworld. It was there that rulers acquired the supernatural power to govern. The tunnel under the pyramid took the city's rulers into the underworld. Vanishing under the earth suggested that they could visit this unknown world, an act which gave them the ability to communicate with the forces of the supernatural realm. The Ciudadela was where everyone in the great city participated in public ceremonies that marked major events in the ritual calendar. It was there, too, that the architects attempted to create the entrance to the underworld.

The ongoing Ciudadela project is no fast-moving search for precious objects, but rather a systematic, painstaking analysis of the meaning of the objects in the tunnel. Everything had a ritual significance – including the way the tunnel had been dug below the natural water table in order to re-create the watery environment of the underworld. The last 30 metres of the tunnel had been made even deeper, so that they were always filled with water, representing the sacred water of the creation.

Investigations at Teotihuacán began a century ago, but the city is so enormous that archaeologists have hardly scratched the surface. The current emphasis is on tunnelling – not only at the Ciudadela, but also under the Pyramids of the Sun and the Moon. Here, further tunnels and rich offerings, as well as sacrificial victims, will help decipher the complex symbolism of one of the greatest cities in history.

CHAPTER 37

Çatalhöyük

The half-size clay figures looked out at me from the museum display case, staring straight ahead. Some were double-headed, perhaps a husband and wife. As I moved around the room, I felt their black-outlined eyes following me. I got as close as I could to one figure and gazed into the cowrie (sea snail) shell eyes. The black bitumen (tar) dots of the pupils seemed to burn deep into my soul. I was hypnotised by the power of a figure buried, with thirty others, in a pit sometime around 8000 BC.

This was one of those rare moments when I have been confronted by the force of ancient beliefs. There have been others: Ice Age paintings in French caves and at Altamira, Spain (see Chapter 14); a few minutes alone in complete darkness in a pharaoh's tomb in Egypt's Valley of the Kings; tracing the ancient legend of the Maya creation, as painted on a clay bowl... But few have been as powerful as the time spent with those figures from 'Ain Ghazal in Jordan – the clay modelled around bundles of twigs, the painted clothing and hair and the tattoos. I felt myself in the presence of the ancestors.

Like other early farmers, the 'Ain Ghazal people buried the decorated heads of their forebears under their hut floors. Kathleen Kenyon had found plastered skulls under 7000 BC houses at Jericho (see Chapter 30). At 'Ain Ghazal, the people also made models of their ancestors, which stood in house shrines. Even looking at them in a museum, you feel as if previous generations of your family are staring out at you, watching over their descendants. The more we learn about early villagers in the Middle East, the more we uncover evidence that respect for those who went before was a powerful force in society. Why was there such concern with earlier generations?

We know from living traditional societies that ancestors are often considered the guardians of the land: they ensure that harvests grow and life continues as before. The same was definitely true in the past. A deep respect for ancestors has been part of human belief ever since farming began – and probably from much earlier in prehistory. The Jericho skulls and the 'Ain Ghazal figurines show that ancestor cults were part of societies that lived from one harvest to the next. Crop failure, hunger and malnutrition were harsh realities for earlier and later generations alike. A concern with the continuity of life was central to early farming societies, which was why ancestors were important. The beliefs about ancestors held by traditional societies today have reached us in the form of spoken stories or songs, passed down through the generations. But what about the beliefs of much earlier societies, such as the first farmers? We can only rely on archaeology and material remains of the past to tell the tale. Fortunately, a Turkish farming settlement named Çatalhöyük and a carefully planned, long-term excavation have shed much more light on the power of the ancestors.

James Mellaart (1925–2012) was the British archaeologist who discovered Çatalhöyük. He had learned his excavation with Kathleen Kenyon at Jericho, and so he knew a village site when he saw one. During the late 1950s, he surveyed the Konya plain in central Turkey in search of Bronze Age sites. Instead, he came across the two mounds of Çatalhöyük, the larger of them 20 metres high.

Mellaart dug Çatalhöyük from 1961 to 1963, uncovering thirteen occupation levels of a settlement that dated to around 6000 or

5500 BC. He thought up to 8,000 people could have lived there at the height of its power. The excavations investigated more than 150 rooms and buildings. It was a crowded place: houses were packed together so tightly that they had no front doors, but were entered through the roof.

The rooms included shrines with clay bulls' heads, plaster reliefs and wall paintings. There were also small female figures. Mellaart believed that the people worshipped a mother goddess, a symbol of fertility. He even suggested that some of the wall paintings were based on textiles, ancient prototypes for modern Turkish carpet designs. But for various controversial reasons, Mellaart had to cut his work short, and his dig was closed.

Mellaart's excavations caused quite a stir. Çatalhöyük covered 13 hectares, making it about ten times larger than most settlements of the period. Many questions remained unanswered, but the Turkish authorities did not permit new excavations until 1993, when another Englishman, Ian Hodder (born 1948), started an ambitious, long-term research project that has continued ever since. Thanks to his carefully designed teamwork, the ancestors are now emerging from the shadows.

Hodder is an experienced and imaginative archaeologist, one of the few with the vision and skills required to undertake such a job. He involved in the excavations not only archaeologists, but experts in all kinds of disciplines. Everyone had to share information freely, including research notes. Right from the start, the team worked closely with the Turkish authorities, who have developed the site as a potential tourist destination.

From the beginning, Hodder thought of the Çatalhöyük project as an excavation concerned with people. He believes that the past was created by people, both as individuals and as members of groups large and small. Just as we do today, the people then interacted with one another, with their society and with their ancestors. Hodder realised that Çatalhöyük had the potential to reveal such interactions. Long-forgotten ancestral beliefs would come down to us in the form of material objects found during excavation: in shrines, temples and elsewhere.

Hodder set out three basic principles. First, we couldn't look at the past purely through ecology (the relationship between living organisms and their environment), technology or ways in which people fed themselves. Second, we must focus on neglected aspects of ancient societies, among them ethnic minorities, women and the anonymous people, often illiterate commoners. Third, we must always consider the wider significance of the research for the public. Many archaeologists had voiced some, or even all, of these three principles before. But no one had embraced all of them from the outset.

Everything depended, of course, on excavation. The team addressed two basic questions early on: when did Çatalhöyük come into being, and what was the first settlement like. Trenches dug down to the base of the East Mound tell of a small settlement that flourished close to a wetland in about 7400 BC. Animal bones and seeds proved that the people had been farmers. They also relied on fish, waterfowl and game from the surrounding landscape.

This small village flourished for 1,000 years thanks to fertile soils, plenty of water and a combination of agriculture and herding. At first, only a few hundred people lived at Çatalhöyük. But as cattle herding became more important, the population grew to between 3,500 and 8,000. This was when the village became Mellaart's small town of densely packed houses. It was now an important place, known for miles around.

The villagers were lucky, for they lived within easy reach of volcanic lava flows, where obsidian (volcanic glass) could be mined with little effort. Shiny, fine obsidian is ideal for making stone tools. Çatalhöyük's inhabitants seized the opportunity to shape thousands of standardised blocks of the material that could easily be carried and then fashioned into small, sharp-edged tools. The obsidian trade was huge and extended as far as Syria and beyond.

Çatalhöyük prospered, so much so that those who lived there rebuilt their houses at least eighteen times over a span of 1,400 years until occupation ended in about 6000 BC. Now Hodder and his colleagues could truly focus on people and their 'voices'. To this end, they have excavated more than 166 houses – not just single dwellings, but sequences of houses, all built at the same location.

The settlement consisted of tightly packed clusters of flat-roofed dwellings, separated from one another by narrow alleyways. The same groups of people occupied and rebuilt the houses on the same spot for generations, suggesting strong kinship ties between neighbours and those who had lived there in earlier times. The glue that held the community together was the close flesh and blood connections between individuals and their families, and with other relatives who lived nearby or farther afield. These connections also linked living people and their ancestors, which was one reason why kinship ties were so important at Çatalhöyük.

The town's inhabitants never built large public buildings, temples or ceremonial centres. Everything happened inside their houses: eating, sleeping, toolmaking and rituals of all kinds. Nor did they bury their dead in cemeteries. Day-to-day life and spiritual beliefs blended together. We know this because the walls of many houses have paintings of humans and animals, such as leopards and vultures. It is as if the ancestors, animal and human, were watching over the living. And many of the houses contained burials, as well as the skulls of wild bulls. Sometimes the heads of the dead would be detached and their faces plastered over. The heads were then displayed and passed on from one generation to the next. All of this speaks of a complex world of myths that gave meaning to daily life.

We know more about this meaning from a small number of houses that were apparently never inhabited. Instead, the dead dwelt there. The average inhabited house contains between five and eight burials. But these special houses contained many more: sixty-two bodies were deposited in one of them over a forty-year period. Their furniture included sacred wild ox skulls and clay models of bulls' heads. The walls bore paintings of bulls, headless people and birds of prey, clearly actors in rituals performed in the shrines.

Each of the uninhabited houses had a history for those who built and maintained them. Sometimes, people would even dig into the floor to recover the prized bull skulls left by earlier generations. They also made a practice of placing teeth from earlier burials into later ones. Hodder calls these few uninhabited structures 'History Houses'. They were places where people could communicate with their ancestors and their history, using familiar rituals employed by those who had lived before them. History Houses may also have witnessed ceremonial feasts that celebrated wild bulls. These dangerous animals had huge spiritual power in farming societies over wide areas of the ancient Middle East.

The people created and maintained this history by living on (and over) the dead, and by recycling body parts, such as ancestral skulls. Ancestors – both human and animal – protected the dead, the house and its inhabitants. Associations between dangerous animals, headless humans and birds of prey shown in wall paintings reinforced the continuity of life before and after death.

Çatalhöyük's farmers lived by a calendar of changing seasons: spring and planting (birth), summer (growth), autumn (harvest) and then winter (death). This was the ultimate reality of human life – the reason why people revered and respected their ancestors. They knew that they would become them one day. This was also why female figures and possible fertility goddesses were respected: they renewed life.

The Çatalhöyük project is far more than just archaeology. Hodder has used the excavations and the research of dozens of experts to create a complex history of a community deeply concerned with its ancestors. This was a place filled with complex relationships and tensions. We look back on a community with many noisy voices.

There is another voice, too: that of the modern local people. Çatalhöyük is part of their history. But it is also far more. Many of the local farmers have worked on the excavations. The site is becoming an archaeological museum, visited by tourists from many countries. Hodder and his colleagues have talked about their discoveries to the villagers living nearby. They have trained museum attendants and guards with the help of Turkish archaeologists. Hodder has even written the life story of one of the site guards.

The archaeologists from many lands – and their work – have become part of the local landscape. This is what we call 'engaged archaeology' – archaeology that is involved with the past and with the modern world. Archaeological research and protection of what is found go hand in hand.

Archaeologists commonly refer to people with an interest in a site as 'stakeholders'. At Çatalhöyük, the stakeholders include the people from the surrounding communities. Also the foreign and Turkish archaeologists who work at the site, and the people who look after the museum. The tourists are stakeholders, too, for Çatalhöyük is part of the common cultural heritage of all humankind. And when we talk of stakeholders, let us not forget the ancestors.

CHAPTER 38

Looking in the Landscape

Antiquarian, lawyer and physician William Stukeley (1687–1765) was obsessed with the stone circles at Stonehenge in southern England. He had a joyous attitude to life and an insatiable curiosity about the past. He was absurd, ingenious and playful. In 1723, Stukeley and his patron, Lord Winchelsea, walked around the top of the Stonehenge trilithons (two upright stones supporting a 'lintel' – a third stone that bridges them). They then had dinner on top of one of them. Stukeley was to remark that someone with a 'steady head' and 'nimble heels' would have space to dance a minuet up there.

For all his antics, Stukeley was a serious scholar who was interested in ancient people. He thought of Stonehenge not merely as a wonder, but as a sacred place within a wider setting. He completed the first survey of the stone circles and dug into a few nearby burial mounds; but most importantly, he walked the landscape.

His perceptive eye spotted long-forgotten earthworks, including what he called an 'avenue', marked by banks and ditches. Two centuries later, aerial photographs traced this about 3 kilometres to the River Avon, near the town of Amesbury. Stukeley also found a pair of parallel ditches marking out what he believed to have been a racecourse (and which he dubbed the 'Cursus'), complete with an earthen grandstand at the eastern end.

William Stukeley's fieldwork was remarkable for its perception and accuracy. Earlier visitors had done little more than describe Stonehenge in a few words. By walking the countryside, Stukeley founded one of the basic approaches of today's archaeology – the systematic study of ancient landscapes.

Archaeologists have always been obsessed with big, conspicuous monuments. And until recently, in the case of Stonehenge, research mirrored this preoccupation. Excavations within and around the stone circles yielded a provisional (not final) chronology, together with lots of speculation about the site's significance. Only in the past few years have investigators raised their eyes – as Stukeley did – and looked properly at the surrounding landscape. While Stukeley traversed the countryside on foot or on horseback, today's archaeologists examine the landscape electronically and from space.

For generations, we have dreamed of ways to explore sites without the backbreaking and expensive effort of excavating them. 'Non-intrusive archaeology' – commonly known as 'remote sensing' – studies sites and their surroundings without disturbing them or destroying them by digging them up. Remote sensing began with aerial photography, which became a serious archaeological tool after the First World War. Nowadays we have Google Earth, satellite imagery, airborne radar and technologies like ground-penetrating radar and other techniques to peer beneath the earth's surface. These allow us to explore entire landscapes.

Some of the best archaeologists in the business no longer really want to dig – they know that excavation destroys archaeological sites. Of course, selective excavation is necessary to provide dating evidence or to answer specific questions. But today's digs are smaller, slow moving and carefully planned – a far cry from Leonard Woolley at Ur in the 1920s and 1930s.

Thanks to radiocarbon dating and limited excavations, we know a great deal more than Stukeley about Stonehenge. The great stone circles were erected in about 2500 BC, though there was ritual activity there at least 1,000 years earlier. But we have always been more interested in the stone circles themselves than in the surrounding landscape. This is the story of what we learned about Stonehenge when remote sensing came into play.

Vincent Gaffney is an expert on remote sensing, who pioneered work on Doggerland, the buried Ice Age landscape under the North Sea (see Chapter 40). He embarked on a four-year study of Stonehenge in 2010, using magnetometers and ground-penetrating radar to produce three-dimensional images of sites under the surface. His team employed the latest technology, mounted on quad bikes and mini-tractors, to map 14 square kilometres of the landscape surrounding Stonehenge. The project has revealed fifteen hitherto unknown stone circles, burial mounds, ditches and pits. It turns out that Stonehenge lay in an elaborate and crowded landscape inhabited by the living and the dead.

Gaffney examined Stukeley's Cursus, just north of Stonehenge – a long strip, marked by ditches, which runs east to west for just over 3 kilometres. Far from being a racecourse, as Stukeley had believed, the Cursus was probably laid out as a sacred walkway, several centuries before construction work began at Stonehenge. Gaffney and his colleagues found several gaps in the ditches. These may have been 'channels' to guide people arriving from north and south onto the east–west axis.

All kinds of mysterious features found in the Gaffney survey await excavation. We do know that many of these features align (line up) with sunrise on the longest and shortest days of the year – the so-called summer and winter solstices. The Stonehenge landscape had intense spiritual meaning. What it meant to those who built its stone circles and earthworks, and what emotions the dramatic sight of Stonehenge stirred in them, must remain a matter of speculation. But there are some questions that we may now be able to answer.

The farmers who built Stonehenge lived in a tough environment, and the passage of the seasons governed their lives. The eternal cycles of planting, growth and harvest – of symbolic life and death – repeated themselves endlessly through good years and bad. These were the realities that governed human life in the

Stonehenge landscape, as they did in many other communities, large and small, including Çatalhöyük in Turkey (see Chapter 37). Fortunately, excavations at Durrington Walls, an earthwork just over 3 kilometres northeast of Stonehenge, have unravelled some of the complex rituals of ancient life there.

Durrington Walls is a great circular earthwork, commonly known as a 'henge'. It was once more than 3 metres high and had a 3-metre ditch on the inner side. The earthwork covers 17 hectares, but there is little to see on the surface today. Next to it, on its south side, once stood a timber circle known as Woodhenge. Two Stonehenge-sized timber circles, known as the North Circle and the South Circle, stood inside the earthwork.

Between about 2525 and 2470 BC, before the earthwork was built, one of the largest human settlements in Europe flourished here. As many as 4,000 people lived in about 1,000 houses with wattle and daub walls (wooden strips plastered with mud). The inhabitants may have been those people who built both Durrington Walls and Stonehenge. There are no signs of a builder's village near the latter.

Until recently, everyone assumed that the two sites were built at different times, Durrington Walls being a few centuries earlier. However, fresh radiocarbon dates show that the two were in use at the same time. But why was Stonehenge built of stone, while Durrington Walls and Woodhenge were constructed of timber? The lintels of Stonehenge's trilithons have joints similar to those found in wooden structures, hinting that the builders were also carpenters.

Michael Parker Pearson is an English archaeologist with very broad experience. Among other places, he has worked in Madagascar, where he visited many tombs and standing stones with Malagasy archaeologist Ramilisonina. Parker Pearson had excavated at Avebury and Stonehenge and arranged for Ramilisonina to visit the sites. Ramilisonina took one look at them and declared that Stonehenge, made in stone, was for the ancestors – the dead – while Durrington Walls, with its wooden uprights, was for the living. Could this have been the case? There were, after all, cremation burials at Stonehenge and burial mounds nearby, but none at Durrington Walls.

Parker Pearson and his team work with huge quantities of data. They like to take a broad perspective. Why, for example, had the famous 'bluestones' at Stonehenge been transported all the way from the Preseli Hills in Wales, about 290 kilometres from the stone circles? Perhaps even more importantly, why was Stonehenge erected where it was, nearly 2 kilometres from the nearest water, on top of a rather desolate ridge? And why go to all the trouble of transporting stone and fashioning it to form a stone circle that imitated wood?

Teamwork was the only way to address these complex questions. Parker Pearson and some of his archaeologist friends assembled a talented research group for a multi-year Stonehenge Riverside Project. Every stage of the work was carefully debated. Thorny questions were thrashed out in the field, in the pub and in the laboratory. What followed was a carefully organised series of excavations and surveys, combined with analysis of even the smallest artefacts. At Durrington Walls, the excavators traced a surfaced avenue about 100 metres across, with parallel banks that led from the south entrance of the earthwork down to the River Avon. The avenue was aligned with the entrance to the south circle. How did this fit into the wider Stonehenge landscape?

One of the team, Christopher Tilley, had previously developed a new approach to exploring prehistoric landscapes called 'phenomenology'. This involves trying to move through landscapes in the same way as ancient people would have. Ground-penetrating radar, maps and other well-established survey devices are all well and good, but there is more to a landscape than that. For a start, the researcher has to ignore modern roads, fields, hedges and paths. How, for example, did the builders of Stonehenge use the natural landscape to approach the stone circles? Tilley walked the avenue and other ancient features, and explored the course of the River Avon, since these were canoe-using societies that covered long distances by river and stream.

While Tilley went to work, Parker Pearson and his team excavated at Durrington Walls. They stripped off the topsoil of their trenches mechanically, exposing the chalk. One house with a chalk floor measured about 25 square metres. Painstaking manual excavation exposed the stakeholes where the clay-plastered walls had once stood. Between the wall and the edge of the chalk floor, the team uncovered shallow grooves that had once held the foundations of box beds and storage bins. The soil on the surface of the floor of five dwellings was sifted through very fine screens in the laboratory.

We cannot understand Durrington Walls without looking at Stonehenge, about which we now know a great deal. For a long time, Stonehenge served as a burial place. Its builders constructed it at the end of a natural geological feature that extended along the axis of the solstice. The first version of Stonehenge was built in 3000 BC. The second stage of construction, when the trilithons and sarsen stones (made of sandstone) were erected, came in about 2500 BC, just as comparable timber circles were being constructed at Durrington Walls. Those were erected in a settlement that housed people who had come from afar with their herds for seasonal feasting in summer and winter.

Most likely, Stonehenge was the place of the dead; Durrington Walls was for the living. We know this from the alignment of the two sites. The surrounding landscape was almost like a giant astronomical observatory. At midsummer, Stonehenge lines up with the sun as it appears at sunrise. The Durrington Walls avenue and the site's southern circle align with the midsummer sun as it dips below the horizon at sunset.

The Stonehenge Riverside Project is a wonderful example of close-knit team research that works on carefully defined hypotheses and objectives. The experts on the team come from a broad range of specialities – some of them far removed from archaeology. The team members take risks, ask bold questions and show an awareness that knowledge is cumulative – it is built up gradually. As such, the project provides a blueprint for achieving a close understanding of Stonehenge in the future.

In many respects, the archaeologists working in the Stonehenge landscape represent the future of archaeology. Instead of just excavating individual sites, we regard them as part of much larger landscapes. We have come full circle – back to what William Stukeley was doing at Stonehenge in the 1720s.

CHAPTER 39

Shining a Light on the Invisible

The research at Stonehenge has revealed the power of remote sensing when studying the past. In a few years, we will have a much better understanding of the sacred landscape surrounding the stone circles. This is archaeology on a far grander scale than ever before. But Stonehenge and Durrington Walls are dwarfed by a different remote-sensing project on the other side of the world.

When I first saw Cambodia's Angkor Wat on a hot, humid day, its sheer size took my breath away. You stumble on it suddenly, in dense forest, its towers stretching up towards heaven. At dusk, the pink of the setting sun casts a soft light on the richly decorated pinnacles. The huge shrine is a spectacle of beauty, wonder and magnificence on an almost unimaginable scale. I could only marvel at the vision of the anonymous architect who built it. This is one of the great archaeological wonders of the world, the historical roots of which extend back over 1,000 years. But the ruins lie in dense forest, which has made the surrounding landscape almost invisible – until now, that is.

Before looking at remote sensing here, we should offer a little background. Angkor Wat lies close to the Mekong River and a giant lake called the Tonle Sap. This lake is unusual: when the Mekong floods between August and October, it swells to 160 kilometres in length and has a depth of up to 16 metres. As the Mekong's waters recede and the level of the lake falls, millions of catfish and other species are trapped in the shallows.

A combination of fertile soils (ideal for growing rice) and this, one of the richest fisheries on earth, created a very productive environment that sustained thousands of farmers. Reservoirs and well-managed canals distributed water over thousands of hectares of farmland and propped up the wealthy Khmer civilisation, which prospered between AD 802 and 1430.

At first, Tonle Sap and its surroundings supported numerous competing kingdoms whose histories are virtually unknown. Then a series of ambitious Khmer kings created a powerful and more stable empire. They considered themselves divine rulers and – at vast expense – built shrines in their own honour. Angkor Wat and a handful of other magnificent palaces and shrines dominate the landscape. Angkor Wat and nearby Angkor Thom are vast: they would dwarf ancient Egyptian temples and the Maya centre at Copán in Honduras, visited by Catherwood and Stephens (Chapter 6).

The rulers of the Khmer Empire created a cult of divine kingship, luxury and wealth. Everything, including the labour of thousands of commoners, was for the benefit of the king. In AD 1113, King Suryavarman II started building his masterpiece, Angkor Wat.

Every detail of this remarkable structure reflects some element of the Khmer mythology. According to the cosmology of the Khmer, the world consisted of a central continent, Jambudvipa, with a mountain, Mount Meru, rising from its middle. The central tower of Angkor Wat soars 60 metres above the surrounding landscape in imitation of Meru's main peak; four other towers represent the lower peaks. An imposing enclosure wall depicts the mountain range that surrounded the continent, while the moat around the enclosure represents the mythical ocean beyond.

Suryavarman II's masterpiece did not last long after his death. It was soon abandoned during a period of political upheaval. Another monarch, King Suryavarman VII, a Buddhist rather than a Hindu, ascended the throne in AD 1151. He built the nearby Angkor Thom, which was as much a capital city as a shrine.

We can easily become obsessed by Angkor Wat. It is, after all, one of the most spectacular archaeological sites on earth. It is also an archaeologist's nightmare: the ruins are so vast and elaborate that they still have not been fully documented. With their scale and complexity, they defy conventional excavation methods.

Suryavarman's shrine measures 1,500 metres by 1,200 metres and is protected by a wide moat. The central block alone measures 215 metres by 186 metres. You approach it across a 1,500-metre causeway over the moat. It is protected by low walls adorned with mythical, multi-headed snakes. Three levels of squares, galleries and chambers surround the central tower. Wall carvings show the king receiving officials and in procession. Battle scenes commemorate conquests. Beautiful maidens dance, promising eternal life in paradise.

Astronomical observatory, royal burial place and temple: everything about Angkor Wat had profound cosmic and religious symbolism. Everything is on an enormous scale. So overwhelming is the site in its complexity and magnificence that it is easy to forget the surrounding landscape. In the past, even archaeologists did.

Research was at rather a dead end when remote sensing entered the picture. Trained as they are in remote-sensing technologies using space satellites, today's researchers ask questions about the surrounding landscape. It was known that Angkor Wat lay at the heart of a huge, densely populated environment that had housed and fed up to three-quarters of a million people. But the surrounding landscape is under dense forest cover, and it is difficult to chart rainforests and thick vegetation because surveyors need straight 'sight lines'. Unless you employ a small army of workers with axes and machetes to cut down dozens of trees, there is not much to be done. Fortunately, researchers have been able to turn to LIDAR.

LIDAR – Light Detection and Ranging – is a form of laser scanning that was originally developed in the 1960s for use in meteorology (the study of the atmosphere). It works by sending out a beam of light which bounces off a target object and returns to the origin; the time taken for the light to travel to and from the object is measured, and the precise distance to the target object can be calculated. LIDAR thus collects extremely accurate, high-resolution, three-dimensional data. A survey produces millions of dots that a computer can then convert into a three-dimensional mesh.

From the archaeologist's point of view, LIDAR is more cost-effective than traditional field surveys. It can even be used on the ground to record individual structures in extremely fine detail. This state-of-the-art technology is perfect for the aerial exploration of large sites that lie in forested landscapes, such as Angkor Wat. Up to 600,000 pulses are sent out by the device each second, allowing it to penetrate leaves and other vegetation and reach the ground below. It can record houses, temples and other structures under thick forest canopy. Rainforests no longer have secrets.

Before 2012, archaeologists Christophe Pottier, Roland Fletcher and Damian Evans had combined a series of small-scale ground-penetrating radar projects with field research. To their surprise, it turned out that once upon a time Angkor Wat had not been surrounded by dense forest, but had been near the middle of a huge urban complex covering at least 1,000 square kilometres, and with an estimated 750,000 inhabitants. The archaeologists uncovered traces of canals and ponds, thousands of rice fields surrounded by low banks, house mounds and hundreds of small shrines. But for all the new knowledge gained, the dense forest cover of today, especially around Angkor Wat itself, made foot surveys almost impossible.

In 2012, frustrated by the lack of progress, they turned to LIDAR since it could 'see' through dense forest. Evans worked closely with the Cambodian organisation responsible for Angkor. Meanwhile, a team of specialist researchers from Australia, Europe, Cambodia and the United States joined forces to work with ground-penetrating radar on foot. They combined the results with carefully targeted excavations within the grounds of Angkor Wat itself. An entire urban landscape emerged from the research.

For well over a century, the traditional view was that Angkor Wat had been a temple city and capital of the Khmer Empire during the twelfth century. The great enclosure appeared to have housed a dense urban population, especially the elite of the ruler's court. Isolated villages were thought to be part of a heavily forested agricultural hinterland. The virtual 'removal' of the forest cover allowed the researchers to map Angkor Wat and its enclosure as well as large tracts of the urban area around the temple.

The new findings were extraordinary. The temple complex was far larger and more elaborate than any archaeologist had imagined. A well-developed road grid had originated in Angkor Wat half a century before the nearby Angkor Thom was built, and had extended far beyond the two great shrines to take in all of Angkor's outlying temples. A road and canal network ran across the sprawling precincts (the suburbs) of the greater Angkor area. This was where most people had lived.

For generations, archaeologists had assumed that ancient cities were compact, densely populated entities like Sumerian Ur or Athens. But Gordon Willey's early studies of Maya landscapes and now these findings at Angkor have revealed spread-out, unwalled cities in tropical regions. The word 'city', traditionally associated with ancient walled places, has many more meanings than we thought.

Those who worked on Angkor Wat used to believe that the elite dwelt there, in the shadow of the most sacred place. But the LIDAR survey contradicts this assumption. The great temple was part of a complex, interconnected landscape that was almost invisible until the laser scanners came along. While Evans and Fletcher examined the LIDAR data, the research team working on the ground used their radar and careful excavation to try to determine how many people had lived close to the temple, and who they were. They were interested to learn that these people had lived in modest dwellings, built mostly of materials that decayed rapidly. The researchers now suggest that it may not have been the wealthy elite who dwelt close by, but temple staff such as priests, dancers and officials.

Once again, remote sensing provided a thorough overview. The ground radar – combined with LIDAR, the collection of soil samples, ground survey and selective excavation – identified a grid of about 300 small household ponds within the enclosure walls.

This was far more than the handful known previously. Using the newly discovered ponds and a description by a Chinese visitor in AD 1295–96, they estimated that about 4,000 people had lived in Angkor Wat's main enclosure.

How many people ran the temple? The team used a Khmer inscription to calculate that the staff numbered about 25,000. But most of them lived outside the main enclosure, probably quite close to the temple. The same inscription records that five times as many people were engaged in delivering food and other produce. Almost all of them must have lived in the suburbs.

The remote sensing provides us with a totally unexpected insight into the scale of Angkor Wat's logistics. Thanks once again to LIDAR and earlier remote-sensing efforts, we know that the major Angkor temples lay in the midst of a huge network of canals, ponds and reservoirs. These managed, stored and dispersed water from three small rivers through the city and into the Tonle Sap. One of the reservoirs alone, the so-called West Baray, is 8 kilometres long and 2 kilometres wide.

LIDAR is becoming cheaper, as fieldworkers experiment with LIDAR-carrying drones. We can now look at the landscapes that surrounded ancient cities in ways quite unimaginable a generation ago. Whether compact or more spread out, these cities depended on the surrounding communities and the agricultural landscapes. Damian Evans, Roland Fletcher and their colleagues have completely transformed our perceptions of Khmer civilisation.

LIDAR is being used elsewhere, too, revealing the scattered settlement patterns of ancient Maya centres like El Mirador in Guatemala. It has been used to plot a colonial-era plantation near Annapolis, Maryland, in the United States.

Within another generation, the traditional symbol of the archaeologist, the trowel, could be joined by various remote-sensing devices, operated from balloons, circling drones or satellites.

CHAPTER 40

Archaeology Today and Tomorrow

Imagine a swampy landscape with a few ridges and low hills, crossed by streams and rivers. Now imagine it 9,000 years ago, with a dugout canoe making its way through a narrow channel in the tall reeds. A strong wind carrying drizzle gusts above, but the black water is still. The woman paddles quietly, while her husband stands up front, barbed spear at the ready. One lightning-quick thrust and a struggling pike breaks surface. Startled birds make a commotion. In seconds, the fisherman has tipped his catch into the canoe, where his wife swiftly kills it with a wooden club. The water is again calm and the fishing continues.

The story may be fiction, but this is no imaginary landscape: it is based on archaeological and climatic evidence gathered from the bottom of the North Sea. Today, a cold and often rough stretch of water separates Britain from continental Europe. But 9,000 years ago, when global sea levels were far below those of today, this was dry land.

Known to geologists today as Doggerland, the area was only a few metres above sea level, For the most part, it was a waterlogged world, whose inhabitants spent much of their time afloat. We know details of this natural landscape from remote sensing. But we know little of the human inhabitants, except for what we can glean from chance finds such as bone harpoons dredged from the shallow sea bed. We know these people were hunters and fisherfolk, for agriculture was still unknown. We also know that they lived in an ever-changing environment, so flat that a rise in the sea level of just a few centimetres could submerge canoe landings or campsites within a generation or even less.

Doggerland finally vanished about 5500 BC during a time of major global warming after the Ice Age. Thanks to archaeology, we know more and more about how people have adjusted to changes in the climate (both large and small) – whether small hunting bands in Doggerland or magnificent civilisations in danger of collapse during major drought. We live in a time of global warming, of climate change triggered by human activity (much of it since the 1860s). We archaeologists provide a long-term historical view of climate change, and this offers a unique background to today's concerns.

Whether we like it or not, we are going to have to adjust to more frequent 'extreme weather events' such as hurricanes or droughts. We're like the long-vanished inhabitants of Doggerland, but on a global scale. Their small bands moved around in the face of rising sea levels. But the populations of today's big cities cannot do the same.

Long before the million-person city, early civilisations were vulnerable to climate change. Ancient Egyptian civilisation nearly collapsed because of failed Nile floods, caused by drought in 2100 BC. Fortunately, the pharaohs were shrewd enough to invest in extensive agricultural irrigation canals and grain storage facilities. Their civilisation lasted for 2,000 more years.

Meanwhile, great Maya cities descended into social disorder and chaos, in part because of major droughts. We learn from archaeology that vulnerability to climate change is nothing new. In this and many other ways archaeology tells us a great deal about ourselves and how we face today's challenges – many of which are also nothing new.

Archaeology has always been about people. What has changed is not the people, but the layers of evidence that we use to study them. We began purely as excavators, out for spectacular finds and (sometimes) knowledge. We preferred, for the most part, civilisations. Today, we're interested in everything from human origins to the Industrial Revolution and First World War trenches. Of course, we still excavate statues and buildings – or an emperor's terracotta regiment; but we're just as comfortable in the laboratory studying pot fragments or animal bones, or discussing the religious beliefs of Maya rulers. Archaeology is being transformed by new technological methods, such as LIDAR, which can expose entire landscapes and sites deep under tropical forests (see Chapter 39). We've become so specialised that there is a tendency sometimes to forget the people.

It is now rare to make a truly 'spectacular' discovery, such as a richly decorated tomb. Tragically, archaeology's precious archives are vanishing before our very eyes. Archaeological sites everywhere are under threat from deep ploughing, industrial development and looters.

Without being aware of it, thousands of tourists – fascinated by archaeological sites and the remains of ancient societies – are eroding the stones of the pyramids and of ancient Angkor Wat in Cambodia. At the same time, the terrorist organisation ISIS (Islamic State of Iraq and Syria) and other criminals have deliberately destroyed ancient Palmyra and Nineveh with gunpowder, and sold looted artefacts from ravaged museums.

Fortunately, there are heroes, too – communities that value their history and realise that they are stakeholders in the past. Archaeologists in several countries have joined forces with non-professionals who use metal detectors. This has resulted in impressive discoveries, including collections of Anglo-Saxon and Viking gold.

Many commercial companies have also helped save sites threatened by their development plans. The Crossrail Project, which is building an underground railway line across London, has paired archaeologists with tunnelling contractors from the beginning. They have recovered more than 10,000 artefacts from over forty worksites along the 100-kilometre line. Remarkable finds include 3,000 or so human skeletons excavated from underneath Liverpool Street Station, a major London terminus. Of these, forty-two came from a single burial ground used during the Great Plague of 1665, the 'Black Death'. A hundred thousand Londoners perished in the plague which swept across Europe from the east. Victims died within days, and sometimes within hours. They broke out in black rashes and often collapsed in the streets. At the time, no one knew what the killer disease was or where it had come from.

The exact nature of the disease was still somewhat uncertain until the Crossrail researchers took DNA samples from the Liverpool Street victims' tooth enamel. These yielded traces of a type of bacteria associated with bubonic plague, which is spread by rats. The DNA settled once and for all what disease it was that had killed so many Londoners.

Crossrail explored centuries of vanished London history. Elsewhere, other sites exposed by industrial activity, and then excavated with the support of the company that discovered them, tell of dramatic moments in the past. For example, some 3,000 years ago, a fire broke out in a small village lying in a marshy setting at Must Farm, near Peterborough, in eastern England's low-lying Fenlands. The flames tore through the tiny, fenced settlement, built on stilts above the bog. The villagers fled the blaze, leaving everything behind them. Within minutes, five huts had slid into the water.

This is when archaeology is at its best: a long-forgotten catastrophe that froze a moment in time; near-perfect preservation conditions in waterlogged ground; and collapsed dwellings, where everything lies virtually unharmed. Thanks to the cooperation of a helpful brick quarry owner, the fascinating and tragic story could be pieced together.

The site was so waterlogged that the archaeologists could sift through the wet mud and fine silt in huts that were preserved so completely that it was as though the researchers had simply walked into them. Parts of the wattle walls were still in place beneath traces of the collapsed roofs. Possessions lay on the floor and by the hearth – even clay pots with food still in them. There were traces of butchered lamb carcasses that once hung from the rafters.

The hut owners had a fine array of bronze axes and swords, as well as bronze-tipped spears (two were found still complete with their wooden shafts – a rare discovery). The mud perfectly preserved textiles made from the bark of lime trees – some of the fibres were finer than human hair. This was a community that spent much of its time afloat: no fewer than eight wooden dugout canoes have been found nearby. Must Farm is Britain's Pompeii.

Some dramatic finds in recent years have revealed long-forgotten natural disasters. Cerén, a Maya village in El Salvador, Central America, was buried by a volcanic eruption in about AD 580. The people had eaten their evening meal but had not yet gone to bed. They abandoned their houses and possessions to flee for their lives.

American archaeologist Payson Sheets and his team have been working there since 1976. They have unearthed two houses, some public buildings and three storehouses. The preservation is so good that they have recovered bean-filled pots, sleeping mats and garden tools, either carbonised or preserved as casts in the ash. The eruption buried fields with young and mature maize plants, and several fruit trees, including guavas.

Like Herculaneum and Pompeii, Cerén and Must Farm are places where we get up close and personal with the people of the past. And when all is said and done, that is the point of archaeology.

Archaeology is about discovery – but discovery today means something very different from even half a century ago. We've traced the history of archaeology from its early days of antiquarians like John Aubrey, William Stukeley and John Frere. Then came the early excavators, who dug up a jumble of artefacts from European burial mounds. Pompeii and Herculaneum yielded dramatic finds. General Napoléon Bonaparte's scientists made ancient Egypt fashionable in 1800. Jean François Champollion deciphered hieroglyphs in 1822 and founded Egyptology.

Then came the adventurers, like Paul-Émile Botta, Austen Henry Layard, Frederick Catherwood, John Lloyd Stephens and Heinrich Schliemann. These were the heroic days of archaeology, when archaeologists revealed unknown ancient civilisations. Meanwhile, Christian Jürgensen Thomsen and J.J.A. Worsaae brought some order to prehistoric times with the Three-Age System during the early nineteenth century.

The era of adventuring and collecting began to fade in the 1870s with the German excavations at Olympia and Babylon. Slowly, archaeology ceased to be an amateur pursuit. In 1900, most archaeologists were men. But a small number of women were in the field, among them Gertrude Bell and Harriett Hawes. The early twentieth century was a time of increasing professionalism and truly magnificent discoveries. Among them was the undisturbed tomb of Tutankhamun, opened in 1922. Leonard Woolley's excavations at Ur in Iraq were one of the last enormous classic digs; his clearance of the city's royal tombs rivalled the Tutankhamun excavation. By the 1930s, a growing number of professional archaeologists taught at colleges and universities.

Slowly but surely, archaeology became global – not just confined to Europe and the Middle East. Gertrude Caton-Thompson's excavations at Great Zimbabwe opened the world's eyes to early African states. Excavations at Pecos Pueblo put the archaeology of the American Southwest (and indeed of North America generally) on a scientific footing.

We have traced the slow development of world prehistory, the debates over the first farming, and have joined the Leakeys and others as they searched for the first humans in East Africa. Archaeology has become an international undertaking, where long-term, slow-moving projects tackle issues like sustainability rather than merely finding and dating sites.

Excavation itself is no longer fashionable, as remote sensing has slowly come to fulfil the archaeologist's dream of being able to see underground without digging. Archaeology is still exciting. It's now highly technical, but that allows us to decipher the medical history of pharaohs and to establish, from the tooth enamel of skeletons, where people once were born and lived. Archaeology helps explain why we are similar and why we are different. It explains the ways in which we adapt. By looking backwards into the past, it helps us look forwards into the future. And every year, new discoveries and technical advances make it easier to peer over the shoulders of ancient people – almost, sometimes, to talk to them.

I remember standing on the ramparts of a 2,000-year-old hillfort in England one cloudy day. I closed my eyes and imagined the battle below in AD 43 between a Roman legion and the local inhabitants – the shouts of the attackers, the clash of sword on shield, the screams of the wounded. . . For a moment, I was a spectator. Then the vision faded and I shivered in the grey chill.

The past is around us for all to experience and enjoy – not only archaeologists. So when you next visit an archaeological site, let your imagination run wild.

Index

'Will make you writhe, ripple
and froth with pleasure.'
—*Stephen Fry*

'Brilliant, irresistible: a
wonderful surprise.'
—*Philip Pullman*

Explore the LITTLE HISTORIES

Illuminating, energetic and readable, the Little Histories are books
that explore timeless questions and take readers young and old on an
enlightening journey through knowledge. Following in the footsteps of
E. H. Gombrich's irresistible tour de force *A Little History of the World*,
the family of Little Histories, sumptuously designed with unique
illustrations, is an essential library of human endeavour.

Which Little History will you read next?

A Little History of the World by E. H. Gombrich
A Little Book of Language by David Crystal
A Little History of Philosophy by Nigel Warburton
A Little History of Science by William Bynum
A Little History of Literature by John Sutherland
A Little History of the United States by James West Davidson
A Little History of Religion by Richard Holloway
A Little History of Economics by Niall Kishtainy
A Little History of Archaeology by Brian Fagan

New titles coming soon!

For more information visit www.littlehistory.org